One Dies, Get Another

Convict Leasing
in the American South, 1866–1928

One Dies, Get Another

Convict Leasing
in the American South, 1866–1928

Matthew J. Mancini

University of South Carolina Press

Copyright © 1996 University of South Carolina Press

Published in Columbia, South Carolina, by the
University of South Carolina Press

www.sc.edu/uscpress

22 21 20 19 18   5 4 3 2

Library of Congress Cataloging-in-Publication Data

Mancini, Mathew J.
    One dies, get another : convict leasing in
the American South, 1866–1928/Mathew J.
Mancini.   p.   cm.
    Includes bibliographical references and index.
    ISBN 1-57003-083-9
    1. Convict labor—Southern States—History.   2. Prisoners—
Southern States—History.   I. Title.
HV8929.S92M36   1996
365'.65—dc20   95-50208

To my son, Philip

Man is a being in movement. He is called to the conquest of freedom.
—Jacques Maritain

When life arises and flows along artificial channels rather than normal ones, and when its growth depends not so much on natural and economic conditions as on the theory and the arbitrary behavior of individuals, then it is forced to accept these circumstances as essential and inevitable, and these circumstances acting on an artificial life assume the aspects of laws.

—Anton Chekhov, *The Island* (1897)

CONTENTS

LIST OF ILLUSTRATIONS

ACKNOWLEDGMENTS

I am grateful for an opportunity to offer thanks to some of the people whose crossing of my path at certain vital moments helped this study become a reality. Crucial to the development of this project were two scholars, two generations apart, one a generation ahead of me, the other a generation younger. The first is Robert E. Gallman, a great economic historian, whose short course on cliometrics, which I took nearly twenty years ago as a young college teacher, permanently changed my outlook on history, and especially Southern history. Not only did my decision to study convict leasing emerge from that course, but Bob Gallman's tireless and discerning criticism helped me to think clearly about it, and to give it a definite shape. The second scholar was, when I met him, a young and very promising graduate student at the University of Pennsylvania, Alex Lichtenstein, whose inquiries into a subject I had, for many reasons, both personal and professional, allowed to languish, gently and persistently led me back into active engagement with it. In 1989 Alex and I participated in a session on forced labor at the Southern Historical Association's annual meeting, which also included Gerald Shenk, Pete Daniel, and Dan T. Carter. I thank them all for their thoughtful critiques of my contribution to that session.

Dan Carter, however, must abide a word of special thanks for the most practical suggestion on research I've ever received.

A vital force in and model for my intellectual life since this work began in earnest has been Stanley L. Engerman, who in countless patient ways perhaps unknown to him helped this study achieve coherence.

I have benefited from professional and clerical assistance of unfailing excellence in a great many libraries and archives while completing this project: the Alabama Department of Archives and History; the Special Collections Department of the Mullins Library, University of Arkansas; the Georgia Department of Archives and History; the Woodruff Library of Emory University; the Monroe F. Swilley, Jr. Library, Mercer University/Atlanta; the Richard B. Russell Memorial Library, the

Hargrett Library, and the Georgia Room at the University of Georgia, Athens; the Atlanta Historical Society (now the Atlanta History Center) Library; the Louisiana Room of Louisiana State University; the Tilton Library, Tulane University; the Mississippi Department of Archives and History; the Southern Historical Collection and the North Carolina Collection at the University of North Carolina at Chapel Hill; the Special Collections Department of the Perkins Library, Duke University; the Archives Division of the Texas State Library, Austin; the Thomason Room at the Gresham Library, Sam Houston State University; the Fondren Library, Rice University; The State Historical Society of Wisconsin; the University of Wisconsin Library; the Meyer Library, Southwest Missouri State University; and the superb libraries at the law schools of Emory, Tulane, and Washington Universities.

But a complete list of all the students, scholars, prisoners, archivists, friends, and family members whose assistance left an imprint or a trace on this work would violate the essential purpose of a preface, which when read at all is read only because of its brevity. Apologizing in advance for inevitable and regretted omissions, I would single out a few who teem in my stirred-up memory as I complete this book:

In 1990 I spent a semester at Tulane University's Murphy Institute for Political Economy, splitting my professional time and attention between Southern convicts and Alexis de Tocqueville. My colleagues there pretended not to mind this duality; especially thoughtful in this regard were Judith Schafer, Peter Schwartz, and Richard Teichgraeber III. An afternoon with LSU's Tom Carleton was worth a seminar in Louisiana culture. Of my exceptionally supportive former colleagues in the history department at Rice University, John Boles, Thomas Haskell, and Paula Sanders have been the most dauntless. Graduate students in my Rice seminar on prisons, especially Jeff Hooton, also raised important questions and opened research opportunities. The outstanding history department at Southwest Missouri State University has earned my heartfelt thanks for their encouragement, patience, and understanding. Dean Bernice Warren of SMSU's College of Humanities and Social Sciences supported crucial late journeys to the archives in North Carolina and Texas, and a Southwest Missouri State University Faculty Research Grant gave me the chance to research and write when the accumulating mass of other academic duties threatened to inundate me.

But this study goes much further back in time, to a period in the mid and late 1970s when I worked at what was then an exciting institution, Mercer University in Atlanta, with faculty, administrators, and students, some of them prisoners, who helped me understand what education is. They included Bill Cleary, Duane Davis, Colin Harris, Deal Hudson, and Jean Hendricks, a great educator whose early support was crucial. I also thank Donna Mancini for steering me in the right direction at the Georgia Archives and for other support when research was difficult.

In Texas, Bob Pierce opened some doors for me, and Jane Gregory accompanied me through them. In Wisconsin, Larry Vanko put me up each night when the Historical Society and the university library had closed. Julius Scott was kind in North Carolina, and converted me into a Durham Bulls fan. Because Paul Finkelman's critical acumen matches his enormous erudition, he helped me clarify what I meant to say.

Why do family members always come last? Because if a writer is lucky they are always there, part of his natural surroundings. It is only when he actively tries to ascertain how he has been helped in specific ways relating to a particular project that their faces crowd his memory. Missy, Phil, Cath, Joe, Tim, Maribeth, Tad, Michael, Jim, and Mary have been, as Immanuel Kant might have put it, the indispensable groundwork for the possibility of getting anything done at all.

One Dies, Get Another

Convict Leasing
in the American South, 1866–1928

INTRODUCTION

A merica has a mania for prisons. It routinely incarcerates a higher proportion of its citizens, it used to be said, than any other nation in the "free world." But once the Soviet Union disintegrated and its records were opened up it became clear that the United States imprisoned more than the Soviets too.

In 1990 the Department of Justice counted three-quarters of a million Americans in state and federal prisons. The incarceration rate for those prisons for the nation at large was 289 per 100,000. If the thousands of jail inmates were to be included in the count—those either doing time in jail or waiting for their trials to commence—the national rate jumped to 426 per 100,000, or over one million Americans behind bars, according to the Sentencing Project. The rate for black American men was 3,109 per 100,000. The incarceration rate for the second most prison-bound society, South Africa, was 333 per 100,000. Third was the Soviet Union (its figures are from late 1989) at 268. European rates varied from 35 to 120. By 1993 the number of state and federal prisoners had reached 883,593, and the Bureau of Justice Statistics calculated that new prison beds were needed at the rate of 1,143 per week.[1]

It may come as a surprise to some readers, therefore, to learn that for half a century following the Civil War, the Southern states had no prisons to speak of, and those they did have played a peripheral role in those states' criminal justice systems. Instead, persons convicted of criminal offenses were sent to sugar and cotton plantations, as well as to coal mines, turpentine farms, phosphate beds, brickyards, sawmills, and other outposts of entrepreneurial daring in the impoverished region. As often as not they were sent to these places directly from the places of their convictions. They were leased—literally, contracted out—to businessmen, planters, and corporations in one of the harshest and most exploit-

1

ative labor systems known in American history.

For in the late nineteenth century Southern penology was overwhelmed by a mighty flood. The swollen waters of fear, greed, and indifference swept along the byways of nearly every Southern hamlet, capital city, and rural courthouse, seeking weak points and sweeping away any lingering attachment to discredited Yankee ideas or practices in the field of criminal justice. When the floodwaters finally receded after half a century they left behind a vile and dangerous residue that lingered for generations. That flood, which grew slowly at first and then amazed observers and participants alike by its sudden rapid expansion, was convict leasing.

Leasing was a method of criminal punishment that reveals much about the economic and political condition of the society that spawned it, and, more important—since leasing just more or less happened at first—that nurtured and cultivated it once it had come into being. The proper office of the historian, according to the theologian Bernard Lonergan, is to discern and elucidate in any given historical epoch that which is going forward.[2] In the convict lease, the late-nineteenth-century South forged an institution that expressed and carried forward some of the deepest impulses of that society. All the major themes of the period in Southern history were clustered together within that institution: fears of a labor shortage, racism, the dearth of capital, hair-trigger violence, the courageous efforts of humane reformers, and, through it all, the struggle to modernize.

An anecdote related by Hastings Hart in 1919 captures much that was singular about the lease. Hart was a well-known social worker at the turn of the twentieth century. He served as the head of the Russell Sage Foundation's Department of Child Helping. From his office at 130 East Twenty-second Street in New York City he supervised numerous social welfare projects. Like many of his fellow social workers to this day, Hart retained the nineteenth-century confidence in the ability of prisons to save people from themselves, and he was a frequent delegate to the cheery conventions of the National Prison Association. As a young man, at the association's 1883 meeting, he heard George Washington Cable deliver a solemn address on the convict lease system. Afterward, a Southern delegate who leased prisoners gave Hart his opinion of Cable's denunciations in terms that summarize the significance of hundreds of statistics, reports, letters, diaries, speeches, laws, and court cases accumulated in a dozen dusty archives. "Before the war, we owned the negroes," the lessee reflected nostalgically. "If a man had a good negro, he could afford to keep him. . . . But these convicts, we don't own 'em. One dies, get another."[3] One dies, get another: no apothegm could better capture the distinctive feature of convict leasing, the origins of its brutality, or, for that matter, the most salient difference between it and slavery.

In spite of its importance to Southern history in general and penology in particular, however, this distinct mode of convict management has never been the object of a full-length study. The source of this neglect is, at least in part, to be discovered in the federal system of government in the United States, which, however manifold its political and cultural benefits, can create serious difficulties for the specialized historian.

For of course each had its own laws as well as customary practices, its own prison (or lack of it), its distinctive population size and mix, distinguishing cultural traditions and regional tensions, its singular combination of factor endowments, and its unique experience with the Civil War, Reconstruction, and Redemption. The more deeply specialized a historian of a particular state becomes, therefore, the more foreign can the ways and histories of his neighboring Southern states be made to seem. With the notable exception of Edward L. Ayers's pioneering work, *Vengeance and Justice*, this tendency to statewide studies has been especially acute in the field of criminal justice, because one of the areas in which states are most distinctive vis-à-vis one another is in the theory and practice of criminal justice. Consequently, state studies have dominated this field, and although some of them are very good indeed, they are often rather insular in outlook and interpretation.

But while some historians have directed their gaze toward individual states, one obvious feature of late-nineteenth-century prison history is in danger of being overlooked. For however great the differences among states' criminal punishments might have been, the commonalities that bound the Southern states together, and that distinguished their prison practices from those of the rest of the nation, were far greater. In other words, if one focuses closely on a single state's policies and practices, those of other states seem altogether different; but if, on the other hand, one examines the United States as a whole, the Southern region leaps out as one with a distinctive way of handling prisoners.

The scope of this book, therefore, is regional, not state-centered. It is an attempt to put between the covers of a single volume, for the first time, both a narrative of the diverse histories of leasing in the Southern states and an analysis of the system as a whole. It is concerned, then, with both causation and meaning—of what happened, why, and why it mattered.

Consequently, this study opens, in part one, with an examination of three crucial issues that must be confronted if leasing as a regionwide phenomenon is to be understood: first, through the use of a comparative method, the definition of leasing as a form of forced labor; second, the nature of the labor convicts performed; and third, conditions and treatment in the convict camps.

But, of course, no careful observer can fail to recognize and record the unique and individual characteristics of the several states, not without doing violence to the motley variety of actual historical realities. Part two, accordingly, consists of a series of brief, mainly narrative, even institutional histories of leasing in each state of the Deep South. Based on the primary sources, several of them also reveal and express an indebtedness to monographs on individual states.

Sometimes in a preface or introduction an author will invite readers to browse among the chapters, or to read them in any order, skipping some and concentrating on others as interest or fancy may dictate. I have never understood that invitation and would make a special point of disavowing such a reading strategy for this book. For as the separate stories of the individual states roll by in part two, I hope the reader will begin to discern the many similar patterns that the states shared—patterns of population growth, cruelty, aborted abolition attempts, rising convict prices, and many others.

In part three concentration is on the single most important question a historian confronted with this arcane and almost unbelievable practice can ask, which is why it ended; or, more specifically, what were the enabling conditions for the replacement of leasing with other modes of using convict labor? For this purpose focus is on the dying days of leasing in Georgia, the state where leasing was practiced in its most unadulterated form, and Alabama, the state where it lasted longest.

Convict leasing was a distinctive practice in the history of the South's treatment of its prisoners. It was a stain on the region, and everyone knew it, but like many such evils, it was much easier to recognize than to remedy. As far as the material conditions of convict life are concerned, moreover, it might be reasonably argued that leasing's abolition had little effect—that prison life was as squalid and perilous after leasing was abolished as it had been during the years of its ascendancy. Although I disagree with that position, I leave it to others to decide. I confess to having slipped at times into a judgmental mode of discourse in these pages, but my primary purpose has been simply to reveal and explain something distinctive, something whose passing constituted an important moment in Southern history, however sorely Southern prisoners continued to suffer in its aftermath. I argue below that what Southern prison reform amounted to was the shift of one kind of forced labor from private to public hands. But that, historically, if not morally, is an important shift indeed.

This book is not an exhaustive survey of every leasing contract that was ever drawn up or of every crew of prisoners who hewed and dug the nation's infrastructure. Rather, it comprehensively examines the practice of leasing in the South in the last third of the nineteenth century and the first quarter of the twentieth. Its focus is a rather wide, but steady, one. States outside the South occasionally practiced leasing. Massachusetts leased some prisoners in 1798. In 1825 Kentucky's Joel Scott leased and worked prisoners within the walls of the state penitentiary in Frankfort. Overcrowding caused Oregon to lease its prisoners in 1859. "The experiment was a disaster," its historian writes. "All the prisoners escaped, the lessees forfeited their contract, and the state resumed control in 1862."[4] California contracted its convicted felons right through the 1870s. Missouri also undertook an on-again, off-again lease from the 1850s to the 1870s, and used prisoners as strikebreakers in 1877. Once again, the experiment proved "disastrous," Gary R. Kremer writes. "A revolt in November 1877 among the 254 convicts working at the Montserrat mines led to three inmate deaths, twenty injuries, and twenty-five hundred dollars in property damage."[5] After that Missouri would keep its convict labor within the prison walls. These episodes are not the concern of the present study. However much personal or political importance these contracts may have in the states where they were entered into, they were in fact peripheral to the great sweep of penological theories and methods outside the South.

II

Even within the South, and in some states on its margins, leasing sometimes occurred in fits and starts but not so thoroughly and so relentlessly as to define the state's entire penal policy. The most prominent state in this regard was Virginia, which, as its prison historian, Paul W. Keve, explains, never became a leasing state: "The lease system, which turned over to a private entrepreneur the whole prison operation, was tried at various times in some Southern states but not in Virginia." Nevertheless, Virginia did at times work convicts on contracts outside the penitentiary.[6] Virginia thus provides this book with a limiting case—that is, an example of a Southern state whose penitentiary experiences were atypical of the rest of the region—and therefore provides a model for understanding what conditions were necessary for a Southern state *not* to undertake leasing after the Civil War. Because several fiscal and institutional factors acted as levees against the flood of leasing in Virginia and protected its prison policy from being completely inundated, Virginia's experience can serve to illustrate disparate trends that converged only later and more slowly in other Southern states, trends that allowed leasing to ebb in the early twentieth century.

First in importance was the simple fact that Virginia had a penitentiary. It was a beautiful building, one of the early republic's most graceful designs, whose architect, Benjamin Henry Latrobe, was one of the great figures in the history of American architecture; it was also damp, unheated, impossible to maintain, and an obstacle to effective surveillance. Nevertheless, Virginia's having been a pioneer in the field of penitentiaries led to its having alternatives at its disposal that other states did not. A second factor was the willingness, however marginal or reluctant, of its citizens to collect and expend some public revenue on prisoners. In 1882, for example, the state added a new floor to the penitentiary building, constructed a wing for female prisoners, and reorganized the workshops inside the prison, while in 1892 an entire new female prison was established. Third, convict hires faced declining profitability, especially in states, like Virginia, that relied on railroad construction for contracts. The railroad boom ended rather suddenly in the 1880s throughout the South. By 1889 Virginia's superintendent, B. W. Lynn, had told the National Prison Association that "our expenses have increased by the hiring of convicts [because of] additional guard hire, clothing, feeding, medical attention, etc. . . . the cost of maintaining these men on the railroads is considerably in excess of the amount received by the state for their hire."[7] Fourth, Virginia purchased a prison farm of about a thousand acres, known simply as State Farm and located twenty-six miles from Richmond.

A final consideration, perhaps the most important one, was political: in the 1870s and 1880s Virginia experienced a remarkable political movement, that of the Readjusters, which held back the pressure to lease convicts. Early in the 1880s the Readjusters gained control of state government and managed to repudiate over half of the state's prewar indebtedness, overhaul the state's revenue structure, lower property taxes, and introduce efficiencies into the internal revenue offices. They also abolished the whipping post and the poll tax, authorized free vaccinations for the poor during epidemics, and attempted to limit child labor. The net effect of these changes was "to revitalize Virginia's impoverished social services, particularly the public schools," explains historian James Tice Moore. "Even the antiquated state penitentiary came in for a major overhaul."[8]

The prison history of Virginia, like that of other states, is the story of the search for a satisfactory labor system. The state had an antebellum precedent for working prisoners outside the penitentiary; in 1857 Gov. Henry A. Wise had persuaded the legislature to empower him to use free-black convicts alongside slaves on public works. Wise sent eighty-three convicts to the James River and Kanawha Company and considered the experiment to be so successful that he soon recommended the extension of his authority to include white convicts as well.[9]

The Civil War terminated this experiment, but in the early 1870s Virginia's convicts were again sent to railroad construction camps, quarries, and canals. The state had been physically devastated by the Civil War, and such infrastructure work was urgently needed. Indeed, the prisoners were furnished free of charge to the James River and Kanawha Company, which was digging canals. Immediately certain trends asserted themselves that would be invariable whenever convicts were set to work outside the prison for contractors, namely soaring death and escape rates, degenerating physical conditions, and fraudulent actions by unscrupulous contractors.[10]

At about the time when Conservative governor Gilbert C. Walker began dispatching prisoners to these railroad and canal construction sites, the debt of the state stood at $45 million. Walker had been instrumental in persuading the legislature to pass the Funding Act, which committed the state to pay off $30 million of that enormous burden. From the moment of the Funding Act's passage, the debt question became the pivotal issue in Virginia politics, for, due to the magnitude of its debt liabilities, Virginia could not pay for even the most vital state expenses. By 1878 fully half of the state's schools were not in operation.

But such public services as schools were not the only state investments that were starved for funds. In the fall of 1877, a deluge wreaked $218,000 worth of damage to the James River Canal. Desperate to make repairs, the company implored the legislature to assign prisoners to the task. Soon every available prisoner was working to restore the canal. While the convicts' labor probably saved the canal, the arrangement cost the state over $65,000.[11] Facing a fiscal crisis in 1878, with a huge debt, an empty treasury, and the state's schools on the verge of shutting down, the legislature approved a measure allowing convict leasing. The law, however, remained a dead letter, since the state received no bids. Such was the prison situation in 1879, when the Readjusters scored an overwhelming victory in state elections and began the task of altering many of the state's priorities.

Readjusters were beholden to black voters. In 1883 their leader, William Mahone, asserted that "the Readjuster party in Virginia is composed of 110,000 colored and about 65,000 white voters."[12] That year railroad officials were complaining that the state was simply not sending them the convicts they demanded—and they were right: convict labor was an important issue to black Virginians.[13] After the Readjuster tide ebbed, Conservatives made more efforts to disperse prisoners to contractors. But by then the profitability of the potential convict labor projects was diminishing, while at the same time workshops inside the prison were turning a profit.[14] Leasing, then, simply could not grab a foothold in the Old Dominion.

All these factors—declining profitability, the presence of a penitentiary, the development of alternative means of using convict labor, and significant political pressure against leasing, often connected with a willingness to undertake social expenditures—would be present in varying degrees in each of the Southern states, permitting public opposition to the practice, which was never far from the surface, to become effective. But only in Virginia were these forces in motion from the beginning of the post–Civil War period. Elsewhere in the South, they would not gather enough momentum until after the new century had dawned. Virginia's experience reveals what factors the post–Civil War Southern states would have to develop before their systems of convict leasing could be overcome. No other state had such a combination of elements (except, in radically different circumstances, Tennessee) before the twentieth century.

But the hold of leasing on the rest of the South is remarkable in its tenacity. The story seems to go on and on, in state after state, despite attempts, some of them actually successful, to outlaw leasing; it persisted in spite of laws, constitutional provisions, court decisions, and executive actions prohibiting it. How and why these things took place is the subject of the remainder of this book.

PART ONE

MAKING SENSE
OF CONVICT LEASING

One

CATEGORIES

J ust as today's corrections experts try to classify prisons and prisoners by degrees of security risk into minimum, medium, and maximum security levels, so also penitentiary managers early in the nineteenth century were concerned to distinguish between competing plans for the convicts' moral reformation. This debate is known to history as the famous battle between the "Auburn" and "Philadelphia" plans. At the Philadelphia penitentiary, prisoners labored in utter silence and isolation in single cells at such tasks as cobblery and harness making, which could be performed by solitary workers, while in Auburn, New York, they worked in communal workshops under strict rules of silence during the day, retiring to their single cells at night.

Between the earliest and the most recent eras of prison management, there arose a different kind of taxonomy that was expressive of the late nineteenth century's concern with systematically organized production. Each of these three modes of classification reflects the social order that produced it, and each one proved in time to obscure more than it illuminated. In the dreary history of American penology, classification reveals more about the preoccupations of the classifiers than about the ostensible object of analysis.

In order to appreciate these late-nineteenth-century classifications, it is necessary to become familiar with some recondite terms in use among prison professionals a hundred years ago. In 1910 an assiduous warden named Amos W. Butler, the president of the American Prison Association, addressed the association's convention on the subject of prison labor. Butler was a careful student of his subject—so careful, in fact, that he comes across as something of a pedant. Of convict leasing he said: "The lease system exclusively is in use in Florida. It is combined with state account in Alabama, with state use in Arkansas and North Carolina, and with both state account and state use in Texas."[1] Five years earlier, the United States Department of Labor had issued a comprehensive study of prison labor, in which were categorized the activities of some 86,034 convicts, on daily average, in 296 institutions in the United States. The study was arranged by the system of labor control in effect in the various prisons, using for this purpose such categories as "contract," "piece-price," "public account," and "state-use."[2]

State account? Piece-price? State use? What do these arcane terms mean? The expression "lease system" may at least be said to possess the virtue of clarity. It is my contention that terms like piece-price and state account, however, which were intended to classify prison systems by distinguishing between types of labor management, serve instead to mislead students of prison labor, since they establish distinctions that are based on false or irrelevant criteria. Essentially these terms indicate different systems of accounting, not of labor, and they helped form the structure of an elaborate hierarchy that, in the fashion of the late nineteenth century, carried a heavy load of moralistic connotations.

In fact, the penological literature of Amos W. Butler's day abounds with these oversubtle distinctions about the use of prison labor. They dominate the discourse of nineteenth-century penology to a remarkable degree. John Peter Altgeld, Illinois's leading reformer and, in the 1890s, its courageous governor, provides a good illustration in his 1886 book *Our Penal Machinery and its Victims.* Under the public account system, Altgeld explained, the state furnished all the inputs, namely raw materials, tools, and labor in the persons of incarcerated felons, and marketed and sold the resulting products of prison labor. As Glen A. Gildemeister has recently pointed out, the public account system was therefore "the antithesis of the lease: that is, the state retained complete control over the convict, setting all standards of discipline, behavior, labor, food, clothing, and medical care."[3]

The most common system in Altgeld's day was called the contract system. Under it, a firm paid the state a fixed rate. The state's only obligation was to house and guard the labor for which the firm was contracting. The company provided the raw materials and any necessary machinery, marketed the product of the prisoners' labor, and took all the profits therefrom. Under the contract system, then, labor and its products were privatized, while monitoring and subsistence remained a governmental function.

The contract system brought an abundance of corruption and fraud in its train. In 1883 the exceptionally thoughtful warden of New York's

Elmira prison, Zebulon Brockway, came up with a new scheme, which was soon emulated in other Northern prisons. Called the piece-price system, it was a means by which the terms of the public account plan—which had always been difficult to achieve—could be modified. Under it, outside firms provided inputs of capital and raw materials but the state controlled the labor of the prisoners. As one student defined it in 1915: "In the piece-price system the power of the employer or contractor extends only to the purchase of the raw material and to the selling of the finished goods, while the direction of the labor and the discipline of the prisoners is posited with the warden and his responsible foremen."

The so-called state-use system was another kind of compromise—"a method of employing prisoners whereby the products of their labor should be withheld from the competitive market and used by the state and its political divisions on public works and in the manufacture of articles for public institutions."[4]

Finally, of course, came the convict lease system, under which the state, after receiving a fixed sum for the privilege, paid no attention to the prisoners whatever, while the lessee fed, clothed, guarded, and worked them to his own profit.[5]

Each of these methods had its detractors. Common to all was the charge that, in Altgeld's words, convict labor "is contracted out at such figures that the honest free laborers are reduced to starvation in the necessary competition which ensues; or, in case the convicts work under the public account system, that their products are sold cheaper than the same kinds of goods can be made by free labor at living wages."[6]

This charge is as difficult to substantiate as it was frequently made. Indeed, condemnations of prison labor on the grounds of its alleged depressing effect on workers' wages can be found as early as the 1820s. Yet, as Gustave de Beaumont and Alexis de Tocqueville noted in one of the earliest systematic examinations of prisons in the United States, prison officials really had no choice other than to introduce labor into the penitentiary if they wished to avert mass insanity. The original Quaker ideal of the penitentiary had demanded utter isolation, silence, and idleness as the triple pillars of convict reformation. The results of this new regimen, however, were horrifying. "In order to reform [the convicts], they had been submitted to complete isolation," wrote Beaumont and Tocqueville. "But this absolute solitude, if nothing interrupts it, is beyond the strength of man; it destroys the criminal without intermission and without pity; it does not reform, it kills."[7] Prison officials responded by eliminating the idleness while retaining the silence. Thus, the element of labor was introduced into the still-evolving institution of the penitentiary as an inseparable component of reformation.

Free workers immediately protested the new regime. The earliest such complaint contained the basic elements of all subsequent arguments against the use of prisoners for remunerative labor. On 17 May 1823 the New York cabinetmakers passed along the text of their resolution "against the employment of prisoners in their art" in a letter to the *Mechanics' Gazette:* "Let no man, who is a mechanic[,] think himself safe, because his business is not conducted in the prison; for he knows not how soon an attempt may be made to wrest from him what must be ever dear to him, a fair opportunity of supporting his wife and children, by the labor of his hands and the profit of his trade."[8]

I have found but a single nineteenth-century rebuttal to this platitudinous substitute for analysis—an editorial in *The Nation* criticizing the 1886 Department of Labor's report on prison labor, a report that was in fact deeply flawed in a number of respects. "The competition of prison labor with free labor is that which is seen," the editor wrote. "It is very minute, being only 54–100 of 1 per cent. of the mechanical labor of the country, but it can be seen, and, what is more to the purpose, it can be heard from. That which is not seen is the fact that if every prisoner were turned into a skilled workman and an honest man, according to the hand-labor plan favored by the Commissioner, and then discharged, he would be 50 per cent. more a competitor than he is now. . . . Would Labor be better off or worse off if all these criminals had learned honest trades and earned an honest living?" The editor's judgment, harsh as it was, was probably correct. As the most thorough recent student of nineteenth-century Northern prison labor has concluded: "it is difficult to assess precisely the impact of prison labor competition on unemployment and outside wage rates. Major variables which entered the equation determining free wage rates and the size of the labor pool—for example, immigration, economic depression, industrialization—affected workers in various crafts and locales to greatly differing degrees."[9]

If Altgeld, the political reformer, demonstrates an ardor for taxonomy that was typical of the early history of convict leasing, E. T. Hiller, a graduate student in sociology at the University of Chicago thirty years later, exhibits the same enthusiasm at the moment of leasing's demise. Hiller wrote two long articles in the *Journal of the American Institute of Criminal Law and Criminology* in 1914 and 1915 elaborately explaining

16

the detailed differences among the systems. In their ornate embellishments they represent a sort of baroque culmination to the style of prison labor taxonomy that was characteristic of the leasing era. Dividing his subject into chronological phases, types of labor control, and disposition of the products, Hiller was exhaustive. His definition of convict leasing does provide a useful starting point for comprehending the practice. "The final stage of the lease system," he explained, "is reached when entrepreneurs appear who are willing to assume the responsibility of employing, guarding and maintaining the convicts without the aid of any public prison, in lieu of the permission to employ this labor in private enterprise."[10]

The defect of this formula lies in its spurious precision. Only a few states, during just a short span of years, fit all of these criteria exactly; the most conspicuous example was Georgia from 1879 to 1899. At any given time in the fifty years after the start of Reconstruction, however, most Southern states would have in place a type of convict labor management that manifested most, but not all, of the attributes so carefully enumerated in Hiller's classification system. What gave Hiller's careful sociological analysis its dangerous character, then, was the ease with which it allowed embarrassed Southern prison officials the opportunity to pretend that the means their state had chosen for the disposition of its prisoners was something other than the almost universally despised solution of leasing them to businessmen for the purpose of mutual profit.

For example, in 1879 Alabama governor Rufus Cobb informed potential lessees that he would reject all contracts that would not conform to two criteria: first, lessees had to accept all convicts, including dead hands; and second, they had to pay the costs of transporting the convicts from the place of conviction to the lessee's stockade. Having undertaken so extreme a form of convict leasing, the state could later cite any minor modification of the contract terms as evidence of the state's having abandoned the practice. And in fact Alabama did make just such a denial, in 1888 of all years: the year in which the Tennessee Coal, Iron and Railroad Company (TCI) entered on a contractual relationship with Alabama that would last for forty years. The ground on which such a remarkable disavowal was based was the fact that the state, rather than the lessees, established the "task" of convict miners.[11]

Further examples abound in the peculiar literature of the nineteenth-century prison. Anyone familiar with the intense struggles associated with the termination of convict leasing in Mississippi, in 1906, would be shocked to read that it ended in 1890. But that is what J. H. Jones, a former chairman of the Penitentiary Committee in the Mississippi House, claimed in 1902. "The final abandonment of the convict lease system in Mississippi was the work of the Constitutional Convention of 1890," he flatly maintained in a triumphal account of Mississippi penitentiary reform. Article 10 of the 1890 Mississippi constitution did indeed forbid the leasing of convicts to "any person, corporation, or private or public board" after 1894, when the leases then in force would have expired. But the article simply remained a dead letter until James K. Vardaman decided to use the convict issue as leverage against his political enemies. At the time Jones wrote, in fact, convicts were laboring on no fewer than nine farms on a sharecropping arrangement between the landowners and the state. Twice as many convicts were leased in 1902 as in 1890. What was different after 1890 was simply that the state, rather than the lessee, hired the guards. Therefore Mississippi no longer met the strictest definition of convict leasing, and indeed it does not appear in several reports as a leasing state. Several later historians took Jones at his word, declaring Mississippi leasing's demise to have occurred in 1894, while the Department of Labor obligingly categorized Mississippi among the states on the public account system in 1895.[12] Gov. Charles Henderson of Alabama, thirteen years before abolition in 1928, also denied that there was any such thing as convict leasing in his state: "The State of Alabama maintains all of its convicts, feeds, clothes, such convicts. Under the state system the lessees simply pay the state for services rendered by the convict."[13]

On several occasions, the United States Department of Labor published compilations of statistics based on these convict labor classifications—statistics which, due precisely to such classifications, are highly unreliable. In 1895, for example, Department of Labor statistics show that the value of products produced under convict leasing had fallen to about two-thirds of its 1885 value. But this apparent decline was chiefly due not to the depression then under way but rather to the Department of Labor's method of counting—in particular, to the fact that only seven states were classified in the "lease" category. Among the states that were thus so brazenly excluded from the South's "barbarous and inhuman" system of convict labor were Mississippi, Texas, and Arkansas. Five years later the United States Industrial Commission simply duplicated the Department of Labor's 1895 figures in its own report on prison labor, thus perpetuating the deceptive impression that leasing was fading. In another misleading federal report, the Census Bureau showed only 4,883 convicts leased in 1880; the actual figure was two and a half to three times that number.[14]

Not only did the classifications allow states to obscure their real practices, but they also permitted the number of leased convicts within leasing states to be undercounted. The Census Bureau's figures for 1890, for instance, showed only 474 of Georgia's 2,938 convicts being leased, with 1,729 in "penitentiaries"—that is, presumably, in stockades of various sorts on the properties of lessees.[15]

Finally, the professional associations also promulgated incorrect information. One illustration of many possible ones comes from the 1873 proceedings of the National Prison Association, where statistics and other kinds of information were assembled on many aspects of life in some forty-five prisons; they included the names of the prison chaplains, the educational levels of the prisoners, and even wardens' opinions "as to the connection between the use of alcoholic liquors and crime." In that report Alabama, Louisiana, and Mississippi, leasing states all, were listed as working under the contract or the state-use systems. The following year E. C. Wines, the association's secretary, reported the lease in effect only in Missouri, Kentucky, Tennessee, Texas, and Georgia.[16]

These taxonomical decoys lured even reformers, like Texas's scrappy journalist Tom Finty Jr., into analytic traps. Finty wrote at times as if he accepted the fine distinction that left Texas outside the venomous ring of leasing states. "At first these contracts were in effect leases," he wrote of post-1883 arrangements, but "within recent years the state has guarded, clothed, fed, and medically attended the convicts." Like many of his contemporaries, he considered the "real" lease period in Texas to have ended in 1883.[17]

Contemporary indications of a recognition of the deceptive nature of these taxonomies are difficult to locate. One appeared in an unsigned article in an obscure policy journal, the *American Labor Legislation Review,* for October 1911. The article contained an admonition that was succinct, accurate, and ignored: "The usual penological analysis of prison labor into lease, contract, piece-price, public account and state-use systems," the author concluded, "is impossible to use in an economic analysis of the labor conditions involved." The other showed up in a rather more popular setting, *Everybody's Magazine,* in an article by a well- known muckraker, Charles Edward Russell. Russell provided a rare and valuable piece of early oral history by interviewing a convict who had been sent to an unnamed brickyard; from the description it is apparent that he is writing about the Chattahoochee Brick Company not far from Atlanta. Russell called the game of labor-classification systems "our quacksalving device of changing names and disguises" and noted that, when "leases" were replaced by "contracts," "though no conceivable difference resulted in any essential particular, the change of name afforded to some persons that soothing relief for the conscience."[18]

Such "quacksalving" relief indeed seems to have been one of the chief functions of these classifications. But the desire to arrange and order has led to unfortunate repercussions for later students of prison labor, as well. Some scholars continue to use the nineteenth-century categories, taking them at face value as descriptive accounts of actual practices,[19] while others take a more promising route to understanding, seeking in analogous forms of coerced labor a means by which to understand convict labor practices.

II

One difficulty for current scholarship stems from the evident continuity between convict leasing and slavery. Certainly the control of black labor was a leading motivation behind every significant effort to establish and maintain convict leasing for fifty years. Just as plain is the similarity between the brutal hardships of convict life and the oppression of slavery times. Finally, the racial character of convict leasing reinforced connections with the slavery regime. George B. Tindall's observation about South Carolina applies to all Southern states in the Gilded Age: "From the beginning it was understood that the system of convict leasing was to be a method of utilizing Negro labor." Only in Texas were black prisoners a minority of the population, and in that state the proportion of blacks in the population as a whole steadily declined during the leasing decades, until it was only 20 percent in 1900—in spite of the black population's absolute growth of two and a half times its 1870 figure of 253,000.[20] In short, convict leasing was partially a response to the demise of slavery.

In light of the foregoing circumstances, it is not surprising that some modern commentators, like their nineteenth- century counterparts, also show some confusion about leasing. But it is important to establish a clear yet flexible theoretical structure in which to comprehend this awful practice. The convict lease system was not, for example, "a functional replacement for slavery." In fact, it is doubtful whether it was even a "system" at all during most of its existence. The presentation of a preliminary theoretical framework is one of the "ground-clearing" functions of the present chapter.

How does convict leasing compare to slavery as a social and economic institution? Orlando Patterson's magisterial synthesis of slave systems is notable in having comprehensively defined slavery; it consists, he contends, in "the permanent, violent domination of natally alienated and generally dishonored persons."[21] Such a conception might serve as a touchstone by which to evaluate other forms of unfree labor. Though forced labor in detention under contract was neither a permanent nor a natally alienating condition, distinctions between it and slavery do tend to fade somewhat upon close examination: as David Brion Davis observed, "if one has been working on a plantation or in a penal camp for most of one's life, it probably makes little difference whether one got there by the legal fiction of sale as a piece of property or as the result of some alleged civil or political crime that has almost faded from memory."[22]

A more conclusive difference arises when one considers the slaves' status as radically dishonored beings, a standing linked to their condition as outsiders. Before emancipation slaves might not have been a part of "society," but Reconstruction endowed the freedmen with the status of citizenship. Post-Reconstruction legislatures expressed their bewilderment and rage at this status by in effect criminalizing Negro behavior. Some illegal behavior patterns identified as specifically "black" were removed from misdemeanor status and reclassified as felonies. Charles L. Flynn Jr. has recently described with relentless thoroughness how Southern "society" was defined as an arena for white people, and blacks as "a racially defined laboring caste": "The equation of whiteness with membership in society was inseparable from the implicit equation of black labor with agricultural labor as a whole and of whiteness with capital. . . . *White* equaled property, equaled capital, equaled society. *Black* equaled poverty, equaled labor, equaled something somehow alien."[23] The social anomaly of citizens being outsiders helps to explain the penological anomaly of convict leasing. In the eyes of Southern whites, blacks' "outsider" status had passed unchanged through the revolutionary events of 1861–65. From the perspective of the nation as a whole, however, their status as quintessential outsiders had ended. Now, more than ever, their own sense of honor mattered. Prisoners, then, cannot be considered "generally dishonored persons"—least of all in the eyes of their own communities, where they often returned from their sentences with enhanced prestige. "The numerous negro convicts," a contemporary observer noted, "seem like heroes to other members of their own race."[24] In respect to Patterson's definition, then, this form of forced labor, however brutal, is something distinctly different from slavery.

But Patterson's concise, almost epigrammatic definition is lacking in specifically economic content. This is perfectly proper in view of the comprehensiveness of his intention. Vast numbers of slaves in world history performed no function whatsoever in respect to production. In the context relevant to our narrower concern, however, economics is of almost paramount importance. Economists tend to understand slavery in terms of exploitation; in neoclassical terms, slavery is that means by which the master captures the difference between the value of the slave's marginal product and what must be expended for the acquisition, subsistence, and reproduction of his workforce. In Karl Marx's formulation, it is the value of unpaid labor.[25] We may thankfully avoid delving into the merits and drawbacks of each of these definitions by noting simply that under convict leasing the rate of exploitation as measured by either model was greater than that under slavery. For those caught up in the web of labor agents, corrupt sheriffs, and businessmen desperate with the fear of a labor shortage, the convict lease was "worse" than slavery. This fact is easily demonstrated with recourse to the neoclassical model, which must be understood as an aggregate measure.

Slave exploitation has to be looked at in the aggregate because the slaveowners' maintenance costs must provide for the subsistence and reproduction of the *entire* slave community, including the aged, the infirm, and children; subsistence means more than simply the cost of maintaining the individual productive slave. Lessees of convicts, by contrast, were concerned in the main only with productive laborers. The sick were refused or, in cases where it was possible, remanded to jails. In January 1888, at the outset of the TCI lease in Alabama, the company declined anyone "who, though able to work, can do no more than enough to pay for their maintenance," as the exasperated convict inspector explained to the governor.[26] Later, in March 1893, the Sloss Iron and Steel Company, a division of TCI, refused to accept Melissa Stewart, who was nursing her infant, protesting that "they had hired no babies" and dispatching her to the Jefferson County jail.[27]

Hence, if the lessees' capital costs are put aside for a moment, it is evident that their outlay was less than that of slaveowners. Even though convict productivity was often valued by contemporaries at about two-thirds that of wage labor, the convict wage bill was often so incredibly low that it more than made up for the smaller surplus value convicts created. Finally, to this brief discussion of exploitation must be added the simple observation that lessees often expended less than what was needed for subsistence in any case.[28]

A second economic consideration involves capital expenditure, and again the difference between slavery and the convict lease becomes clear when the two are juxtaposed. While each individual slave represented to his master a certain capital outlay, convicts in the main represented a capital expenditure only in the aggregate (here as elsewhere it must be borne in mind that practices varied widely from state to state and even within states). These differences can be represented graphically in a simple matrix:

Expenditures from the Perspective of Owners or Lessees

	Slaves	Convicts
As labor:	aggregated	individual
As capital:	individual	aggregated

The individual convict as such did not represent a significant investment, and his death or release, therefore, not a loss. When considered as a source of labor, then, slaves received a "wage" best thought of as aggregated, convicts one that was individual; as a form of capital, by contrast, slaves were individually significant, convicts collectively so. This does turn out to be a relevant distinction rather than a metaphysical exercise, for the consequence was an economic incentive to abuse prisoners. These two economic factors—the subsistence or lower-than-subsistence "wage" the convicts received and their status as aggregated capital—served to reinforce one another and to make leasing, from the point of view of the economic definition, "worse" than slavery.

Indeed, the high rate of exploitation was often seen as a potential benefit to the state by politicians who wished to abolish the lease. As James K. Vardaman, the nemesis of Mississippi's lessees, put it in 1906: "If the State can make money working a private individual's land and giving that private individual half of the products of the convicts' toil [on shares], I cannot understand why it cannot make more money working its own land and keeping the entire products of the convicts' toil."[29]

23

The fact that the lessee's capital cost was fixed while the number of convicts was variable meant that convict labor was a perfect commodity for speculation. This, too, differentiates convict labor from slave labor, since slaves were usually purchased for use rather than speculation.[30] As the pioneer black historian George Washington Williams wrote of Southern prison labor, "Just as great railway, oil and telegraph companies in the North have been capable of controlling legislation, so the corporations at the South which take the prisoners of the state off of the hands of the government, and then speculate upon the labor of the prisoners, are able to control both court and jury."[31] When the number of convicts rose from twelve hundred to seventeen hundred in Georgia between 1879 and 1890, the per capita rate of hire fell from $20.00 to $14.50.

Convict leasing, then, was sometimes a form of commodity speculation, and several leasing companies were "organized to speculate in convict-labor futures."[32] Indeed, the only loss on such an investment in "fixed capital" would occur as a result of, in the words of Louisiana governor S. D. McEnery in 1886, "supporting them in idleness at periods of the year when they could not be employed in such work."[33] And in fact it was just such a condition which contributed to the demise of convict leasing in the first decade of the present century.

It is imperative, then, to be rid of the sloppy and imprecise notion that convict leasing was some form of slavery or even a "functional replacement" for it, whatever such a formula might mean. For, in some sense, of course, all kinds of coerced labor are substitutes or replacements for slavery, as slavery is for them. There is a subset within a larger category, labor, that comprises varieties of forced labor. That slavery and convict leasing are two components of the subset does not make them functional equivalents.

It is also important to maintain the distinction between leasing and the other means of racial and economic domination that were endemic to the postbellum South. It does make some sense to interpret the South's economic and social arrangements as an interconnected "system" and the masses of the South's poor population, and particularly its poor blacks, as entangled in an oppressive matrix of law, custom, and politics whose operations they could neither understand nor control. But such a blending of separate practices obscures the fabric of daily life as it was experienced by those caught up in that "system."

For example, Christopher R. Adamson, who calls leasing a "functional replacement for slavery," also conflates sharecropping, the Black Codes, and convict leasing, because, he argues, they shared a common objective, namely the denial of wage-earning status to the former slaves. Yet a number of historians have convincingly shown that planters would have liked nothing better than to have seen the freedmen working for wages, and that most of the opposition to such an arrangement came from the freedmen themselves, who staunchly resisted any attempt to "turn them into a working class."[34]

James L. Roark comes much closer to the mark when he writes of planters in the postbellum period: "The dominant theme in [their] lives became the search for a substitute for slavery." For a "substitute" is, or can be, a far cry from a "functional replacement." Slavery was much too complex and ramified an institution to be easily reproduced. Still more to the point, in terms of understanding labor history, is Roark's judgment as to why this search became central. "Emancipation," he writes, "confronted planters with a problem their deepest convictions told them was impossible to resolve—the management of staple- producing plantations employing free black labor."[35] Among the multifarious debilitating legacies of slavery was the conviction that blacks could only labor in a certain way—the way experience had shown them to have labored in the past: in gangs, subjected to constant supervision, and under the discipline of the lash. Since these were the requisites of slavery, and since slaves were blacks, Southern whites almost universally concluded that blacks could not work unless subjected to such intense surveillance and discipline.

What emerged over the decade after Appomattox was something new, though something neither modern nor traditional—a "peculiarly southern free-labor system," Harold D. Woodman called it. Pete Daniel similarly refers to a "metamorphosis of slavery" that emerged "in the middle ground between slavery and freedom."[36] Convict leasing was not slavery, then, and yet it was unlike other forms of prison labor, before or since. It took root in a society just emerging from the violent overthrow of its slave system, a society that both resented and depended upon the more economically and technologically advanced region that had defeated it.

To raise the question of the status of convicts under the law is to be reminded of the frequent disparity between empirical fact and legal theory. For it would appear that the actual conditions convicts faced were often the worst in the states whose courts exhibited the greatest solicitude for their welfare. And conversely (although this is far from being a rule), their treatment was somewhat less inhumane in states that had the harshest judges. Two pertinent examples of this disparity come from Virginia, which barely dipped its toe in the floodwaters of leasing, and Georgia, where leasing reached a level of development almost unmatched elsewhere in the region. Virginia's courts viewed convicts with pronounced harshness, while Georgia's showed considerable concern for their rights.

Woody Ruffin was working on the Chesapeake and Ohio Railroad in Bath County, Virginia, in July of 1870 when he made a break for his freedom. Ruffin killed Louis Swats, whom the railroad had employed as a guard, in his escape attempt. Tried and convicted by a Richmond jury, and sentenced to hang, Ruffin thought he found a loophole in the state's constitutional guarantee of a felony trial "by an impartial jury of his vicinage [local community]": he should have been tried in Bath County, Ruffin contended. Judge Christian of the Virginia Court of Appeals was not sympathetic to the argument and dismissed Ruffin's appeal. But in doing so he went beyond the immediate issue to express a broader judgment concerning the relation of prisoners to the law. It is a judgment that echoes classical defenses of slavery. "The law in its humanity punishes [the convicted felon] by confinement in the penitentiary instead of with death," he affirmed. "He has . . . not only forfeited his liberty, but all his personal rights except those which the law in its humanity accords to him. . . . He is *civiliter mortuus* [i. e., in a condition of civil death]; and his estate, if he has any, is administered like that of a dead man." The state's bill of rights, he went on, applies only to a society of freemen, and not to felons. "Such men have some rights it is true, such as the law in its benignity accords to them, but not the rights of freemen. They are the slaves of the State."[37]

The doctrine that prisoners are state slaves would seem at first to accord well with the notion that convict leasing was a form of slavery. But this idea is not consistent with the evidence—or indeed with itself: for if convicts were slaves, then such would be their condition irrespective of the mode of their labor; any form of prison labor, not just leasing, would be slavery. But, more to the point, the severe ruling of Judge Christian is anomalous. Nothing like it appears elsewhere in the volumes of Southern decisions for half a century after it was issued. On the other hand, Southern judges did make several rulings that contradict *Ruffin*.

One of the most antithetical of such rulings stemmed from a tragedy in Georgia. Cleveland Westbrook, a murderer, killed a convict who was chained to him and eight or ten others on the same "squad chain" in Tift County. Westbrook was a troublemaker who, when found with a knife, was confronted by the warden, J. M. Davis. Davis declared he was going to have to punish him. "No, sir, you won't," retorted Westbrook. Davis replied, "I reckon I will; you are not running this business." "I know that, but you aint going to whip me," Westbrook warned. The warden's testimony continues:

> The boys [on the squad chain] began to get scared and pulled away, and this chain tightened up on Cleveland, and Cleveland starts to stick the knife in the boy next to him. He started, and I raised the strap; I said "Stop, I will hit you—don't cut that boy." Then he held the knife back in shape to stab at me. They kept tightening the chain, and he started at him again, and I struck him in the face to stop him. He turned at me and was cutting at me, and I kept striking him in the face to stop him. He couldn't get to me, the chain stopped him. The boys got scared and kept tightening the chain. He just wheeled and took into the crowd and the first boy he came to was this James Davis. He struck him in the breast the first lick, and he was still trying to get to me. When he stabbed him the first time he fell, and he turned back [to] give two or three more licks at me. In that time this boy was on his all-fours, and he just stabbed him in the back.[38]

Cleveland Westbrook was as dangerous and vicious an individual as Woody Ruffin had been, and he, too, was sentenced to die for first-degree murder. But Justice Atkinson of the state's supreme court ordered the case returned for a retrial. His reasoning was that the warden's administration of corporal punishment amounted to an assault; it was more than was strictly necessary to maintain good order, and as such was illegal. But then Atkinson went further—only in a direction opposite to the one that Christian had taken. "A convict stands upon a different footing from a slave," he wrote. "He is not mere property without any civil rights, but has all the rights of an ordinary citizen which are not expressly or by necessary implication taken from him by law. While the law does take his liberty, and imposes a duty of servitude and observance of discipline for the regulation of convicts, it does not deny his right to personal security against unlawful invasion." Consequently the jury should have been instructed that Westbrook could have the charge against him reduced from first-degree murder to manslaughter.[39]

The key difference between *Ruffin* and *Westbrook* was that, whereas the former averred that prisoners were deprived of all rights whatsoever except those which the legislature might decide to bestow by positive statute, the latter asserted that they retained all rights of citizenship except those which the legislature might choose to revoke by law. Without question, the trend of Southern courts ran in the direction of *Westbrook* rather than *Ruffin* during the late nineteenth and early twentieth centuries. "One under sentence of imprisonment for life is not civilly dead," ruled the supreme courts of both Texas and Florida in identical words.[40] Only Alabama accorded the status of civil death to lifers, and that was by positive legislation.[41]

III

It is helpful to journey outside the United States in search of forced labor systems with which to contrast convict leasing. The convict system of nineteenth-century Australia offers one useful example. Recent studies by Australian historians have forced a radical rethinking about convictism in Australia—in ways that might provide a fruitful source of comparative analysis for persons interested in convict forced labor in other areas of the world. A new picture is now emerging of Australian convicts and of the treatment they encountered after their transportation.[42]

A sentence of transportation to Australia must have been a shock of scarcely imaginable dimensions. Prisoners sentenced, for example, in Scotland were herded onto prison vessels in Perth in lots of about twenty. They then sailed to the Thames where they waited some months more for the ship to fill up. They then set off on the three- or four-month voyage. Upon arrival in Australia, the convicts would until 1840 be "assigned," that is, handed over either to free settlers or to the government for gang labor. It could be a gamble for the private master; as Robert Hughes writes, "The average 'dungaree settler' was likely to end up with an unskilled, resentful cuckoo of a convict who had been born and raised in a city and could not tell a hoe from a shovel."[43] Those assigned to the government worked most often on road construction. The system thus bore resemblances to the slightly later practice of leasing convicts in the American South and its successor, the state-run chain gang.

The portrait of these convicts that is now emerging constitutes a distinct revision of the former supposition that they were denizens of a Dickensian underworld. Stephen Nicholas has recently argued that

Australian convicts were not habitual criminals; they possessed considerable work skills, and they arrived in a healthy physical condition that they were able to maintain as convicts. Likewise, the Scottish historian Ian Donnachie examined a cohort of 112 men sentenced from Scotland in 1828 and 1829 who disembarked in New South Wales in 1830. He found that one-third were twenty or younger, and 48 percent were in their twenties. Ninety-five percent were literate, and 69 percent could both read and write. They came, he found, from the ranks of Scotland's "labouring poor"; only 10 percent were agricultural laborers. Only half had prior convictions, and two-thirds were sentenced for theft.[44] In a comparable study for England, Nicholas and Peter R. Shergold found that "transported convicts were broadly representative . . . of the non-criminal working class."[45] The contrasts with a state such as Georgia are illuminating. In 1897 some one-fifth of Georgia's convicts had life sentences; it was the single most frequent sentence handed out and was twice the Australian rate. Forty-seven percent were under twenty-one years of age, over half were completely illiterate, and 1,848 of 2,235 were listed as laborers or farmers.[46]

As important to the newly emerging portrait as the class and skills background of the convicts while they were in Britain is the new evidence about their treatment as workers after their arrival in Australia. L. L. Robson concluded in 1965 that Australian convicts assigned to a settler were not subject to constant supervision, and especially after 1840 the lash was but infrequently employed. "Incentives and rewards were an integral part of the extraction of work from public labour," Nicholas contends, "and there is little evidence of a society terrorized by corporal punishment." In sum, "the convicts received good treatment, nutritious food, decent housing, adequate medical services and reasonable hours of work relative both to other forced and free workers."[47] Among Southern leased convicts, of course, the whip was a constant presence. Statistical evidence is hard to come by, and that which is available is not trustworthy. For example, the so-called "whipping reports" that Georgia camp bosses had to submit can be shown to have been false in other respects, so their whipping figures are surely dubious as well. But the overwhelming impressionistic and circumstantial evidence shows flogging to have been frequent. As an Alabama committee reported in 1889: "Records show an immense amount of whipping is done."[48]

It seems that a key variable for overseers in forced labor systems in determining the "right," that is the most productive, mix of rewards and punishments is the relative degree of care and attention demanded by the task at hand. Care-intensive—and especially skilled—in contrast to labor-intensive work was perceived to be somewhat more effectively motivated by rewards; while effort–intensive work, like that performed by Southern convicts everywhere, relied more heavily on physical pain and the threat of pain. While a combination of rewards and punishments was employed on Australian assigned servants, many of whom were skilled or semiskilled,[49] the types of work as well as the perceived appropriateness of the lash for a population of over 85 percent black convicts led to "the immense amount of whipping" in the American South.

Still, the whipping, as the Alabama committee noted, was mostly "for failure to get task"—and the task system itself was a modified form of incentive system. Convict miners were expected to produce an output somewhere between two-thirds and three-fourths of that of an experienced free miner. "Making task" gave the convict miner a sliver of time and space to call his own.

A second, related contrast between the Australian and the Southern convict forced labor experience concerns wages: what it cost a contractor to command the labor of another. In 1792 Australia's first governor, Arthur Philip, established the practical rule that prisoners could not be expected to labor after 3:00 in the afternoon—ten hours after they had been mustered from their bunks. Subsequently, assigned convicts could be found hiking along rural roads and town lanes on their way to after-hours jobs. Soon, however, masters found themselves bidding with their neighbors for the after-hours labor of their own assigned servants. In 1800 the governor directed that masters would have the first call on the afternoons of their servants, who were to receive an annual wage of ten pounds. Since most convicts who had received seven-year sentences were eligible for tickets-of-leave after four years—an arrangement whereby they had control of their own time but were subject to supervision—they could enjoy two concrete incentives: the prospect of commanding their own time and cash money with which to begin their lives in freedom.

For Southern convicts, of course, it was a far more dismal story. Because of the structure of the contracts binding the prisoners to the lessees, lessees in many cases actually had an economic incentive to abuse their prisoners. The rate of exploitation, defined as the difference between the value of the convict's marginal product and the lessee's contract, monitoring and maintenance costs, was enormous in all states (although the gap narrowed rapidly in the 1890s as leasing lost its shield against market forces). In Georgia in 1882, with a prison population of 1,243 and an annual contract price of $25,000, the per capita per work-day cost of convict labor was six and a half cents. Over time, the per capita figure declined still further as the population soared and the cost of the lease contract remained fixed, so that in 1896 the total per-convict cost, including capital as well as maintenance expenditures, was about six cents a day.[50] What is more, Southern convicts were replaceable. New prisoners were constantly arriving to answer the insatiable demand for such labor.

This difference points to one of the most salient contrasts between the two systems. The Southern convict labor supply was much more elastic than Australia's. In the South, convicts could be much more eas-ily replaced if they were released, were pardoned, or died, while Australia's assigned convict population was fairly inelastic, dependent as it was on prosecutions far from the scene of needed labor and then on the long, slow voyages from Britain. As late as 1831 there were only 13,400 assigned convicts in all of Australia. But Southern convict popu-lations grew steadily. In 1869, for instance, the Louisiana legislature ap-propriated funds for two hundred looms for use in the prison. Although some 550 hands were needed to run them, there were only 350 on hand. But the next year's penitentiary report showed a population of 574 male convicts. North Carolina's convict population was 121 in 1870 and 1,302 in 1890. Florida, with 125 prisoners in 1881, had 1,071 by 1904. Between 1871 and 1879 Mississippi's population quadrupled, from 234 to 997. Alabama's records show 374 convicts in 1869 and 1,878 in 1903.[51] No comparable responsiveness to labor demand can be found in Australia.

Here can be seen the nub of the larger problem of the allocation of this scarce labor resource. In Australia, Nicholas explains, "landowners did not have private property rights in convicts; ownership rights over convicts were vested in the government." Hughes elaborates: "This put the assigned servant in an odd relationship to his or her master. . . . The government strictly monitored a master's treatment of his assigned ser-vants because each master was its agent in the scheme of punishment. The assignment system was not just a way of using the labor of people whose crimes had already been expiated by transportation. Assigned labor was their punishment."[52] Masters, of course, were often slow to grasp this fine point of the law and resented having to drag their ser-vants in front of a magistrate before subjecting them to a punishment that would, according to the reasoning of the masters, be more effec-tively meted out on the spot.

31

Little of such solicitude characterized the history of convict leasing. Although some states maintained the fiction of state control, others simply turned the convict population over to lessees lock, stock, and barrel, with an admonition to treat the convicts humanely. An example of the first kind of arrangement appeared in Mississippi. In December of 1888 the state took formal responsibility for guarding the prisoners, and consequently claimed not to be a state where leasing was practiced. Alabama too watched over its convict miners by establishing the task—which was in reality lower than that of free miners. It was because of such evasions that the U.S. Department of Labor placed only five states in the "leasing" category in its 1895 survey "Convict Labor." Clearly, however, the Southern leasing states in practice showed no sense that lessees and convict camp bosses were their agents. The U.S. commissioner of labor Carroll D. Wright expressed the situation accurately in 1887: "The great advantage of the [lease] system lies in the fact that the state has no care beyond the receipt of the amount stated in the lease."[53]

In the last analysis, this complete abdication of the state's authority may contain the seeds of the other differences between the two systems. When twenty-seven-year-old Woodrow Wilson wrote a cogent piece on leasing for the *New York Evening Post* in 1883, he contended that the chief objection to the practice lay not just in its brutality but in its surrender of public duty to private profit. "Who can justify a policy which delegates sovereign capacities to private individuals?" he asked. "Who can defend a system which makes the punishment of criminals . . . a source of private gain?" In retrospect, there was something inevitable about both convict leasing and Australian convictism—for, as Alexis de Tocqueville wrote toward the end of his life, "political societies are not what their laws make them but what they are prepared in advance to be by the feelings, the beliefs, the ideas, the habits of heart and mind of the men who compose them."[54]

IV

A third comparison might be of assistance in understanding convict leasing—a comparison much favored by contemporaries. In the late nineteenth century, Southern prisons were frequently compared to Siberia—not Siberia the place, but Siberia the institution, the desolate wasteland used by the czars for the punishment and physical removal of Russia's criminals. One significant example of this conventional metaphor was the sensational, not to say salacious, memoir of J. C. Powell, the Florida camp boss, who wrote *The American Siberia* in 1891, immediately upon retirement from fourteen years of gruesome service. The image of Siberia as a forlorn expanse where undesirables were sent to political exile is familiar to most Americans in the post–Cold War period. But knowledge of Siberia also had a currency, almost a cachet, in the United States a century ago. This awareness owed much to the popularity of the famous travel books of George Kennan, the great uncle of George F. Kennan, the renowned Soviet scholar and ambassador to Moscow. In two books, *Tent Life in Siberia* (1878) and especially *Siberia and the Exile System* (1891), Kennan disclosed to an avid reading public the exotic horrors of a land he knew better than any Westerner. The chapters comprising *Siberia and the Exile System* appeared serially in *Century Magazine* in 1888 and 1889. "Its effect," writes George F. Kennan, "was fortified by the lectures which Kennan, a forceful speaker, delivered in many parts of the country. The impression created by all this on the educated public of that day was profound. Few of its members remained ignorant of Kennan's experiences or unmoved by his tales."[55]

Thus, parallels with Siberia needed little explanation to the educated American public at the time. Nevertheless, in the preface to Powell's book his publishers did make the analogy explicit. "The countless thousands who have read George Kennan's sketches of exile life in Siberia with awe and interest will be surprised and shocked to learn that the terrible cruelties he there depicts have their counterpart in the convict-lease system of one of our Southern States," they somberly explained. "Were it not for climatic and race conditions the reader could easily fancy that 'The American Siberia' is taken from Mr. Kennan's writings so far as working, feeding, sleeping, guarding, and punishing the prisoners are concerned." Powell referred to Kennan in such a way as to reinforce the resemblances: "I will beg the reader's indulgence at this point to call attention to a parallel. . . . In Mr. George Kennan's celebrated papers upon the Russian exile system, he fully describes the 'Kameras,' or cell-houses, in use in Siberia, and his articles are accompanied by numerous illustrations. I will venture the assertion that if any Floridian convict was shown these pictures without the accompanying text he would be prepared to swear that they were ruins of the camp in this state."[56]

While Powell's account of the Florida camps has a concreteness and authority that impart an undeniable validity to much of what he has to say, the circumstances of his book's publication should serve to warn readers to approach it critically. It was published in the same year as Kennan's volume, which was eagerly awaited by the reading public after its serial publication in *Century*. In both content and form it imitates Kennan's work, including in the placement, size, structure, and content of its curious and exotic illustrations. Although his work has considerable intrinsic literary interest, its use as historical evidence might best be limited to instances that can be corroborated by other data.[57]

In 1891, while both Powell's and Kennan's books were in press, Anton Pavlovich Chekhov was struggling in Moscow with the composition of a different kind of prison/travel volume—one based upon his arduous and perilous journey the previous year to a place that was remote even by Siberian standards, a place that was a kind of ultima Thule of Siberia itself: Sakhalin. His volume about the island and his journey is one of the world's classics of prison literature.

Sakhalin Island, in the northwest Pacific off the eastern shore of Siberia, was czarist Russia's most desolate and remote prison, the place where convicts were sent for very long sentences of hard labor. It came to symbolize for Chekhov, and, through him, for his readers, all that was cruel, stupid, and pointlessly despotic. Peculiar as it may at first appear, the observations of Chekhov about this far-off island cage are as relevant to the realities of the convict lease as any comparative penal practice of his or our own time.

Chekhov's was both a physical and spiritual journey to the remotest corners of human habitation and most obscure of Russian institutions. It took him nearly three months to reach the outpost of Alexandrovsk, a journey that was itself Kennanesque in dimension. On the last leg, crossing the Tatar Strait from the Siberian port of Nikolayevsk, Chekhov relates: "The captain . . . does not believe the official maps and follows his own map, which he draws and corrects each trip." The chartless captain could symbolize the entire convict system.

Chekhov found that system to be astonishingly crude and unproductive, and the practice of hiring out prisoners to the island's settlers to lack penal, economic, and moral justification. In Sakhalin he entered a sealed-off world where even time was conceived in terms of that world's own peculiar rhythms rather than by seasons or as a progressive, diachronic sequence: "'When did you come to Sakhalin?' I asked a settler [a freed convict]. 'I came in the same group with Gladky,' he answers uncertainly, looking at his friends. . . . Or they say, 'I came in the year when they killed Derbin,' or 'Mitsul died that year.'"

The entire island was both product and producer of convict labor: "Convict labor on Sakhalin is extremely varied. The labor is not specialized; it does not depend on coal- or gold-mining, but encompasses the entire range of Sakhalin life and is spread throughout the populated areas of the island. Digging out stumps in the forest, building houses, draining swamps, fishing, mowing, loading and unloading cargo on ships are all types of convict labor which have necessarily merged with the life of the colony to such a degree that they cannot be isolated." The same could be said, mutatis mutandis, of the South—as Captain Powell and his shrewd publishers surely recognized when they read the popular works of Kennan.

In a work that is almost completely given over to sober observation, and in a style that is at once detached and appalled, Chekhov made but few general observations, but among them is this judgment on the convict system: "When life arises and flows along artificial channels rather than normal ones, and when its growth depends not so much on natural and economic conditions as on the theory and the arbitrary behavior of individuals, then it is forced to accept these circumstances as essential and inevitable, and these circumstances acting on an artificial life assume the aspects of laws."[58]

Yet another type of forced labor—besides slavery, Australian convictism, and the Siberian exile system—that could be useful in forming a comparative analytical framework for understanding this form of primitive accumulation would be the condition of helotage in classical antiquity. The helots of ancient Sparta were an oppressed community of state laborers whose status, while close to that of slaves, nevertheless was different from slaves' in a number of important ways. As Orlando Patterson points out, they retained "rights of birth, however attenuated, including custodial claims in their parents and children. Their status as Greeks was never lost; it was only politically suspended."[59] The great classicist M. I. Finley, in assessing the place of slavery in ancient Greek civilization, noted slavery's close connection with "progress"—a theme that David Brion Davis would later explore with great range and subtlety in *Slavery and Human Progress*. Slavery, Finley noted, was decisive for economically and politically more advanced societies; helotage appeared in the more archaic. Slavery, therefore, was found in Athens, helotage in Sparta. Slavery was the more "flexible" of the two forms of coerced labor, he pointed out, and thus helotage was more suitable for "agriculture, pasturage, and household service." This penetrating observation is directly relevant to the present study, for convict leasing can be thought of as a kind of helotage, a regression, in fact, from slavery—so long as the terms *progress* and *regression* are shorn of normative content. In other words, slavery is a system the moral repulsiveness of which can be disentangled from both its economic function and its relation to political complexity. Until the end of the eighteenth century, as Davis has shown, slavery was always linked intimately with societies at the forefront of history's forward motion—with classical Greece and imperial Rome, the great maritime powers of the Age of Discovery, the empire builders of the seventeenth and eighteenth centuries, the dynamic United States in the nineteenth century.[60]

After the Civil War, when states turned to convict leasing, it was a retrograde step in a specific sense. With slavery shattered and the former slaveholders uncompensated for the dissolution of their "property," the South, insofar as it adopted convict leasing, moved in a direction opposite not merely to that of the North's expanding industrial capitalism, but even to its own "progressive" prewar labor system.

Of course, slavery itself had been replete with precapitalist or prebourgeois elements. But even Robert William Fogel and Stanley L. Engerman, who make the strongest case for the capitalist nature of North American slaveholding, contend that it was prebourgeois in at least one significant way, namely that the state yielded a great deal of legal authority to the planters, in contrast to Europe where the rise of capitalism was accompanied by a demand to centralize political authority in the state and weaken it in the manor.[61] Here is further evidence of the retrograde nature of convict leasing, for even scholars who argue as to the relative importance of bourgeois or capitalist elements in slavery will agree about its being anomalous within a capitalist regime insofar as it involved an abdication of elemental state authority to private control—which is precisely the definitive characteristic of convict leasing.

As is so often the case, Chekhov went to the heart of the matter, identifying this abdication of state authority as a form of feudalism. "Permitting convicts to be used as servants by private persons is in complete contradiction with evaluating punishment," he surmised. *"This is not penal servitude, it is serfdom*, since the convict does not serve the government but is in the employ of a private individual who has no connection whatsoever with corrective measures or with the concept of proportionality of punishment."[62] Convict leasing is the prebourgeois form of coerced labor par excellence.

A few contemporary Southern observers grasped the quasi- feudal nature of leasing. To one Georgia reformer, Hooper Alexander, convict leasing was an atavism that harked back to the old tradition in English law to farm out government duties on contract. The practice went back to the days when "the very structure of the English government was a system of feudal franchises." Young Woodrow Wilson gave more than a hint of the direction of his future positions when he inquired, apropos of convict leasing, "Who can justify a policy which delegates sovereign capacities to private individuals?" Reformers and even prison officials struggling to articulate their dismay and indignation at the lease often resorted to the metaphor of medieval bondage and arbitrary, despotic power. More recent scholars, too, in casting about for comparisons, have resorted to the feudal analogy. Fletcher M. Green refers to two very different kinds of oppression in trying to explain what leasing was like. The system, he writes, "left a trail of dishonor and death that could find a parallel only in the persecutions of the Middle Ages or in the prison camps of Nazi Germany."[63]

The labor-camp analogy is a tempting one, because from all indications, convict life was closer to the experience of the concentration camps than was slavery. The phrases "relic of barbarism" and "form of slavery" are ubiquitous in the camp inspectors' and legislators' reports, as was the frustrated acknowledgment that people who have not witnessed cannot comprehend: "We found a system of cruelty and inhumanity practiced at this camp, that it would be hard to realize unless it could be seen and heard direct."[64]

The analogy, however, cannot be pressed. For one thing, many convict camps were virtual sieves. Perhaps the only statistic in excess of mortality rate would be escape rate. But more important, it remains as true as ever that, as M. I. Finley remarked almost forty years ago, "Nothing is more elusive than the psychology of the slave"—in spite of the wealth of evidence available to scholars, for which no parallel exists in the case of nineteenth-century convicts. Therefore, the consequences of leasing on the personality are even less understood than those of slavery or the Third Reich's labor camps of central Europe.

Of all the factors that distinguish convict leasing from slavery, however, none was more economically important than the fact that the lessee had only a minimal capital investment in any individual convict. This reality combined with a relative—to be sure, also variable—abundance of supply to produce a level of oppression that, taking convict leasing as a whole, can be said to have been "worse" than slavery during the period of the convict's sentence. The phrase *worse than slavery* may seem surprising, even shocking. But the word *slavery* itself is, as many scholars have argued, often used imprecisely to refer to a kind of absolute oppression. Thus, however appalling the material conditions of life may have been for British industrial workers in the mid nineteenth century, for example, they were seldom thought of by British or American abolitionists as the objects of ameliorative reform measures, for as "free" individuals they enjoyed critical liberties, most notably the liberty of contract. Yet as Orlando Patterson points out, "The distinctive feature of slavery is not the degree of oppression involved; were this the case, the British proletariat at the middle of the nineteenth century would have been as much slaves as the blacks of the U.S. South, not to mention the countless millions of the Asian rural poor."[65]

An awareness of the disposable nature of convicts' lives can be gleaned occasionally in comments by contemporaries of varying degrees of sophistication. A guard in Alabama's Red Diamond mine remembered being given orders to shoot to kill, since "a dead convict didn't cost nothin'." In 1879 South Carolina's prison superintendent T. J. Lipscomb reported 153 dead and 82 escaped in two years. Perhaps, he said, if the convicts were property, "then the contractors, having more interest in their lives and services, would look after them with greater zeal, and not leave them . . . to the ignorance, inattention, or inhumanity of irresponsible hirelings." Georgia's principal keeper noted in 1875 that "casualties would have been fewer if the colored convicts were property having a value to preserve. Then the proprietors would look after them." And a North Carolinian, with brutal simplicity, noted that convict conditions were so poor because "if [a convict] dies it is a small loss." Slave owners in the antebellum years also made distinctions among laborers that anticipated those of the leasing era. For example, Irish wage hands were sometimes used in ways that protected the capital investments of slaveholding whites. One slave owner explained how he hired Irish laborers for unhealthful work like clearing swamps—exactly the kind of work that would later be performed by prisoners. "A negro's life is too valuable to be risked at it," he pointed out. "If a negro dies, it's a considerable loss, you know."[66]

Two

LABOR

J ust as convict managers spoke routinely of "first-, second- , and third-class" hands, so also they used categories of labor discipline that derived from slavery times—categories like the "gang" and "task" systems. Other terms had arisen in the postwar years, like "squads." While the evidence is less abundant on the organization of labor than on the classification of convicts, it does appear that most leased convicts were worked by "task": that is, they were required to meet an output quota each day, whether of turpentine, coal, bricks, or cordwood. These quotas could be the source of terrible suffering.

Without question, the reintroduction of a system of gang labor reminiscent of slavery was the aim of planters in the immediate postbellum years. Gang labor was a highly interdependent, brutally efficient, and immensely productive way of organizing a labor force. The opinion of planters, and of Southern whites generally after the war, was that only under such a system could production with black labor take place. Under slavery, the most common method of organizing work routines was the gang system, under which "the field-hands were divided into gangs commanded by drivers who were to work them at a brisk pace," Kenneth Stampp explains. "The purpose of the gang system was to force every hand to continue his labor until all were discharged from the field in the evening."[1] Work gangs achieved their high efficiency levels by means of a cruel, assembly-line pace. Large plantations usually divided field laborers into two gangs, the hoe gangs and the plow gangs. The labor of each put pressure on the pace of the other, and it was in part from this interdependence that the high production levels of the slave era were achieved.[2]

The other major scheme of production under slavery involved the setting of specific "tasks." "Under the task system," Stampp explains, "each hand was given a specific daily work assignment. He could then set his own pace and quit when his task was completed. The driver's job was to inspect the work and to see that it was performed satisfactorily before the slave left the field." Stampp quotes a planter's succinct statement of the task system's advantage: "As . . . the task of each [slave] is separate, imperfect work can readily be traced to the neglectful worker."[3]

After slavery had ended, however, in the late 1860s and 1870s, a remarkable socioeconomic tug-of-war occurred in the South, one that has been portrayed with great cogency by Jonathan Wiener, Ralph Shlomowitz, Harold D. Woodman, Roger L. Ransom and Richard Sutch, and many others: it was the struggle between planters and freedmen over the terms and conditions of the freedmen's labor. The upshot of this prolonged struggle was the sharecrop system, a means by which the former slaves achieved a treasured amount of independence from supervision, as well as family-based work arrangements, while landowners traded off somewhat lower output levels for lower supervision costs.[4]

The conflict began immediately upon emancipation. Herbert S. Klein has summarized the collective behavior of newly freed slaves not only in the United States but throughout the Western Hemisphere: They "would work on the old plantations for their ex- masters only if they could not get access to their own lands or if they could find no alternative employment, urban or otherwise. If given no opportunities or land, they still refused to return to the old plantation working conditions. They demanded immediate withdrawal of their wives and daughters from field labor, an end to gang-labor arrangements, payment in money wages for all labor, and access to usufruct land for their own cultivations."[5] In response, as Wiener contends, white landlords had to abandon their dream of black gangs working under both the labor contract and the lash.[6]

Between the gang and the sharecrop, as Ralph Shlomowitz and Gerald David Jaynes have argued, there appeared a transitional mode of labor control, the "squad system." Planters often contracted with squads or teams of laborers, usually six to ten in number, for specific assignments. According to Jaynes, "the gang system on cotton plantations was an institution of the past by 1868."[7]

As the relations between laborers and landowners settled into a routine that, however oppressive, was one in which black laborers retained a measure of control over the conditions of their work, both the gang and the squad passed away from the contract-labor scene. But both would be reincarnated in the South's convict labor practices.

The evidence shows that what happened under convict leasing was a fusion of the most slavelike means of labor control, the gang and the task systems. However, there were many local variations on the theme, as well as different types of labor organization for different products of convict labor. On plantations the gang predominated, while in the mines convicts were worked by task. The hybrid quality of convict leasing emerges when one inspects the matter more closely, however, for gangs on the prison plantations of Texas and Mississippi had to meet a quota, while task-driven miners in Alabama and Tennessee worked in small gangs usually referred to by officials as "squads."

Two essential tasks await the person or institution that wishes to mobilize forced labor—whether it be a slaveholder, a lessee of prisoners, or a feudal lord mustering his serfs for the corvée. First, one has to get the labor force assembled in the right place at the time they are needed; and second, one must then simply get them to do the work. These two fundamental problems, of mobilization and of incentives, can be seen to have shaped the conditions under which leased Southern convicts worked in the late nineteenth century.[8]

The first order of business was accomplished not only by the machinery of criminal justice but also through corrupt networks of sheriffs and labor agents. The criminal justice apparatus was systematically geared for the collection of labor. While black Southerners certainly were responsible for a considerable measure of lawlessness and crime, it is also the case that the laws themselves were biased against what was perceived as "Negro" behavior, and that the enforcement even of ostensibly neutral statutes worked to incarcerate blacks in numbers far out of proportion to their numbers in the society at large. Southern states rewrote the criminal law and created such "Negro crimes" as incitement to insurrection and criminal trespass. In Georgia hunting and fishing were made seasonal, and in several other states what had been minor acts of theft were changed to felonies. As Atlanta sociologist Monroe Work wrote in 1906, "Laws as to vagrancy, disorder, contracts for work, chattel, mortgages, and crop liens are so drawn as to involve in the coils of the law ignorant, unfortunate, and careless Negroes and to lead to their degradation and undue punishment, when their real need is inspiration, knowledge, and opportunity."[9]

Furthermore, the same behavior that could be lauded when engaged in by whites could result in convict labor for blacks. What was initiative for a white man would be impudence for a black man. Arguing with or even questioning a white man could result in a criminal charge. And laws on such subjects as vagrancy, civil disorder, or liens were effectively means of entrapment. The judicial process contributed as well: in South Carolina in 1901, for example, 80 percent of blacks who were arrested were convicted, in contrast to 60 percent of whites. For every white arrested, 4.3 blacks were. That year 1 black for every 306 in the population was convicted and sent to prison, while the proportion for whites was 1 to 856.[10]

The second problem in forced labor, incentive, is more complex yet, for it concerns the enigmatic realm of human motivation. It is the task of establishing a means of getting work out of men and women whose labor is utterly disconnected from their own interests except insofar as adequate performance delivers them either from punishment or from the conditions of the forced labor itself. The problem of motivation under conditions of forced labor is usually considered in terms of rewards and punishments—in effect, of the relation between positive incentives and physical abuse. Furthermore, scholars are beginning to understand the relation between incentive and punishment systems, on the one hand, and the types of labor that persons are required to perform, on the other. Stefano Fenoaltea, using a simple transactions-cost model, has examined a variety of slave tasks and concludes that "slaves in care-intensive industries will tend to be motivated by rewards," whereas in cases where "the worker's productivity depends overwhelmingly on his brute effort and negligibly on his carefulness . . . a shift to a system that eliminates the supervisor and lets the worker retain his marginal product would *not* yield a reduction in total labor costs." In other words, where care and attention to the details of the work being performed are paramount, greater output can be expected with positive incentives rather than physical punishment. Where the worker's muscles are all that is of interest to the person who commands the labor, however, punishment will tend to predominate as a means of ensuring the continued stream of output. What gives Fenoaltea's model particular usefulness is his linking of effort-intensive and care-intensive kinds of work to specific inputs. "In general," he concludes, "land-intensive activities are effort-intensive rather than care-intensive." Thus, extractive industries like mining and farming (land- intensive activities) place a premium on brute effort, while capital intensivity characterizes those tasks for which attentiveness to detail is more productive.[11] The activities of leased convicts, of course, were almost entirely extractive, the prisoners working in coal and phosphate mines, turpentine farms, and cotton and sugar plantations.

Stephen Nicholas found this pattern confirmed in his examination of Australian convict labor. "Care-intensive workers were motivated largely by rewards; effort-intensive working by fear of pain," he contends. Australian convicts worked either in large gangs of chiefly unskilled workers or in smaller squads Nicholas calls "teams," consisting of convicts with some skills. He concludes that "pain incentives . . . were least effectively employed against skilled or team workers and most effectively to unskilled labour gangs."[12]

Another factor that conditions the nature of the reward-and-punishment structure is the relative scarcity or abundance of labor. "In the relatively labour-scarce Australia," Shlomowitz points out, "assigned convicts were given considerable autonomy as they mostly worked as shepherds . . . in the more labour-abundant postbellum United States South, leased convicts were treated much more harshly when they worked in gangs constructing railroads."[13] Shlomowitz's correct observation inadvertently highlights yet another way in which convicts were trapped. From the point of view of land- and capital-owning whites there was a labor shortage, and this fear helped greatly increase the incarceration rate. But on any single given convict-labor project there was an abundance of labor. Again it is clear that every incentive existed both to round up convicts and then to mistreat them once they were sent to the labor gangs.

Turning from the theoretical to the empirical, one can see how convict leasing kept alive some of the labor practices of slavery days, but often in new combinations. First, on some convict labor enterprises the gang system was actually combined with the task system. Second, a modified gang-task system, what might be called a squad-task system, was applied to several kinds of work, but especially mining. Third, in still other tasks, such as certain stages of brick making, jobs were set for individual convicts. Finally, some convict bosses worked men in squads but without tasks. But in almost all the examples available from contemporary documents, convicts are seen to be working to meet some sort of a quota, either in small squads of three to eight or in larger gangs.

"The following is generally the actual method of carrying out contracts based on a part of the crop," explained a Southern farmer in 1871. "The freedmen are divided into squads of four, six, eight, or ten, as the case may be, and a certain portion of land is assigned to each squad and planted in cotton, corn, potatoes, peas, etc., and the produce divided according to the special terms of the contract, when the crop is gathered."[14] This is an excellent depiction of the squad system, which, as the 1870s wore on, faded from the Southern free labor scene, to be replaced by sharecropping. But it was kept alive in the more coercive situation of convict labor. T. E. Durham, the sergeant at a Hill County, Texas, share farm, described the way labor was mobilized: "Have 148 convicts here now. Have sixteen regular guards. Have fourteen trusties. Have all classes of men, some first, some fifth, boys and men, good and bad. Cotton and corn is principal crop. Eight to ten men constitute a squad." With 16 men to guard 148 convicts, an average squad in Hill County comprised 9.25 men. Although one or two guards would have been left behind when the squads marched or trotted out to the fields in the Texas dawn, a trusty or two would also be assigned limited lookout duties, maintaining the eight-to-ten-man size of the plantation's squads. Ben A. Nabours, a guard at the Watts farm in Milam County, likewise spoke of an eight-man squad: "Get men out to work by daylight. Usually get them in by dark. Never trot men on turnrow. Men sometimes gives guards trouble. Sometimes men do not work as well as they ought to. . . . My squad of eight men are all able bodied men. Don't always have the same squad." Nabours's statement suggests that his men were not working on a task. Sometimes they did not do as much work as they were supposed to, but he does not specifically mention punishment for such shortages. Durham flatly disavowed the task: "Don't task the men," he claimed.[15]

Elsewhere, however, even on plantations, the task system was combined with the squad. An anonymous Arkansas prisoner writing around 1910 described a squad-system. Squad number one was expected to pick four hundred to five hundred pounds of cotton per day, squad number two, three hundred, and squad number three, two hundred pounds— the squads were based on the convicts' work classifications. They were whipped for not completing their tasks.[16]

From the beginning, Alabama's convict miners were also separated by strength and ability according to the old slave categories. In 1882 Warden John Bankhead reported the state receiving twelve dollars per month for first-class miners, eight dollars for second, and four dollars for third-class hands. There was no mention of squads. Tasks in Alabama were established by law in 1883. Later in Alabama's leasing history the tasks were divided by squad and ranged from ten to fourteen tons per squad.[17] This suggests small squads of from three to four miners, since the task as reported elsewhere in TCI mines was three to four tons per man. "The task assigned . . . at this mine [Coal Creek] is about four (4) tons of coal per day," reported a Tennessee House investigating committee in 1885. The task per first-class hand in Alabama was given in 1889 as four tons. In 1893, however, Superintendent J. W. Kirk testified that the average output at Tracy City was only about two and a half tons. Of course the "average" could well differ from the official task, and tasks themselves would vary with the quality of the seam, but the figures are in conformity with other data about mining tasks (and production figures at Tracy City would rise dramatically when convicts were given more positive incentives there).[18]

A combination of task and squad was used in the brickyards of Georgia. The onerous nature of brick making, and its combination of extracting and manufacturing, made it a peculiar hybrid. But by and large it was simply numbing, back-breaking labor that required little of workers besides muscle power. There were at least five different squads assigned to the various stages of brick manufacture.[19] The first stage apparently did not use a squad; it was the extraction of clay from clay pits adjacent to the brickyard itself. Digging the clay was pick, shovel, and wheelbarrow labor, like the mining of phosphate . Some thirty prisoners mined the clay and loaded it onto cars. Mules then hauled the cars into the brickyard. Next was a milling stage in which the clay was mixed with rock and forced into molds. Then the squad-task system came into play. A squad of six had the daily task of hand-carrying 140,000 bricks to the kiln for drying, and crews were whipped for not making task. According to one convict, the squad removing bricks from the drying belt was composed of female convicts.[20] Another squad, this one comprising six men, carried the newly dried bricks to ferociously hot kilns where they were deposited in clamps; from these clamps they were transferred to the oven itself by yet another squad of six. Lastly, a squad of boys loaded the finished product onto railroad cars for transport to the company's many customers in and out of the South. The number of squads of the same size—a size considered ideal by students of labor economics—make the brickyards a particularly clear example of convict labor management under leasing. No evidence exists for positive incentives in this land- and labor-intensive portion of the Southern economy.

Another locus of the task-squad system was the piney woods of Georgia, Alabama, and especially Florida, where men coaxed the sap

South Carolina prisoners mine phosphate, 1880s. Julian Ralph, "Charleston and the Carolinas," *Harper's New Monthly Magazine,* vol 90, issue 536 (January 1895), p. 223

from scarred pine trees. Turpentine work was as harsh as any of the arduous, lonely, and squalid forms of labor performed by Southern convicts. It was a kind of labor that had to be executed rapidly and with persistence. In winter, convicts cut V-shaped gashes about a foot wide on longleaf pines, then attached cups known as "boxes" below the incisions, into which the sap, aided by gutters, would flow come spring. Usually two prisoners would work together in slashing the trees, often trotting from tree to tree, and their task was about ninety trees each day. When the sap began to rise in March, and for nine months thereafter, during the fiery Florida summer and fall, turpentine workers went to every cut tree each week to chip the face of the tree in order to stimulate the flow of the sap. Every three weeks or so the worker would dip the gum from the cups with an implement called a "spoon" or "dipper" and pour it into a bucket, hauling the ponderous container from tree to tree. "Each branch of the work is done by different squads," relates Captain Powell, "and they are worked as nearly as possible in lines—'drifting,' it is called, and the word well expresses it—through the timber, some cutting, some chipping and some dipping. The guards follow at a little distance behind."[21]

When the bucket was filled the convicts would tote it to a mule-drawn cart loaded with thirty-nine-gallon wooden barrels, there to empty it before setting back out into the woods again. Besides being exhausting, parts of the process were dangerous as well, involving the skilled use of uniquely shaped, razor sharp implements called "hacks."

Although the task of the convict turpentine workers was grueling and hard to attain, it was less than the output of the most skilled free laborers. Florida lessee E. B. Bailey testified in 1901 that free workers in turpentine (when they could be found) could make as much as two dollars a day by cutting boxes at 1.5 cents per tree. These figures compute to an average of 133 trees, or 43 trees more than the convict task—nearly half again as many. This testimony reinforces yet again the point that the most important feature of convict labor was not its productivity but its reliability. "The value of the convict labor was that you could have regular work all the time while there were times you could not depend upon free labor," Bailey declared. Sugar plantation managers agreed. Convicts were essential to the success of the Texas sugar business, claimed Calvin Blakely, manager of the Harlem Farm, "because of the uncertainty of free labor." And, as Joseph E. Brown, then a senator, said in Congress about leasing in 1883: "No matter what goes wrong you have no labor strike."[22]

Perhaps equal to turpentine work in the physical and mental demands it made on convict workers was chopping wood. The wood- cutting camps of Texas, usually run by railroad companies, were singled out more than once as the site of the toughest work convicts had to perform.[23] Woodcutters worked in squads, first to chop the tree down and then, standing shoulder to shoulder, to hack the felled log into cordwood size. Woodcutters had tasks, too, and although they were described on a per-man basis, the likelihood is that they were actually handed out per squad. In 1879 Assistant Supervisor D. M. Short described a task of one and one-quarter cords of wood per day "for the best choppers"—testimony confirmed by convicts.[24] The figure of one and a quarter cords per man suggests that the actual task was five cords per four-man squad. One and a quarter cords is a stack four by four by ten feet. For four men to cut and chop a pile of wood four by four by forty in a single day, day in and day out in the Texas heat and humidity, was a numbingly arduous demand.

Because of the relative abundance of labor in any given project worked by leased convicts, the mix of punishment and incentive that lessees resorted to was seldom in any sort of balance. The stress always was on physical punishment. Over time, however, there did occur a shift toward time and money incentives as well as punishment, as bosses had to learn yet again what is seemingly the most easily forgotten principle of human behavior: that even under the most oppressive labor system, some measure of positive incentive can amplify the output.

The earlier years of leasing were characterized by a drive for economy and coercion at all costs. In 1882 Alabama's Bankhead said of the prison stockades in his state: they are "built, in most cases, with a view to the strictest economy"; while Georgia's convicts before the twenty-year lease were, in the words of the principal keeper, "managed by hirelings, selected generally for the ability to drive with severity, rather than to hold securely."[25] In Tennessee an 1885 House minority report said, "convicts are whipped for various causes, the most common of which is for not getting their tasks done each day. Convicts are compelled to do the labor of an experienced miner the third week after they are sent to the mines." Even when their quotas were met, prisoners in Tennessee had to stay down in the mines until the whole workday had ended, so that they all came up in a body.[26]

But some modification of this unrelieved harshness began to take effect in later years. Starting in 1886, for example, Tennessee miners were allowed to leave the mines after making task. And by 1893 flogging was no longer the daily lot of the prisoner who could not meet his assignment. "The usual custom had been to whip a man when he fell behind and call that square," the warden explained, but after 1893 a man who fell short one day could make it up the next. Tennessee's convict managers knew how to respond to a sudden imbalance in factor endowments. In 1893, undoubtedly spurred by a need for productivity increases in light of the massive defection of free miners, the TCI also sweetened an apparently preexisting system of money incentives. Beginning April 20, convicts were paid eight cents per car for every car over their quota. The average output shot up from two and a half to four and three-fourths coal cars per convict (each car averaged one ton).[27]

The evidence suggests, however, that this monetary incentive was actually a reinstitution or even a modification of a practice that prevailed earlier in the Tennessee mines. As early as 1878 mining magnate James Bowron, after visiting Tracy City, noted in his diary: "Shook . . . invited me to see Tracy City mines. He had convicts working over 100 bush[els] per day. [He] gave them [a] bonus of five [cents] . . . [every] sixteen bush[els] . . . [of] extra work beyond their task." (Sixteen bushels filled approximately one car.) Shook himself testified in 1885 that he considered these incentives superior to flogging as a means of increasing production, and even claimed that convicts had earned $4,000 per year by exceeding their quotas.[28] The estimate sounds accurate: at a nickel per car and 320 workdays per year, miners in the aggregate were putting out some 250 cars a day over quota. Tennessee's penitentiary report for 1886 shows 313 convicts working at Tracy City;[29] allowing for individual variations in the strength, skill, and health of the miners, then, the average "first-class" hand could and apparently did mine about one ton per day over quota (sixteen bushels=one car=one ton). When this money incentive was increased in 1893, from five to eight cents per car, so also did output. In 1923 the elderly Bowron was still taking pains to point out the benefits of tasking prisoners. The task at Belle Ellen mine, by his account, was four tons a day after four months in the mines. "The task is easily performed and by 2 or 3 P. M. the men are finished and ready to come out. . . . If they prefer they may continue to cut and load coal for which they receive [the] *same payment as any free miner*."[30]

Alabama's convict miners also worked on Sundays, a practice specifically upheld by that state's Supreme Court in 1898. The Sunday work, for which squads of prisoners were paid the going rate that free miners received, deepened the ambiguities involved when forced labor was mixed with voluntary incentives. In 1926 the *New York World* reported that convict "check-runners" compelled fellow prisoners to work on Sundays and drove them with a severity comparable to that of the guards.[31]

In general, the performance of the South's convict coal miners provides confirmation of the Fenoaltea-Shlomowitz hypotheses about the relationships among the variables of brute- effort and skill required for the task, labor and capital intensivity, and relative labor scarcity in determining the mix of physical punishment and positive incentive under conditions of forced labor. Mining is an extractive industry that nevertheless requires the application of capital, and one that takes brute effort and yet attention to the task at hand. As labor became scarcer miners were offered greater positive incentives, and the threat and the reality of brutal physical discipline diminished somewhat.

Notable, too, is the use of monetary incentives on sugar plantations. Of course the demand for labor varies considerably in any agricultural setting, but this is particularly true in the case of sugar during the processing time, which in Texas started in December and lasted through the spring. Getting the harvested cane from field to mill and then rolling, boiling, and curing the cane took not only great quantities of labor but also high levels of skill and care. The sugar mill itself represented a large capital investment as well. As Sidney Mintz describes these circumstances, sugar making was a drama both of misery and of marvelous skill and danger:

> Boiling and "striking"—transferring the liquid, and arresting its boiling when it was ready—required great skill, and sugar boilers were artisans who worked under difficult conditions. The heat and noise were overpowering, there was considerable danger involved, and time was of the essence throughout, from the moment when the cane was perfect for cutting until the semicrystalline product was poured into molds to drain and be dried. During the harvest the mills operated unceasingly, and the labor requirements were horrendous.[32]

In the latter part of the nineteenth century technological improvements on the mill combined with the construction of railroad lines to increase greatly the demand for cane.[33] Plantations worked by convicts, therefore, would demand enormous labor inputs.

Georgia prisoners as early as 1870 were being paid in tobacco for Sunday work.[34] Texas penitentiary ledgers show convicts receiving extra pay for working nights and Sundays, especially during harvest and processing time. The rate was 50 cents per day and 50 cents per night. For "Work in Harlem Plantation during Sugar Rolling" in the 1889 season, for example, Dave Washington earned $16.50 for working twenty-six nights and seven days, while Steve White worked four nights for $2.00.[35] Although Harlem farm was a state-owned rather than a leased farm, the practice of paying for extra work was also customary on the lease and share farms. Given the size of the labor requirements, however, it may be questioned whether this extra work, like that of the Alabama coal miners, paid or not, was entirely voluntary. Certainly Fred Shackey, a convict at Dunovant Camp Number 2 in 1901, did not think so. "Last fall during the cane season I was forced to work all day each Sunday and every other day during heavy rains and regardless of weather conditions," he protested. "I was worked all day Christmas." The pay by 1901 had risen to 62.5 cents a day during cane season, but Shackey claimed he had yet to receive the money. Shackey's complaint about working in all sorts of conditions during the season was confirmed by a number of other prisoners: "In cane cutting season we work in all kinds of weather." "During cane cutting season last fall we had to work Sundays and through heavy rains." "I worked on Sunday during cane season and got 62 1/2 cents per day for such work. I worked on Christmas day and got nothing."[36]

For their part, states considered prisoners as assets and the loss of their "time" and "services" through escape to be an expense justifying compensation. This notion is most clearly expressed in the South Carolina Supreme Court's ruling in *Lipscomb* v. *Seegers* (1883), wherein it enforced a critical distinction between a fine and damages: "We cannot regard the fifty dollars per annum, stipulated to be paid for each convict allowed through negligence to escape, as a technical penalty to be recovered by suit on the statute, but we consider it rather compensation for the time of the convict thus lost to the State by his escape . . . compensation only for the services actually lost to it by the escape."[37]

Although evidence for monetary and other rewards for exceeding production quotas is clear, equally obvious is the sheer durability of harsh punishment, from the earliest to the last days of convict leasing—especially in states where leased convicts worked on tasks that required "brute effort." At the camp of the Georgia Midland Railroad on 19 August 1886, whipping boss C. C. Bingham ordered a young prisoner, Hardy Mobley, to drop his pants. Positioning Mobley across a barrel and ordering four convicts to hold him down, one at each hand and ankle, Bingham proceeded to whip him until streams of blood flowed down his legs. Occasionally Bingham would pause in his cruel business to soak his whip in water, then drag it in the sand. Bingham—silent, deeply tanned, with a weatherbeaten, furrowed face and deep-set eyes—was the "best convict man in the state," one of his defenders asserted when his penitentiary company was brought to trial for violation of the lease statutes. Such an opinion reflected the strong belief in the absolute necessity of the lash in Georgia penology. It would be impossible to have discipline in the camps or to get any work out of the convicts without it, T. J. Smith, Bingham's defender, testified. Besides, "if you whip in time, it is not necessary to whip them much."[38]

The durability of these practices, which formed part of the routine, almost ritual behavior of convict bosses throughout the South, can be seen in the tragic case of Abe Winn. In 1906, fully twenty years after the torture of Mobley, an alcoholic whipping boss at the Durham camp with the incongruous name of Captain Goode whipped sixteen-year-old Abe Winn to death. According to witnesses Winn received an astonishing sixty lashes. During the application of this gruesome flagellation, Goode would place the whip under his foot and drag it through the sand. A Tennessee boss, Dewitt Carter, son of the Tracy City warden, likewise spread prisoners prone on the ground and stood on their necks in order to deliver his licks.[39]

In another routine that became almost a ritual, prison investigators would ask abused prisoners to lift their shirts and show their backs. Daniel Longs of Georgia, fourteen years old, testified to being whipped "75 licks," sometimes twice a day for not "working good enough." For an investigating committee Daniel "pulled off shirt and exhibited his back showing numerous very large scars on it."[40] Texas examiners did the same. "The chairman and I both examined this negro, and he is terribly cut up and scarred"; "I saw at least twenty cuts on this man's person"; "I saw these scars"—these observations punctuate the testimony of prisoners in another shameful report.[41]In sum, while Southern convict labor practices in the leasing era varied considerably, they yet shared certain common features, among which were a task system and positive incentives, albeit alongside physical punishment.

One of the enduring refrains about postbellum Southern convict labor, among both nineteenth-century lessees and some twentieth-century scholars, was that it was a response to a labor shortage. Another was that it depressed wages in the region, as indeed it was intended to do. When C. Vann Woodward wrote, concerning the rebellion of free miners in the Tennessee coal fields against (among other practices, to be sure) the use of convicts in the mines, that "the Tennessee struggles involved more men and deeper issues than the contemporary Homestead strike," he presumably was referring to the miners' charge that the use of convicts deprived them of their livelihood, or at a minimum lowered the general wage rate to such a level as to drive them from the field.[42] How accurate are these beliefs? Did convict labor achieve a critical mass such that it depressed the wage levels of Southern free laborers? What effect did convict leasing have on the Southern labor market?

Certainly the lessees thought leasing had a major effect. The conservative *Birmingham Age-Herald* put the argument directly in 1889: "Employers of convicts pay so little for their labor that it makes it next to impossible for those who give work to free labor to compete with them in any line of business. As a result the price paid for labor is based upon the price paid convicts."[43] As indicated earlier, this was a nearly unanimous opinion. More recently, however, the amount of impact convict leasing had on the Southern labor market has been questioned. Gavin Wright, for example, argues that the numbers of leased convicts were never great enough to have a substantial impact on wage rates. Market forces were just too strong, he contends; this strength is clear in the fact that industrial wage differentials between blacks and whites were minimal in the South generally. It was not racism or other forms of oppression but the market that dictated wage levels. "More important than the policies or attitudes of individual employers," he argues, "was the effect of the market. So long as blacks and whites had relatively open access to the farm labor market, and so long as labor flowed freely between sectors, industrial wages for unskilled labor could not deviate widely from the farm wage. . . . in effect, the labor market accomplished the mill owners' goal: obtaining white labor at the black wage. In this way, industrialization and competitive profit-seeking firms were perfectly consistent with continued segregation by race." And elsewhere he amasses copious evidence to show that "even the most notoriously oppressive postbellum labor institution, the convict-lease system, operated primarily to preserve the competitive market rather than to obstruct market forces. [Convicts] were never more than a tiny fraction of the labor force, and even in mining, the primary functions of convict labor were to break up strikes and attempted labor organization. That is to say, convict lease was used to maintain the competitive labor market."[44]

In another, elegantly conceived and executed study, Jennifer Roback shows that even though convict leasing and the legislation that nurtured it were exploitative by any standard, its effect on blacks' economic position generally was insignificant. Her analysis leads her to deny the widely held proposition "that whites were so powerful economically that their private preferences could be translated through the market into segregation and discrimination against blacks."[45] Her position is not, of course, that whites did not segregate and discriminate against blacks, but that such actions did not come about by means of their manipulating market forces.

Thus there have been two prevailing views about the impact of convict leasing: the first, that it lowered wages for free workers and distorted the South's labor market; and the second, that no matter how objectionable convict leasing was in moral, social, or political terms, its economic effects on wages and markets was negligible.

Between these two is a third possible analysis, outlined by Edward L. Ayers. "The precise impact of convict labor in the South is impossible to measure," he sensibly observes. However, "convict labor took on an exaggerated importance in the South more because of its context than its mere size. . . . Because the region had so few industries, because those industries were concentrated in relatively small areas, because the products of those industries, especially coal, were so crucial to the growth of the Southern economy, and because Southern labor was relatively unorganized, convict labor could in fact disrupt the wage scale and working conditions of entire Southern industries."[46] Ayers's appraisal has the merit of directing attention away from the Southern economy in the aggregate and toward specific, strategic components of it.

For there were several kinds of industry that were simultaneously important for Southern economic development and for which it was difficult to find labor. The shortage that postbellum Southern planters and other employers complained of was a reflection of the fact that wages were not high enough to attract a sufficiency of workers to perform the tasks that were needed at the time they were called for; the wage, in turn, was a function of the market price of the commodity the workers were turning out—whether it be sugar, turpentine, cotton, or cordwood. The term *labor shortage*, then, can be a slippery one. Any activity—including turpentining, woodcutting, and brick making—will draw laborers, providing the wages are high enough. Turpentine work furnishes a good example of an industry Southern employers would consider suited to forced labor. As Captain Powell recounts: "In addition to the reasons that appeared upon the surface, there was another, and a potent one, for the employment of convict labor in the turpentine woods. The work is severe to a degree almost impossible to exaggerate, and it is very difficult to control a sufficient quantity of free labor to properly cultivate any great number of trees. The natives follow it more as a make-shift than a vocation, and are only too glad to abandon its hardships for any other character of work that comes to hand."[47] Such expressions of shortage were typical in other sectors of Southern industry, both extractive and infrastructure- building. It is not hard even today to imagine the difficulties confronting a contractor who wishes to mobilize labor to construct levees or railroad beds in the swamps of Alabama, Mississippi, or Louisiana, or cut sugar cane on the Brazos, or dig coal on the banks of the Arkansas. It was in part, at least, this unpleasant reality that was responsible for the fact that most of the South's pre–Civil War infrastructure—its railroads, canals, harbors, turnpikes, plank roads, and ferries—were built, dug, dredged, and worked by slaves. According to Robert Starobin's estimate, over twenty thousand slaves were owned by Southern railroads. One canal superintendent advocated using slave labor in 1854 in terms that would be repeated almost verbatim forty years later to promote the use of convicts: "1st because of the difficulty, trouble, and expense to the company of hiring [laborers] even at exorbitant rates . . . 2ndly because of the great savings to the company as an economical measure." (Forty years later, of course, the economies would be even greater, capital costs being much lower for convicts than for slaves.) In Tennessee, Arthur S. Colyar, later a leasing baron, first put slaves to work in the Sewanee Mines in 1861. Most antebellum railroad construction in that state had also been completed by slave labor.[48]

At war's end the anxiety about "shortages of labor" centered around the organization of labor. Seeking to fill the gap produced by blacks' refusal to submit to prewar patterns of control, some employers and planters resorted to the importation of immigrants. Like former masters throughout the Atlantic world, some in the American South tried Asian contract laborers. Chinese were working Louisiana's sugar plantations by 1870, while immigration agents scoured Italy and Iberia for workers. Early in the 1870s Thomas O'Conner's Tennessee railroad construction projects were in the uncertain hands of Chinese, Italian, and Irish, as well as black, laborers.[49]

One by one, however, these efforts to supplant the former slaves fell out of practice. Mostly the failure stemmed from the magnitude of the adjustment both sides were being asked to make. As one sugar planter wrote concerning the Chinese laborer in Louisiana, "He can't plow, he can't run a cultivator, he can't steer a mule, but otherwise, his performances are admirable!" Moreover, "there have been many *conspicuous successes* with free negroes, and *not a solitary one with any other.*"[50] Convict forced labor was ideally suited to this situation, where free men and women refused to conform to the old patterns of labor organization, and substitute schemes foundered on the myriad of difficulties they entailed.

Over time, however, as Wright and others have shown, and as was argued above, convict "wage" rates in most industries rose to a rough equilibrium with the cost of free labor. Even the disagreeable turpentine industry, which was jump-started by convict labor, was far from dependent on it. Captain Powell's analysis of the turpentine labor shortage was made just before that industry entered a decade of considerable expansion. The number of turpentine workers grew 174 percent in the 1890s, so that by 1900 some fifteen thousand men worked in the industry. Yet in Florida in 1903 only three hundred convicts labored in the turpentine camps. The impact of having convicts supply 2 percent of an industry's labor force would be minimal in any case, but in Florida by 1903 the sublessees of those three hundred convicts were paying about ninety cents a day for their labor, which was about two-thirds as productive as the best free workers' labor. The combined effect of these various components on wage rates was infinitesimal. In Alabama that same year the governor could report, "the contractors are now paying [the state] per ton practically what free miners are paid"; while eight years later Governor Comer spoke of the high convict wage rate as official policy: "It is the policy of the State to maintain the labor price commensurate with the earning capacity of other laborers."[51]

Alabama's contracting policy provides a sharp contrast to the situation in Georgia of the 1880s, for example, where under the enormous twenty-year lease convicts were available for a few dollars a month, or Florida in the 1890s, where contractors worked men in phosphate mines for $26.40 per year. Over time, these figures would change dramatically, however, as market pressures greatly increased the price of the lease contracts. Just how much the subleasing spiral both raised prices and made tracking the convicts a baffling task is evident in a 1906 Georgia case, *Hamby & Toomer* v. *Georgia Iron & Coal Company*. Hamby and Toomer leased Georgia's convicts in 1904, then sublet them to Dean Brothers, who sub-sublet them to Pritchett Turpentine, who in turn sub-sub-sublet them to the Georgia Iron and Coal Company. Then Hamby and Toomer wanted the convicts back! The state Supreme Court denied the original lessee's request, ruling that the sublessee's "right to the convicts becomes authorized by law" when the contract is transferred.[52]

Thus it would appear that one of the factors that made convict leasing viable was the political strength to overcome market forces, though this could be done only temporarily; a second was the use of convicts in tasks for which free labor was hard to come by. Indeed, where there *were* men wanting to do the work convicts performed, as in mining—that is, where there was an actual "labor market"—convict leasing either lost its grip, as in Tennessee, or gave the state enough leverage to raise the hire rate to roughly the free worker's level, as in Alabama.

The question remains, however, whether such an investment in forced labor, in cases where alternative sources of labor were available, was a profitable one. For—conceding one or two counterexamples—the available evidence shows the productivity levels of convict labor to have been considerably lower than those of free workers. Most contemporary statements on the question place convict output at somewhere between two-thirds and three-fourths that of free labor. The U.S. commissioner of labor, exhibiting, to be sure, a certain statistical legerdemain (he actually reported that it took 51,172.2 convicts to produce goods that required but 32,801.1 free laborers to make), estimated in 1905 that prison labor was three-fifths as efficient as free labor. The task of Alabama's convict miners was two-thirds that of free miners. That state's humane and reflective prison commissioner, R. H. Dawson, reckoned that former convict miners "do about twice as much work after they are free as they did when they were convicts."[53]

Noteworthy in this context is Anton Chekhov's estimate on the output of Siberian convict miners (in the following quote 1 sazhen=7 feet; 1 arshin=28 inches; 1 pood=40 pounds):

> The convicts work in the new mine, where the height of the coal strip is about two arshins; the width of the shafts is the same. The distance from the mine entrance to the present mining area is about 150 sazhens. A worker dragging a sled weighing a pood crawls up along a dark and dank corridor; this is the most difficult part of the work. . . . Each convict must crawl up with his sled not less than thirteen times a day, and here we deduce a lesson. In 1889–90, each convict mined on the average of 10.8 poods a day, 4.2 poods below the norm established by the mining administration. . . . [Free laborers] live at their own expense, in premises far worse than the prison. In spite of all this, their labor is more productive than that of the convicts by 70 and even 100 percent.[54]

Although the actual output of mining entirely by hand with virtually no capital investment was pitifully small, that of convicts was only about two-thirds to three-fourths of the output expected by mining officials, and as little as half of that of their free counterparts.

In 1886 the U.S. Department of Labor did pass along from Mississippi a statement to the effect that "convicts do 30 percent more work than free laborers,"[55] as misleading a sentence as appears in all the illusive documents of leasing. Taken literally it was certainly true, as convicts worked sunup to sundown with short dinner breaks, full Saturdays, and no sick days. But this statement should not be taken as evidence that convict *productivity* was any higher. The rather cavalierly offered statistic suffers from one other major weakness besides its spurious precision, namely that it is itself simply an assertion unsupported by any empirical evidence. In truth, convicts worked more to produce far less than free workers. Even the convicts' quotas under the task system were generally significantly lower than their free counterparts' normal production levels.

Why, then, did employers pay relatively high wages for lower productivity? As indicated earlier, they were willing to do so, above all, because of the reliability factor. "The advantage of this convict labor is that you have it all the time from Monday morning until Saturday night," said Florida's Bailey. TCI president George Crawford stated the same principle in broader terms: "The chief inducement for the hiring of convicts was the certainty of a supply of coal for our manufacturing operations in the contingency of labor troubles."[56] Convicts were exploited in that their wage was less than the value of their marginal product, and in some cases even less than the cost of their subsistence. Yet lessees ended up paying as much for them as they did for free workers, because leasing created two layers of profit—the lessee and the state—rather than one, and because they wished to secure the gains of reliability. From the lessees' viewpoint, the costs of maintaining convicts at the ready, costs including poor work and low output, were, for a time at least, justified by the avoidance of risk.

Three

CAMPS

Convict leasing camps were for the most part sealed-off Chekhovian universes—although to be sure they were considerably more permeable than the island Chekhov visited in 1890. Their chief function was to house a labor force at the margins of the state's populated areas, but at important points of its economy—its forests, farms, and nascent railroad lines. Sometimes these camps were picked up and moved several times a year. A few literally moved on wheels. Others were attached to permanent installations like plantations and mines. Certain camps housed as few as a single squad of ten men, while others were full-fledged penitentiary-stockades where several hundred prisoners lived, slept, and ate.

For good reasons, the mobile bunkhouses, those "great rolling cages" used in railroad and, later, road construction work, captured the attention of later historians. C. Vann Woodward brilliantly evoked the camps in a single sentence: "The South's 'penitentiaries' were great rolling cages that followed construction camps and railroad building, hastily built stockades deep in forest or swamp or mining fields, or windowless log forts in turpentine flats." Mississippi historian Vernon L. Wharton wrote, "Out over the state, in great rolling cages or temporary stockades, on remote plantations or deep in the swamps of the Delta, the convicts were completely at the mercy of the sub-lessees and their guards"; while Blake McKelvey portrayed convicts housed in moveable iron coops modeled after circus cages: "These crowded cages, constructed with two layers of bunks so that it was impossible to stand erect in them, and provided with only one night-bucket, were filthy enough for sleeping purposes, but as living quarters from Saturday noon until Monday morning they were unspeakably vile."[1]

In fact, contemporary interest in these rolling cages was also high. In 1898 W. L. King of North Carolina patented a "Jail for Sleeping Convicts" that contained thirty bunks and could be "easily moved from place to place by 6 mules."[2] Convicts in Columbus, Georgia, slept in a "portable bastile [*sic*]" that contained two tiers of bunks, a stove, and a toilet, as well as a small compartment for two guards. The *Columbus Ledger* was quite taken with the new arrangement:

> It may not be known, but there are ways and there are ways of stowing away a crowd of convicts at night. . . . It is now proposed to stow away the convicts, when the shades of darkness fall, in a movable prison—a small sized jail, that can be transferred from one point to another. . . . While new for this section, the plan has been tried with success in other places. A small prison house, about the size of a half box-car, is placed on wheels and rolled about over the country roads, being used as a sleeping place for the convicts. . . . The cab is really a cage, the wood work being covered with steel bars. Thus, the little house is virtually a prison cell.[3]

Columbus ordered three of the little houses.

As Illustration 2 shows, the mule-drawn workhouse was cramped and must have been insufferably hot in summer, but it was much more secure than the previous means of keeping small squads of convicts at night—namely, by herding them into tents under the not always vigilant lookout of a night guard. Another version of the moving cage can be seen in Illustration 3. Although this photograph depicts a chain-gang camp in 1910, after leasing had ended in North Carolina, it is useful for showing the general setup of these moving camps, complete with cooks, dog guards, sergeant, and trusties. Two of the whites were brought in to pose for this photograph. One was J. Z. McLawhon, Pitt County's superintendent of chain gangs; the other was the sheriff of Pitt County. This leaves a sergeant, an assistant sergeant, a dog guard, and three trusties, one of whom was a "dog-boy." Each cage held twenty-four convicts. They were obviously worked in gangs, since the squad system required a guard for each squad of eight or ten. (The chain gang really was a gang, in the sense understood by students of labor systems.)

Another type of moving prison camp, not surprisingly, was the converted boxcar used to house railroad construction gangs. Railroad work was yet another notorious sentence for Southern convicts, and the railroad camps appear to have remained among the worst convict quarters for ill treatment, poor sanitation, overcrowding, and bad food. As late as 1912, Arkansas governor George Donaghey was startled to find convicts "herded in box cars at night," twenty-four to a car (as in the North Carolina cages), "where they slept amid filth and vermin."[4]

Front View

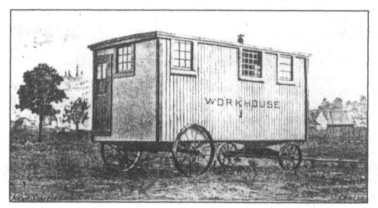

Rear View

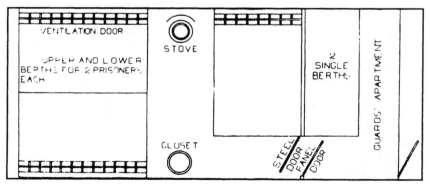

Floor Plan

Portable work house. From "What Shall We Do With Our County Convicts?" (Chattanooga: Converse Bridge Company, c. 1897. Southern Pamphlets, Rare Book Collection, University of North Carolina at Chapel Hill).

Convict chain gang in mobile prison wagons, Pitt County, North Carolina, 1910 (Library of Congress).

Evidence from more than one source makes it clear that railroad roadbeds became the final resting places for many prisoners. One gang was said to have lost two hundred men in two years; most were buried along the railroad right-of-way. However improbable such a figure seems, that "many of them died along the railroad tracks"—most from heat exhaustion—was incontrovertible.[5]

Other kinds of living quarters ranged from the mining or brickyard stockade with its "dark, dilapidated, and most filthy huts," to the log sheds of piney woods Florida. These latter, typically, were simply rectangular containers, with bunks against each wall and a single narrow aisle in the center. Often the prisoners were shackled by short chains to a long chain running the length of that aisle. As for the mining stockades, an English visitor left a useful description of the Tracy City, Tennessee, camp in 1877: "The outside walls consist of a very high strong timber pallisading; within are two or three large wooden halls or chambers; in the first [the convicts] were sitting down to their evening meal of bread and molasses. . . . Their cribs, or dens, or berths, were in another shed-like building, one tier above another, with a gallery around the upper one. Two men were consigned to a berth." Most leased convicts ate either in their cages or huts, or, more often, would take their

Convicts constructing the Western North Carolina Railroad, late 1870s (Special Collections Department, Perkins Library, Duke University).

meals outside, sitting on the ground. Those meals were endlessly repeated versions of the same basic pattern—beans, cornbread, molasses, and, in season, some vegetables—potatoes, turnips, beans—and even fruit. Meat was often included in an unappetizing stew that, convicts throughout the region complained, was often undercooked.[6]

By the turn of the century all states had regulations for maintaining basic standards of sanitation in the camps and for minimizing the mistreatment of the prisoners. Sunday work, for example, was universally prohibited unless it was voluntary, as in the Texas sugar fields. In Georgia the earliest leasing legislation required the convicts to attend services on Sunday. Black preachers often showed up on the Lord's day to perform that act of charity. Given the remoteness of most convict camps, however, these rules served more as ammunition for the system's defenders than as protection for the camps' inhabitants. For instance, Sunday labor was sometimes extracted anyway. In Texas convicts testified to being forced to work Sundays during cane season, while in Florida an 1899 investigation revealed that convicts in Citrus County were punished harshly for refusing Sunday work.[7]

Hours of work was another aspect of convict life that was universally regulated and just as universally subject to local variation. Generally, prisoners worked while there was light to see by. Miners worked ten hours a day. For some railroad construction crews in Mississippi the workday began at "4:30 o'clock A. M. . . . They are then worked until after sundown, and as long as it is light enough for a guard to see how to shoot."[8] Texas convicts were roused from their bunks in the dark, in order to be in the cotton and cane fields by sunup. One guard gave a description that was typical of his comrades': "Ring men up at 5:35. Have thirty minutes to prepare for breakfast. Go to work by good daylight. Get men in before dark. Fartherest point to camp from where we work about two miles. Have dinner sent to men when this far from camp. Have water hauled to men twice a day when in field." This account summarizes the lives of thousands of prisoners in hundreds of camps. Most were at least some distance from the site of the labor. In Alabama turpentine camps men rose at 4:00 and had to walk five to six miles. Some sergeants made the men trot to work; some let them walk.[9]

The rules also dictated sanitary standards: usually a change of clothing once per week and soap for the weekly bath. The bath itself was hardly a leisured relaxation following the prisoners' week of arduous labor, though; as in the North, when bathing was available, it was a matter of the convicts scrambling into a large water tank and making the best of it. All too often, however, bathing was a distant memory, and the "filth and vermin" of the convict quarters were as ubiquitous as they were constantly condemned. The *Knoxville Journal*, as leasing was coming to its end in Tennessee, somewhat sensationally depicted convicts "insufficiently clothed and fed, confined in coal banks by day and pestholes by night, infested with vermin. . . ." The following year Georgia's assistant keeper, R. F. Wright, reported equally "inhuman and barbarous" conditions: vermin, awful food and not enough of it, tattered clothes, poor ventilation, no physician, no records kept.[10]

Clothing was in constant shortage. Alabama convict miners literally never changed their clothing. As late as 1924 this fact had not been ascertained by the best-informed state officials outside of the prison department. When the state fire marshal, Chester E. Johnson, investigated a deadly fire at the stockade of Flat Top Mine in 1924, he inquired about the convict miners' oily, grimy suits, aptly called "muckers" by prisoners and guards alike. "The muckers . . . are nothing but grease," Thomas Dunkin, the yard-sergeant, testified. "You handle coal enough and you get full of grease." Later Johnson asked convict Robert Blanchard, "How often do you draw your suits?" "As a rule you draw a pair of pants, and that pants lasts 90 days," Blanchard replied. Johnson thought Blanchard might have misunderstood the question. "I mean change, for washing or cleaning?" "You don't change muckers at all," Blanchard responded. "Just wear it out." "Wear it out and when you do that, they give you another suit."[11] A Mississippi sergeant gave a balanced report of sorts in 1899: "Health of camp *very* good. . . . Crops clean and in fine Shap. Convicts allmost nude. *All needing clothing badly.*"[12]

The food and sanitation at the best of camps would be unnerving by modern standards. Here again, however, the evidence shows some improvement over time (always making allowances for wide local variations). The following testimony about conditions in a Texas cotton plantation is typical of others produced by the same investigation: "Closets [toilets] cleaned once per day, twice on Sunday. Disinfect with lime daily. Empty tubs about two hundred yards from building. Use artesian water." By the turn of the century, many permanent camps had outhouse facilities, and the night bucket faded. In more mobile quarters, however, the bucket was still an essential component of camp life.[13]

A major reason for the squalor of the camps was their isolation. The least remote of Florida's twenty-eight camps in 1903 were two miles from any town, however small, and many were as far as fifteen miles. Moreover, convicts were often transported directly from place of conviction to place of toil, without passing through any intermediate stage requiring a layover in town. In some states, too, there were so many camps that convicts were thinly scattered in small groups. Arkansas reported sixteen such camps in 1895, while Texas had over fifty in the 1880s.[14] There were some exceptions to this seclusion, however. Lessees sometimes hired free men who worked at or near the same location as convicts. At Sugarland, Texas, free workers performed much of the processing work, while convicts supplied the raw cane. One anonymous black former prisoner recalled the plantation he worked on being about half peon and half convict: "The only difference between the free laborers and the others was that the free laborers could come and go as they pleased, at night—that is, they were not locked up at night, and were not, as a general thing, whipped for slight offenses." Mining provided another case of intermingling. Many former convict miners stayed around the mines after their release in order to secure or retain employment. An inspection of the Briceville mine in Tennessee in 1891 revealed remarkable fraternization: "Fourth left entry—first room being worked— John Bertree, convict, and D. B. Cash, a free man, were found working together as 'buddies,' or in partnership. . . . Any man who works in [such dangerous conditions] does so because he is compelled to, either through fear of rules and regulations, such as the convict rests under, or the necessity of getting something to make a living at, as in the case of this free man."[15]

The isolation, the semifrontier conditions of the rural South, the drive for profits, and the miserable penury of the lessees—all combined to produce terrible health problems, sometimes of epidemic level. They could result in soaring death rates for some years. Mississippi recorded an 11 percent annual death rate over the entire period from 1880 to 1885— a total of 482 convicts. Fifteen of 120 died in the Alabama mines in 1877; 45 of 182 died on the Cape Fear and Yadkin Valley Railroad two years later. In states where convicts were held in jails rather than being transported to their labor camps directly, mortality was higher, and officials did not hesitate to assign blame to jail conditions. North Carolina's physician estimated that 14 percent of its convicts were "unsound" when they arrived, while in 1888 almost half of Alabama's were ill upon arrival—33 percent of them with chronic, incurable diseases. R. H. Dawson ascribed these high levels to the state of local jails. Mississippi's penitentiary board observed in 1891 that "a large number of convicts sent to the penitentiary come here diseased, especially the negroes from the jails, and among those hired out, there are a number who should be worked at some lighter employment than they find with the parties to whom they are hired." Texas's Thomas Goree likewise placed a burden of guilt on the jails when 256 men, mostly in woodcutting squads, died between 1878 and 1880. The population of the prison in that period was 1,930—which means an annual death rate of over 6 percent in those years. Indeed, one of the reasons for the purchase of state prison farms—and hence for the decline of convict leasing—was the high number of convicts who were not "first-class," and consequently could only be leased with difficulty or at a poor rate of return. As Goree told the National Prison Association when Texas hosted the convention in 1897, on the newly purchased prison farm "we work second-class labor, negroes, old men, boys, cripples, such men as we cannot hire out for first-class labor."[16]

In truth, the diseases appearing in the work camps constitute a virtual catalog of dreaded medical catastrophes: smallpox in the bayous below Houston, 1875; scurvy on the Texas farms that same year; syphilis, everywhere; typhoid fever, "continued fever," diarrhea, influenza throughout Georgia in 1893. But the habitual condemnation of jail conditions cannot cover up the appalling sanitation in the work camps themselves. Certainly death rates fluctuated wildly, and some historians have given disproportionate attention to the most sensational years, but it is far from mere sensationalism to note that 10.4 percent of Arkansas convicts died in 1885—and that the rate did not significantly diminish for the next two years; that the death rate in Mississippi in 1887 was 16 percent; that in Louisiana in 1881 it was 14 percent.[17]

L. R. Massengale testified concerning a camp in Coweta County, Georgia, about the fate of one tubercular convict:

> There was a negro that had the consumption out in a little house where they kept provisions for the mules. He was lying in the middle of the floor, I think he had something under his head; I asked the guard why they kept him there, and he said he didn't know what to do with him; he was sick and looked like he wouldn't live long and they said they couldn't give him proper treatment.
>
> Q. Did the guard tell you how long he had been lying there?
> A. I think he had been there about a couple of weeks.
>
> Q. Have any covering?
> A. Yes sir, I think he had a quilt; the room was piled up with the stuff they

kept there for the horses and mules, it was as cold as the mischief and they didn't have any way to heat it, it was just a little open space in there.[18]

Besides death, the other constant of the leasing camps was escape. Records show that literally thousands of escaped convicts must have inhabited the late-nineteenth-century Southern landscape. The figures for Georgia are especially complete and informative; they show 1,174 convicts having escaped in the lease's forty years, and for five of those years escape figures are unavailable. The mean annual attrition rate was nearly 6 percent (see table 1, p. 85). Arkansas reported 463 escapees at large as early as 1892. In other states escapes were equally frequent, and in several spectacular years almost defy explanation. One Georgia lessee was ironically described by the principal keeper as "a noble old gentleman and most excellent citizen, indeed too good a man to handle convicts. As a consequence seventeen [out of one hundred] escaped from him in less than four months."[19] Such judgments, delivered with either caustic scorn or alarmed concern, are another ubiquitous feature of the leasing records. In Texas escapes were so numerous that one year Goree confessed himself "gratified" to be able to report that a mere 110 had successfully fled. His figures are staggering:

> I again am compelled to report a large number of escapes, but am gratified to show some improvement is being made in this respect.
> The two years ending December 1, 1878
> showed escapes 495
> December 1, 1878, to November 1, 1880 366
> November 1, 1880, to November 1, 1882 397
> November 1, 1882, to November 1, 1884 273
> Since November 1, 1883, only. . . . . 110[20]

Between 1876 and 1899, according to the official count, more than three thousand Texas prisoners escaped from their work camps.[21] Over the same period 1,715 escaped from the plantations and levees of Mississippi lessees. Of these, 735 were recaptured, leaving 980 prisoners at large over a twenty-three-year period.[22]

Prisoners would have been foolish to place any faith in the officials, inspectors, legislators, and grand juries who, responding to periodic leaks of corruption or inhumane treatment, came to see the camps. Often these inspections were sincerely motivated, but the obstacles to abolition or even real reform were enormous. At other times the investigations were cursorily or incompetently conducted. During the otherwise thorough 1908 Georgia inquiry, for example, the inspectors refused to enter the mines. Moreover, there were structural impediments to the emergence of the truth. Georgia's prison commission left the investigation of the monthly reports to its clerk, who complained that he did not have time to read them, and that, besides, he trusted the inspector. But the chief inspector was seventy-three years old and inept; he was one of those who had, probably wisely, declined to descend into the mine. He, in turn, trusted the reports of the wardens, who were, illegally, in the pay of the lessees.[23] It was the same in Arkansas; when awful conditions were revealed at Coal Hill, the *Arkansas Gazette* reported that the penitentiary board had "relied for inspection on the lessees, who sent the new rules to their subordinates, whose reports . . . were accepted without question by the state board and the lessees."[24]

In the dozens of investigations of prison conditions that took place, then, few had any success in getting the convicts to speak about their circumstances. Generally the prisoners, overwhelmingly black, would feign satisfaction to placate their interrogators. A grand jury committee that visited a camp near Augusta in 1880, for instance, dutifully sought to obtain complaints from prisoners who were too cowed or too savvy to respond. "The convicts were afforded full opportunity to make complaints to us, but without exception they expressed themselves satisfied with the treatment they received," they reported. A Florida committee had a similar experience in 1903. Making an effort to induce confidence in the convicts by questioning them apart from the lessees and guards, they nevertheless "did not hear a single complaint with the treatment that they were receiving." Yet in 1887 Mississippi investigators were astute, and courageous, enough to note: "We find that instances of cruelty are not uncommon, as the testimony shows; and some, very probably, do not come to light on account of a system of intimidation that seems to be general in the camps." Mississippi's superintendent, David Johnson, was equally frank. "It made no difference how cautious I would be in visiting a camp," he recounted, "by the time I could make my inspection the report of my coming would reach all the camps on the line; this in a great measure prevented me from getting such information as I otherwise might have gotten. So I have reason to believe that convicts have been intimidated, or, in other words, threatened with punishment if they reported anything detrimental to the foreman in charge of them." The same signs of intimidation can be found in any number of other investigations. Texas convicts report: "Since I have been here the treatment has been fair"; "I have no complaint to make as to the treatment here. I am not abused"; "I have been here about two years and have no complaint to make of this place." This was the finding of a conscientious inspector of a Tennessee mine: "When [the convicts] reach the stockade, after their day's work is over, tired, wet, and dirty, they are compelled, in some instances, to sleep on the floor without any change of clothing, sleeping in the same clothes that they have worked in during the day. Some of the convicts have not had a change of clothing since they arrived here. Upon some of the convicts being questioned on these points, they stated they were true, but begged that their names would not be mentioned for fear that they would be flogged for giving any information on this subject." Alabama's R. H. Dawson, a sensitive and conscientious prison official, detected on more than one occasion some unsettling but indefinable troubles that convicts kept from him. "Inspected the Cunningham place," he wrote in his diary on 3 June 1883. "No sick, but there is evidently something wrong here. Examined the men separately and together, but could get nothing. No complaints about anything." And a month later, on a return visit: "Have grave doubts about the treatment but cannot get satisfactory data upon which to act."[25]

Mississippi legislators unearthed hellish conditions in their 1887 investigation, but some members of the committee investigated more thoroughly than others, and cooperation from frightened prisoners was not always forthcoming. At Ledbetter's camp in Coahoma County in February, the investigation consisted of the following questions, posed by the lessee himself:

> Were any of you ever treated unkindly or abused while in my employ? To which they all, save four, answered—We were not. He then asked if his orders had not always been to you to report any unkind treatment by either his manager or guards, and that you should not be punished for so doing? To which they answered—Yes.

The four who chose to answer, however, took advantage of their opportunity to describe working without shoes at Christmas. Bill Long reported: "Toes and fingers frosted down at Capt. Townsend's, just before Christmas, during the snow; walked from Townsend's to Friar's Point; was frosted before I left Capt. Townsend's." Mose Mullins said: "First two nights after I left Townsend's I stayed in jail at Friar's Point; no shoes on my feet when I left Capt. Townsend's camp; I walked from

Friar's Point to Fisher & Yerger's camp; my feet hurt me while I was walking . . ." A local citizen affirmed: "During the month of November I saw two convicts go to Capt. Hardy, ask for a pair of shoes, (they had none on) frost was on the ground at the time. Capt. Hardy paid no attention to them, both of those convicts have since escaped."[26]

Some Texas prisoners, almost certainly whites or, less often, Mexicans, also raised their voices to complain of rough treatment, overwork, and bad food. One frequent grievance was that guards cursed and struck the prisoners; this was the kind of behavior that, while forbidden by the strictest interpretation of the rules, was nevertheless impossible to enforce in any consistent way. Cussing and quirting fell far below the kind of punishment that required permission from the prison commissioner, as flogging with the famous "bat," or Texas strap, did.

The air over the convict camps was blue with the vilest oaths and obscenities, as prisoners and guards routinely cursed and insulted one another. "Guards curse and abuse the men. I have seen the assistant sergeant quirt men in the field," Joe McAfee related; while J. D. Frazier, a forger, told Judge John Henderson, "The sergeant and the guards abuse the men all the time, calling them all kinds of sons of bitches. The assistant sergeant nearly every day strikes some of them while they are at work with his quirt." Mexican prisoners in Texas were usually referred to as "niggers," "greasers," and the like: "Guards call me 'Negro, Mexican, greaser'; don't call me by name, curse me; make me work all the time," complained Antonio Ochoa. But of course the profanity was mutually applied, as the prisoners tried to give as good as they got in the way of insults and other indignities. A field guard, W. D. McMillan, testified: "Have seen the sergeant whip two different convicts in the field . . . one of the men was a Mexican, and he cursed me is why the sergeant whipped him; he said, 'Chingio cathrone,' and they told me that meant 'Damn s. b.'"[27] But poor Mr. McMillan was misinformed. The Mexican prisoner's curse means "go fuck a goat"—and a he-goat at that.

A moral squalor that was proportionate to the physical also characterized the convicts' lives. For example, while rape is a subject seldom encountered in the reticent documents of this repressive age and region, on occasion it breaks through the surface of its stifled discourse—often, by way of a rhetorical compensation, perhaps, in rather purple prose. An Arkansas convict recalled being surrounded by five convicts immediately upon his arrival at the prison in Little Rock. "Make ready for a feast," they jested to one another. "You are too purty to come to the penitentiary," added the deputy warden. A Knoxville paper reported convicts "exposed to deadly and contagious venereal diseases, practicing unutterable abominations upon each other"—reported with good reason: an investigating committee had estimated that half the black and one quarter of the white convicts suffered from venereal diseases. Texas convict Fred Smith witnessed five floggings in as many months, two of which were "for indecent offenses."[28]

Women unfortunate enough to be sentenced anywhere in the South, whether in leasing camp or penitentiary, faced the constant danger of sexual assault. While, to be sure, not all sexual activity on the part of prisoners should be ascribed to violence, nevertheless it must have been especially frightening for a woman to contemplate incarceration in the late-nineteenth-century South. In Tennessee, as in all Southern states prior to the late 1890s, women prisoners, while usually segregated, did not have their own separate buildings. In Nashville women and men were housed within earshot and eyesight of each other. The warden flatly stated in 1883 that "no woman should be sentenced to the Tennessee penitentiary until the State makes better provision for their care," while the chaplain, perhaps not the most impartial of sources on such matters, deplored what he saw as "their conversation obscene and filthy, and their conduct controlled by their unrestrained passions."[29]

It would be too astounding to be believed but for its appearance in the official documents, but early in the history of leasing, one report in Georgia disclosed "men and women chained together, and occupying the same bunks. The result is, there are now in the penitentiary [that is, the leasing camps] 25 children." One woman testified that at Grant, Alexander, and Company, the earliest lessees, women "were whipped on the shoulders and on the rump, getting from one to fifteen lashes; clothing dropped to the waist and whipping over thin underclothes." There were other children born in the camps; Susan Gilbert had more than one child at the Chattahoochee Brick camp, and two others at Chattahoochee also gave birth. In 1869 Georgia's principal keeper called for special treatment for women: "There are only a few females in confinement, and they are all colored but one, and all are worked without any discrimination with the male convicts," he explained. In Arkansas at about the same time, women prisoners had to pass through a room where 15 or 20 men were confined in order to get to their own quarters. A child was born to one of the women. A second child was born in Arkansas in 1874 and four in Mississippi's prison in 1875. At President's

Island just below Memphis, Civil War legend Nathan Bedford Forrest, "The Wizard of the Saddle," worked leased convicts on a plantation. He housed 117 of them in a single shed that had several separate "apartments": one for black and white women, one for white men, and one for black men. However, segregation of women became the rule in the 1890s, following the construction of the South's first female prison, in South Carolina. In Texas and Georgia most of the relatively few women worked on farms. In Georgia some were also sentenced to the brickyard at Chattahoochee.[30]

At least some of those women hated their Chattahoochee camp so much that they burned it down. Its complete destruction in December 1900 was a huge loss to the state, which had made no fire protection provisions whatsoever and had neglected to purchase fire insurance, even though the buildings were entirely made of wood. At the time, it had been "perhaps the largest convict camp in the south," the *Atlanta Constitution* reported. Although three women—two black and one white—were charged with arson in the case, they were acquitted by a jury that was evidently fed up with convict leasing. Two years later a new women's prison—built of stone—was constructed by convict labor.[31]

In most instances the authority of the lessees in the day- to-day running of the camps was paramount, and sometimes made a mockery of the attempts at state supervision. The managers at Georgia's railroad camp number nine wrote to the principal keeper in a tone that borders on arrogance: "We have found it necessary to enlarge the Branch camp . . . at Chickamauga and have appointed Mr. N. T. Pope, to inflict punishment in said camp. Please be kind enough to have his commission issued at your earliest convenience." A former Texas inmate said of the responsible state official: "Major Whatley is the superintendent, but his case can be dismissed in a line—he turns it over to Capt. Smither." Indeed, the widespread perception that many states' politics were in the hands of a nebulous "penitentiary ring" was in many respects a true one. Only through continual vigilance by the best officials, such as Dawson of Alabama and Goree of Texas, did the state assert other than a pecuniary interest in prison affairs.[32]

Below the responsible state officials were the men on the scene, the sergeants and guards who had to put up with the daily tensions of overseeing an unruly, resentful population at a far remove from any penitentiary walls. Young, green, poorly paid, unsure, and armed, they compiled a miserable record of escapes. Evidence about guards is sporadic but almost always negative. In Texas the lessees hired them, and they were usually eighteen or nineteen years old. Because there were not enough, the commissioners explained in 1876, when small numbers of prisoners were hired out they often went unguarded. Eleven were contracted to work at a saw mill, for instance; seven escaped. Indeed, some three hundred prisoners walked away from their work camps that year. It is "hard to get guards of *any* kind, and especially good ones," Goree said in 1880. Three years later the problem persisted. The penitentiary board noted the continuing problem of hiring convicts as servants in Huntsville, where the prison was located. The board suggested that they should only be hired when the number was sufficient to hire a guard for them. Goree's solution to the whole problem was to have the state recruit and pay them.[33]

In some respects the job of guarding prisoners was itself a perfect candidate for convict leasing: it was difficult work at very low wages, and thus it was hard to attract a labor force for it. And, to a certain extent, the lessees reacted to it in the same way they did to similar shortages—that is, by using convicts to guard convicts. The trusty system was quite widespread in the earlier years. Black Arkansas prisoners guarded their fellows in the 1870s, and Georgia also used trusties. When Georgia law forbade the trusty designation, some lessees ignored the law. One of the formal charges against Penitentiary Company number two in 1886 was that they placed convicts in positions of trust over other convicts. Perhaps even more surprising is the persistent use of black guards, a practice that, it might be supposed, existed during Reconstruction but faded in later years. Yet in 1888 convict inspector J. C. Kyle reported that "guards are made up promiscuously of whites and blacks" in the slovenly camps under the control of the Gulf and Ship Island Railroad.[34]

The pay for guards in Florida was so poor that, at first, only blacks were so employed. As late as 1903 Florida guards' wages ranged from $18 to $25 a month plus board and lodging. By 1915 base pay had risen to $25; it was $35 if the guard provided his own horse. A captain, on the other hand, received $150. In Mississippi lawmakers concluded that a "frequent cause of the maltreatment of convicts is the class of guards employed. They work for twelve dollars and a half a month, and we submit that such a price for such a service can only command a very cheap order of man." By 1902 the pay had risen only to $20 a month, with sergeants commanding $50. Texas guards were receiving $50 by the turn of the century, although some of the sergeants there received extra salaries from the contractors.[35]

Guards may have been young, inexperienced, poorly paid, and incompetent, but if the blame for leasing's astronomical escape rate was theirs, accountability for its record of immeasurable cruelty belongs to their superiors—the "Captain" who oversaw each camp or, in some states, the "whipping boss": a designated agent whose job was to inflict punishment. "The object of torture is torture," says O'Brien in George Orwell's 1984[36]—and the dismal history of the brutal and ingenious punishments that leased convicts were forced to undergo provides powerful confirmation of such a view. Many punishments often bear no discernible connection to production or even security, but in the end seem mere expressions of hatred, self-disgust, and a will to power.

Michel Foucault's conception of torture is, somewhat surprisingly in view of the Nietzschean wellsprings of his brilliant and disturbing work, quite different from O'Brien's. Foucault argued that torture was connected with an era in which labor power did not have the utility it commands under industrialism.[37] His formulation of the problem of torture, however much it serves to illuminate the development of a society of ever finer gradations of surveillance, assessment, and judgment, misses a fundamental aspect of convict leasing—namely the license it gave for the display not of a sovereign's but of a petty camp boss's power. Leasing allowed the accumulated reservoirs of human cruelty to overflow in the isolated camps and stockades.

Of course, a distinction must be made between punishment and torture, the latter of which is a kind of spectacle, a display of a sovereign's power, not some sort of "negative reinforcement" intended to produce a particular pattern of behavior. But while the punishments of convicts were often linked to production, at least ostensibly, it is equally clear that the violence visited on prisoners in the late-nineteenth-century South was often inexplicable in terms of the output of their labor. In the convict leasing camps of Mississippi or Georgia or Florida, the distinction between punishment and torture started to blur.

Of all forms of punishment, the lash was the most frequently used. Its ubiquity in the camps would have disturbed few people then, although it shocks us now. Whipping was the preeminent form of punishment under slavery; and the lash, along with the chain, became the very emblem of servitude for both slaves and prisoners. Texas, which had no system of rewards and punishments (except for those related to the performance of extra work) until 1941, relied solely on flogging. The whip there was called the "bat." Arkansas had the "one pound leather," six feet long and four inches wide. Mississippi convicts called it the "beaver's tail." In Tennessee prisoners faced the "strap," nicknamed "Old Suzie." Legislators reported that "it consists of two plies of sole or harness leather, about twenty to thirty inches in length."[38]

Whipping is a punishment not just of insupportable pain but of deep humiliation as well. Few men or women can bear it in silence. The vulnerability of the recipient and the power of the boss who metes it out are underscored by the ritual nature of the chastisement. The convict—man or woman—would be held over a barrel or a sack and held down by other convicts—for the boss often required convicts to participate in the doling out of the punishment to their fellow convicts. Often the offender would be stripped. The results were sometimes debilitating, and occasionally fatal. As late as 1915 Alabama investigators were still finding convicts whose skin was literally whipped off their backs; while in Arkansas at about the same time one witness recounted a punishment in which the prisoner's "body bounced like a rubber ball. His flesh was torn off along with his clothes."[39] Such episodes occurred often, and, indeed, these two examples are statistically unremarkable. What sets them apart is only that they occurred in the second decade of this century.

However painful this punishment was, however, several somewhat mitigating features of it ought to be borne in mind. First, in most instances about which there is direct evidence, it is apparent that the instrument of this punishment was a sort of strap of wide leather, not a whip such as most readers might envision—that is, some sort of modified bullwhip. Still less was it a version of the infamous cat-o'-nine-tails familiar to every British jack-tar.

Second, states did take measures to control the amount of flogging, the reasons for administering the punishment, and the conditions in which it was administered. In Texas the orders had to come from the inspector, who made his determinations on his monthly rounds. Sergeants and guards would submit requests on each visit, and these requests would occasionally be refused. After the 1890 reforms, Mississippi camp sergeants recorded punishments with the care of accountants. Sergeant Nance reported Calvin Cummings's punishment of "10 L[icks] Strap" for "Sorry plowing" and Henderson Williams's for "Sorry hoeing" on the Shelby place in July 1899. As early as 1881 the Tennessee

Supreme Court, in the case of *Cornell* v. *The State,* set strict limits on flogging county convicts. The punishment could only be inflicted under regulations specifically drawn up for that purpose by the county commission or the courts, the court concluded.[40]

The actual value of such a decision as *Cornell* v. *The State* may, of course, be called into question. At precisely the same time as the *Cornell* case the Georgia legislature established its "whipping boss" system, which, in its misguided attempt to circumscribe cruelty, actually served to institutionalize it. And stories of the indiscriminate use of the lash continued to appear into the 1920s. Nevertheless, restrictions on whipping did begin to take hold by the turn of the century.

It is also important to remember that the lash did not have quite the connotations of shocking cruelty it has today. Flogging, in fact, was a common feature of early-nineteenth-century discipline in the family, in the classroom, on the farm, in the factory, at sea. Writing of English, not American, society, Stephen Nicholas nevertheless makes a relevant point when he argues that the whip was commonplace in that society and adduces the examples of the army, the navy, prisons, bound labor of all sorts, and children in nineteenth-century English factories. Likewise, J. B. Hirst reminds us that in the first half of the nineteenth century, "under English common law masters could still beat their apprentices, masters of ships their sailors, and teachers their students."[41] Of course, such punishments had disappeared by the time of the Civil War, but older Americans in the late nineteenth century could recall them. In writing for the Court in the *Cornell* case, Justice Cooper conceded that "our sturdy ancestors not only allowed it in the case of criminals, sailors and soldiers, but considered it a proper discipline for their wives and children," although he went on to assert that "It cannot be denied . . . that this form of punishment has fallen under the ban of modern civilization, as tending to degrade the individual and destroy the sense of personal honor." That the whip would be a recognized feature of nineteenth-century Southern convict life would have disturbed few who bothered to consider the fact.

But there were a myriad of other punishments in the leasing camps, punishments at once clever and mindless, and seemingly unrelated to production requirements. They ranged from the minor harassment to the hell of the dark cell. One night guard told investigators: "Punishment is by strap. For light offenses such as misconduct in the building, convicts are required to carry boxes on their shoulders from thirty to forty minutes. We find this a good way to correct for minor offenses." At the other end of the scale were the stocks. These were wooden planks with holes for neck and arms. But they were not merely placed over the convict's head and left there. One guard, J. W. Richardson Jr., a former saloon keeper, testified about the use of stocks in Texas in 1879. A prisoner, he explained, would be fitted with the stocks and then "lifted . . . so as to stand on his toes." The effect was excruciating. With toes grazing the floor and joints straining, men sweated uncontrollably and sometimes lost control of their bowels as well. Richardson "did see a man stocked until he ~~shits~~ committed a nuisance," reads the manuscript record of his testimony.[42] These refined tortures were not exclusive to Texas but, like many aspects of Southern prison culture, were practiced elsewhere, with appropriate modifications for local conditions. Florida's C. W. Ellis, for example, liked to hang convicts by their manacled hands over a tree branch, so that their feet would not quite touch the ground.[43]

Southern convict managers had learned much about the physical abuse of blacks from slavery, and their memories were long. As late as 1908 one can find examples of slavelike means of immobilizing itchy feet. Some convicts at Muscogee Brick Company near Americus, Georgia, had spikes attached to their ankles, such as one could have found on those of slaves sixty years earlier. When a trusted black convict, John Rutherford, escaped for the third time in 1891, "an iron ring was placed about his neck. To this ring was fixed a spike, curving inward, so that rapid running was impossible."[44]

In brief, punishment in the camps, like leasing itself, had an archaic, nonutilitarian character that existed side by side with more traditional means of securing surplus value from brute labor. And the squalor and disease of the camps themselves were in their way part of the same regime of punishment. Eventually, however, the archaic system became too much of a burden for a modernizing society and economy. Yet its abolition did not bring appreciably better conditions to the forced labor gangs who built the majority of the South's infrastructure.

PART TWO

CONVICT LEASING IN THE STATES

Four

GEORGIA
THAT SUNDOWN JOB

I

In 1932 a radical folklorist named Lawrence Gellert spent some time with a chain gang near Augusta, where the convicts sang a cheerless ballad called "Joe Brown's Coal Mine." Gellert wrote it down with the phonetical exaggeration that passed for dialect transcription in those days:

> Sez ahm boun' to Joe Brown's coal mine
> Sez ahm boun' to Joe Brown's coal mine
> An' it's Lawdy me an' it's Lawdy mine
> Sez ahm boun' to Joe Brown's coal mine.
> Sez ahm goin' ef ah don' stay long
> Sez ahm goin' ef ah don' stay long
> An' it's Oh me, an' it's Oh mine
> Sez ahm goin' ef ah don' stay long.
> Dat's the train dat ah leave heah on
> Sez dat's the train dat ah leave heah on . . .
> Sez ahm boun' to dat Sundown job . . . [.]

Curious about the song, Gellert asked a lot of questions but could ascertain little about its provenance. "Joe Brown's coal mine, I learned, uses mostly convict labor leased from the State," he recorded. "Could learn nothing about it beyond it was notorious for the ill treatment of workers. And was located somewhere in Virginia."[1]

Thus is history transformed by folklife. As any convict, or indeed any citizen of Georgia just two generations earlier, could have told Gellert and his convict friends, Joe Brown's coal mines were located not in Virginia but on Raccoon Mountain in north Georgia, they were the foundation of one of the South's largest fortunes, and they were worked by leased convicts. The particulars of time and place had shriveled in the memory, leaving a husk of endured suffering in the lore and culture of convict workers.

Joseph E. Brown, Civil War governor, United States senator, lawyer, judge, and redoubtable member of Georgia's iron-fisted ruling "triumvirate" of Brown, John B. Gordon, and A. H. Colquitt, founded the Dade Coal Company in 1873. Brown was already at that time president of the state-owned Western and Atlantic Railroad and had large interests in Rising Fawn Iron Company and Walker Iron and Coal. By 1886 Dade Coal owned the other two and more besides. Until the seams of coal were worked out in the early twentieth century, "Joe Brown's Coal Mine" was the destination of many a Georgia convict.

If Alabama was the state where leasing lasted the longest, Georgia is where it achieved the status of a Weberian "ideal type." Or, as E. C. Wines trenchantly wrote in 1880: "The lease system of convict labor seems to be carried to its last limit—its *ultima thule*—in Georgia; and where that system prevails it is useless to write about other things."[2] Georgia's leasing history shows the practice in its least diluted form.

As had been the case not only in Alabama but also in Mississippi, Louisiana, and South Carolina, the decision to "farm out the penitentiary," as one early inspector termed it, was made by the state's military government immediately following the Civil War. Georgia had no penitentiary; Gen. William T. Sherman had seen to that, and had thus helped to pave the way for the prison labor policy for which the state would later be mercilessly castigated by distant philanthropists.

Georgia's first lease was awarded on 11 May 1868 by Gen. Thomas Ruger, the military governor, to William A. Fort, who proposed to work the convicts on the Georgia and Alabama Railroad. Ruger was acting under legislation that had been passed in December of 1866.[3] The year-and-a-half hiatus between the enabling legislation and the first lease suggests that Georgians were slow to recognize the potential of this labor pool. The terms of this first lease called for 100 black convicts for $2,500. Later in the year 134 were sent to work on the Selma, Rome and Dalton, and 109 were shipped to the Macon and Brunswick line.

Georgia placed oversight responsibilities on an officer quaintly termed the principal keeper of the penitentiary, a title that brings to mind

Voltaire's famous quip about the Holy Roman Empire, since the principal keeper was never more than a tertiary figure, he could not care for his scattered charges, and there was no penitentiary. Many keepers, however, seem to have been men of integrity who tried to bring the corruption, cruelty, and abuses of leasing to light. The first principal keeper, Overton K. Walton, warned in his first report that things were not going right. Sixteen convicts had died on the Selma, Rome and Dalton. "I am fully satisfied that a humane treatment of them is entirely ignored," he wrote. And—a complaint that would be heard over and over throughout the years of leasing—"Notwithstanding my repeated and urgent requests to the contractors to make weekly statements to this institution of the number of escapes, deaths, pardons, &c., as well as the number on hand, they have failed to make but one report."[4]

The next year the state had a new principal keeper, John Darnell, and he expressed the same concerns as had Walton. Indeed, his agitation is palpable in his first report. Expressing "considerable embarrassment in the discharge of my official duties, owing to the conflicting construction of the law between the lessees and myself," he found that the information demanded of him by law was unobtainable, since "the convicts are almost invariably sent direct to the railroad on which they are employed. . . . It is confidently believed there are a good many convicts in the hands of the lessees of whom no record can be found." He was convinced that "a good many convicts have escaped, died, and a few been killed, of whom no account has ever been made to me." He disclosed with mounting dismay episodes of overwork, shootings, excessive whipping—all unreported. The first Georgia report on the full-blown system called for an official investigation, because, as Darnell said, "I am impressed with the belief that the General Assembly did not anticipate the very demoralizing consequences of 'farming out' the penitentiary, or it would not have been done."[5]

But it was already too late. In 1869 leasing became the fate of all 393 prisoners. They were sent to build railroads for Grant, Alexander and Company. Eight of them died. Like the contemporary leases in Alabama, Arkansas, and Mississippi, this one in Georgia was also free.

The law, at least, was solicitous of the convicts. The prison rules called for forty minutes for breakfast, which would be dished out about a half hour after dawn. Dinner, at 12:30, was to last fifteen minutes and supper, at sundown, forty minutes. Prisoners were required to attend services on Sunday, a day on which, the regulations also said, swearing was prohibited.[6] Diet and clothing allowances were also reasonable. Convicts were supposed to have a half-pound of meat, two pounds of bread, and one pint of syrup a day, as well as vegetables, milk, "fresh beef or mutton once a week if it can be procured," and peas, turnips, and potatoes in winter. They were to be issued two cotton suits for summer, two woolen for winter. They were permitted to change their clothes after the weekly bath.[7]

After a brief improvement in treatment in 1870, the lessees soon sank back into their old patterns. John T. Brown, the principal keeper in 1873, a former contractor and overseer of state slaves, once again complained: "I find many names of convicts on the monthly reports of the lessees which are not entered on the register." Out of 550 prisoners working on railroad construction that year, 21 died and 5 were reported "killed"— with no further explanation. Twenty-six others escaped.

With the current lease about to expire, however, the penitentiary had become a source of considerable revenue for the state, bringing in $35,213.65 in the eighteen months since 1 April 1872. The enormous expense of constructing a prison seemed like folly in light of the state's indigence and the receipts of convict labor.

New leases went to seven contractors. "Lively Bidding for the State Convicts. All Taken and a Thousand More Wanted" reported the black *Atlanta Herald*. "The governor found only enough convicts to satisfy a small portion of the bids made."[8] The largest of the seven leases went to J. T. and W. D. Grant, former associates in Grant, Alexander, and Company, the previous lessees. The Dade Coal Company appeared for the first time, leasing ninety-one convicts on 1 April 1874. Between April and December the lessees would receive many more. The lease rate was eleven dollars per convict per year.

The legislation establishing this second phase was passed on 3 March 1874. Brown's Walker Coal and Iron Company was chartered on 2 March—a textbook example of how legislation can actually create a market. The deadline for lease bids, Gov. James Smith announced, would be 24 March. Brown's bid was submitted on 25 March—a textbook example of political corruption.[9]

So it was that in 1874 the first of a generation of convicts became familiar with Raccoon Mountain, site of the mines which Brown had opened in anticipation of their labor. In the early 1870s, as the railway system matured, adequate rail linkage and an ample supply of previously unavailable coal cars made extensive mining operations at Rac-

Deaths and Escapes during the Georgia Lease

Year	Convicts	Deaths	Death Rate	Escapes	Escape Rate	%Attrition
1868	259	16	6.18%	NA	NA	6.18%
1869	393	8	2.04%	NA	NA	2.04%
1870	385	17	4.42%	NA	NA	4.42%
1873	550	26	4.73%	26	4.73%	9.45%
1875	1114	49	4.4%	53	4.76%	9.16%
1876	1108	58	5.23%	44	3.97%	9.21%
1877	1448	55	3.8%	NA	NA	3.8%
1878	1417	27	1.91%	NA	NA	1.91%
1880	1186	80	6.75%	32	2.7%	9.44%
1882	1291	22	1.7%	26	2.01%	3.72%
1886	1652	68	4.12%	51	3.09%	7.2%
1888	1618	81	5.01%	NA	NA	5.01%
1890	1891	107	5.66%	40	2.12%	7.77%
1892	2110	107	5.07%	63	2.99%	8.06%
1893	2274	62	2.73%	44	1.93%	4.66%
1894	2409	63	2.62%	19	0.79%	3.4%
1896	2486	78	3.14%	1	0.04%	3.18%
1897	2361	56	2.37%	70	2.96%	5.34%
1898	2316	51	2.2%	37	1.6%	3.8%
1900	2357	54	2.29%	45	1.91%	4.2%
1901	2352	75	3.19%	32	1.36%	4.55%
1902	2419	67	2.77%	37	1.53%	4.3%
1904	2530	117	4.62%	98	3.87%	8.5%
1905	2501	64	2.56%	157	6.28%	8.84%
1906	2476	53	2.14%	89	3.59%	5.74%
1907	2634	62	2.35%	108	4.1%	6.45%
1908	2760	94	3.41%	102	3.7%	7.1%
TOTAL		1617		1174		
MEAN		62	3.61%	56	2.22%	5.83%

coon Mountain feasible. Such operations proved in time to be enormously profitable. Brown, whose fortune could be estimated conservatively at $1 million, personally netted $98,000 from Dade in 1880 alone.[10] By 1886 Dade Coal was a parent company, owning Walker, Rising Fawn, Chattanooga Iron, and Rogers Railroad and Ore Banks and leasing Castle Rock Coal. An 1889 reorganization resulted in the formation of the Georgia Mining, Manufacturing and Investment Company—a conglomerate founded on leased convict labor at eleven, and later about fifteen, dollars per man per year.

Although an inspection report maintained that the company had built stockades with "good and comfortable quarters for all classes of convicts, white, black, male and female," the highest mortality rate occurred on Raccoon Mountain, where 13 of 181 died.[11] In the coming years Brown's operations would be exonerated in no fewer than four separate investigations. But his power and reputation, not to mention his dispensing free passes on the Western and Atlantic for prison investigators and his arranging a dinner to honor the head of one investigating committee, certainly served to deflect effective criticism.[12] It is also reasonable to surmise that Brown destroyed much of his correspondence relating to leasing, since he was careful of his reputation and had plainly been involved in many shady arrangements.[13]

The chaos and brutality increased along with the revenue. Out of 1,114 convicts in 1874, 53 escaped and 49 died. At the Grants' operation some 26 out of 309 died, all of whom had been sublet to other labor contractors.

Two leases had to be canceled in 1875. Wallis, Haley and Company had leased one hundred convicts to work on the railroad but took half of them to a plantation—probably that of Gen. John B. Gordon, the "Hero of Appomattox" and commander-in-chief of the United Confederate Veterans. The principal keeper—who was Gov. James Smith's brother-in-law—had to intercept them. Governor Smith personally set aside the lease of George D. Harris. "[The convicts'] physical condition . . . was deplorable," he found: they were racked with scurvy and other diseases. Forty-one of them were then leased for $162.75 to John Howard, who promptly allowed thirteen to escape in five months.[14]

A small number of women and a much larger number of boys were caught up in the lease in this first decade. Henrietta Green, Amanda Riggins, and Elizabeth Sciplin were sent to Dade, where they worked as cooks and washerwomen and were confined to separate lockups—a precaution that did not prevent the camp from having a birth rate. And "the very large number of negro boys, from ten to fifteen years of age" was noted as early as 1875.[15] The trend toward a younger population would intensify. By 1896 just under half of the total number of prisoners sentenced were minors.[16]

The second half of the 1870s saw considerable legislative and political jockeying over convict labor. In 1876 the Georgia General Assembly passed a momentous piece of legislation intended as a long-term solution to the difficulties of working prisoners. The legislature established a twenty-year lease—the only one of its kind in history, and the policy that represents the distilled essence of leasing. The law stipulated that the lease would be awarded to a corporation, and that prisoners with more than a five years' sentence would be sent to the mines. It tightened reporting procedures and penalties for escapes and provided the Macon and North Georgia Railroad with 250 convicts free of charge. Finally, and almost as a means of accentuating the intent of the legislation, the General Assembly repealed the ten-hour- maximum workday. The principal keeper was pleased: now the state would not even have to lay eyes on the convicts when they were sentenced, he observed, for they would go straight to the camps.[17]

As the 1874 leases approached their expiration, there was a flurry of financial and political activity. In December of 1878 a harsh report from an investigative committee chaired by Robert A. Alston caused a sensation. Privately Alston said that the report did not tell half the story and that he was collecting material for a speech that would really shake the public. He never lived to give it. Alston was fatally shot by Edward Cox in the State Treasurer's Office on 11 March 1879. His murder was more complex than it first appears, however; Alston was not simply a courageous reformer done in by corrupt and unscrupulous business interests. His murderer, Cox, was a sublessee in a company owned by John B. Gordon; Alston, who had power of attorney in that company, had been trying to dispose of the convicts elsewhere.

Cox was convicted and sentenced to the Dade coal mines. There he found a compassionate taskmaster in Joseph E. Brown. Brown sympathized with Cox, partly because Alston had condemned the lease on which Brown's profit margins depended and partly because Cox could be pumped for information on Gordon, Brown's antagonist. He was given an easy outside job tending livestock. A benevolent Gov. Alexander H. Stephens, in one of his last public acts, pardoned Cox in 1882.[18]

Three corporations (not the single company the legislature had apparently intended), chartered especially for the purpose, took control of all the convicts pursuant to the 1876 legislation. Penitentiary Company number one, chartered in Dade County in northwest Georgia, was essentially Dade Coal. Its owners were Joseph Brown; his son Julius; John T. and William D. Grant, the earliest lessees; and Jacob Seaver, a Boston investor.

B. G. Lockett, J. W. Lockett, W. B. Lowe, and John B. Gordon owned the second company. It would later be the largest lessee and, after reorganization, employ most of its convicts in making bricks. It was chartered in Dougherty County in south Georgia.

Company number three's owners—John W. Murphy, William D. Grant (again), W. E. Simpson, Thomas Alexander (again), and John W. Renfroe—chartered their firm in rural Greene County, about halfway between Atlanta and Augusta. Many would be leased to a prominent planter, James Monroe Smith (not the James Smith who was governor).[19]

The contracts reveal just how much authority the state had abdicated. Lessees were to "pay all expenses of said convicts as required by law, and shall pay all expense of transporting convicts . . . shall Keep them securely without expense to the State, . . . and shall in all respects discharge their duty under the law touching the management, control and keeping of said convicts."[20]

But contracts and laws alone cannot tell the story of convict leasing, for the daily realities of convict life lay in their violation as much as in their fulfillment. An 1879 investigation revealed the principal keeper delivering convicts at a cost of twelve dollars apiece—a cost that was supposed to be borne by the lessees. Meanwhile, J. W. Renfroe, a lessee who was also the state treasurer, had to resign after admitting, "I have received some commissions on the State's deposits." "I am . . . perhaps not as careful a student of our present Constitution as I ought to have been," he ruefully acknowledged. (However, Renfroe did not have to grieve for long, for in 1883 he was appointed assistant to the president of Dade Coal.)[21]

What was the system like when the great lease began? In 1880, 80 out of 1,186 convicts died. The physician Dr. Thomas Raines blamed much of the death rate on deplorable jail conditions. "We have lost ten men from the jails that never did a moment's work," he complained. As this remark indicates, Dr. Raines was hardly a paragon of the Hippocratic virtues. One day in 1883, for instance, he showed up drunk at Raccoon

Mountain and certified twelve prisoners as "able-bodied" even though they had been carried in on stretchers.[22]

Most convicts were sentenced for theft and burglary. The 1880 data show 43 percent of all sentences being for larceny and burglary. The median sentence was five years. Just two years later, while burglary and larceny were still the most common crimes recorded, the number of murderers rose from 50 to 100, comprising 8 percent of the 1,243 convicts on hand.[23]

If they were joining labor gangs at earlier ages, convicts were leaving prison life as old men, for prison sentences became fearfully long stretches of time after leasing was introduced. Table 2 summarizes the sentencing data of the "ideal-typical" Georgia lease. The number of men who had been sentenced to terms of more than ten years had comprised only 2.5 percent of the total population before the Civil War. In 1890 that percentage had increased ten times. Another of the many interesting consequences of the change in sentencing patterns was the greatly increased likelihood of receiving a life sentence. Early in the history of leasing it became about as common as a fifteen-year sentence had previously been. Later it would be even more frequently handed out than the fifteen-year sentence.[24]

Under the terms of the 1879–1899 lease, which called for installments of $25,000 per year *regardless of the number of convicts,* and with a prison population of 1,243 in 1882, the annual payment per capita amounted to $20.11, or six and a half cents per workday. Over time, of course, the per-capita figure declined still further as the population soared and the cost of the lease contract remained fixed. There were 2,357 convicts in 1896, yielding a per-capita, per-day cost of about three cents. As for the state itself, its own rate of return was small, making its experience in this as in other ways quite distinct from Alabama's. According to the Georgia reformer and gadfly Rebecca Latimer Felton, Georgia's profit was virtually nonexistent anyway, since "a gang of supernumerary officials, who are generally 'go-betweens,' are paid nearly half [the contract amount]."[25]

II

The year 1886, the midpoint of leasing's history in the state, is a good point at which to take stock. In 1884 Joseph E. Brown had acquired the lease of W. D. Grant and used Grant's convicts to replace the remaining free laborers at Rising Fawn. The following year saw the incorporation of the Chattahoochee Brick Company in Atlanta. Its president, James W. English, who was also Atlanta's police commissioner, would eventually become the lessee of two-thirds of the state's convicts. With George W. Parrott, English controlled a reorganized Penitentiary Company number three. Re-leasing the convicts from Penitentiary Company number three to Chattahoochee Brick, English and Parrott enjoyed an annual return of 380 percent in leasing fees alone. In addition, and more to the point, they guaranteed a stable labor supply for the grueling process of making brick. In time Chattahoochee Brick became one of the largest firms of its kind in the United States.[26] It seemed that leasing's tentacles were multiplying even as their grip tightened.

But a freeze-frame of 1886 reveals other important developments in the making, as well. First, the National Prison Association (NPA) held its annual convention in Atlanta that year, and on the subject of convict labor its delegates had to confront the attitude of shame mixed with defensiveness so characteristic of Southern self-consciousness. Second, that summer witnessed a potentially disastrous revolt at the Dade coal mines. On 12 July 109 men refused to go to work at the coke ovens in protest against excessive work, overuse of corporal punishment, and bad food. They were, as one of their number declared, "ready to die, and would as soon be dead as to live in torture." But the principal keeper, John R. Towers, starved the convicts out, and the mutiny collapsed after three days.[27]

Third, in Macon during the same month as the convict strike, Mrs. Felton led a drive at the state Women's Christian Temperance Union (WCTU) convention to support the separation of women prisoners and the establishment of a juvenile reformatory. Shortly afterward the WCTU also sent the legislature a petition written in the unmistakably cantankerous Felton style. Containing little evidence or documentation, the petition compared the lease with Georgia's famous Yazoo Land Fraud of the 1790s and castigated the convict system as "a subterfuge, a cheat, a fraud on the tax-payers . . . a cankerous sore on the body politic." Mrs. Felton then mounted a fierce attack on leasing in a widely noted article in *The Forum*. "Every prison official appointed by the State," she noted, "holds his place by lessee influence."[28]

The prison statistics for 1886 should also be a part of this snapshot. The convict population of 1,527 represented a per diem cost of a nickel. Sixty-eight prisoners died and 57 escaped that year, rates of 4.1 percent

Georgia Convict's Sentences Under the Lease
PERCENT SENTENCED TO EACH TERM

Year	1-2 yrs.	3-4 yrs.	5-6 yrs.	7-10 yrs.	11-15 yrs.	16-20 yrs.	LIFE
1816-1853 (all prisoners)	18.8	46.8	20.6	11.5	0.8	0.6	1.0
1870 (all prisoners received)	24.5	19.1	21.8	15.4	2.7	9.1	7.3
1875 (sample:80 of 320 received)	10.0	22.5	31.2	22.5	3.7	5.0	5.0
1880 (sample:90 of 360 received)	15.5	17.8	21.1	22.2	7.8	8.9	6.7
1886 (sample:145 of 583 received)	24.1	22.1	20.7	18.6	4.8	1.4	8.3
1890 (sample:73 of 294 received)	19.2	26.0	16.4	13.7	4.1	6.8	13.7
1896 (sample:78 of 308 received)	24.7	20.8	19.5	16.9	0	2.6	15.6

and 3.4 percent respectively. According to the United States census of 1880, 816,906 whites and 725,133 blacks resided in Georgia. The lessees' prison camps contained a population of 1,378 blacks and 149 whites. These figures represent .02 percent of the state's white and .2 percent of its black population. In other words, while 1 of 500 Georgia blacks was a convict, 1 of 5,000 whites was. Blacks were represented in convict labor gangs at a rate ten times greater than their distribution in the population of the state as a whole.

In November 1886 Henry Holcombe Tucker, a prominent Baptist clergyman, former chancellor of the University of Georgia, and former president of Mercer University, mounted a vigorous defense of leasing before a clearly antagonistic audience at the NPA convention. It was a repugnant performance by any standard, and the discomfort and misgivings of Tucker's audience are almost palpable on the pages of the *NPA Proceedings* for that year. Tucker began by hiding behind the smoke-screen of the lease statute's literal provisions. The law provided full protection for convicts in Georgia, he contended, since the governor could cancel leases and sue and recover for cases of inhumane treatment. In fact, convicts themselves could bring action for damages in both the civil and criminal courts. Hours of labor were restricted and Sunday reserved for rest. Rules for cleanliness, bedding, clothing, blankets, hospital accommodations, diet, even cubic feet of air—all, he pointed out, were prescribed by law. Tucker concluded this inventory by declaring: "In fact, almost nothing is left to the mere discretion of the lessees."

Furthermore, he said, "Lessees are almost sure to be men of character, men who are known to be worthy of respect and confidence; and they are almost sure to be men of business, and men of large capacity." He pointed out: "Another advantage of the plan is this: that it provides for the poor convict somebody who is interested in him." For all of leasing's cruelty, it is hard not to imagine laughter in Tucker's audience at this point of the address.

The ugliest portion of Tucker's speech clearly exposed the racism behind leasing. White convicts, he argued, actually suffered more deeply than their black counterparts, since blacks were used to a similar kind of life and were actually better off in the camps with respect to their clothing, diet, and the like. Their only distress resulted from their having been deprived of "liberty, liquor, and lust." The white convicts' afflictions were greater, because they were forced to mingle with the blacks.

The law, Tucker concluded, "lays on the Caucasian a dreadful grief, which the African does not feel. . . . The fact remains, and will remain, that there is a psychological repulsion between races, horrible to one but not the other."[29]

It is likely that Tucker's speech, which occupied a central place in the NPA's program and was delivered in the host city where critics might hesitate on grounds of etiquette to protest, was intended as a definitive defense of a system most delegates considered indefensible. If so, it was a complete failure. Vigorous rebuttals followed this opéra bouffe performance. Particularly effective was a reply, apparently delivered extempore, by Dr. P. D. Sims, chairman of Tennessee's prison board, in which he compared death rates of leasing and nonleasing states. He was followed by a warden from a nonleasing state who pointed out that Georgia statistics published in 1882 revealed "one hundred and eighty-two died in six years; and there is not an average population of quite twelve hundred. There are thirty to the thousand dead; and you can't bring them to life."[30]

In sum, then, what this still photograph of 1886 reveals is mounting criticism, deepening institutional entrenchment, ideological defensiveness, worsening conditions, and the first signs of concerted convict resistance. The history of the next twenty years largely comprises a working out of these themes.

III

In June 1886 C. C. Bingham, boss of the convict camp on the Georgia Midland Railroad, submitted his almost completely inaccurate "Whipping Report" to the governor. Such reports invariably extolled the conditions in the work camps and the treatment the convicts received. In Bingham's report not a trace of cruelty appears: "The condition of the camp is good—I allow cruelty practiced [sic]—The diet consists of _lb Bacon per day to each convict—milk once each day . . . Syrup & Flour bread twice a week ..'Fruit'—that is ripe peaches all they can eat." He also recorded whippings for various offenses: disobeying rules, failing to work, "swaring," resisting.

The following examples are also characteristic of the bosses' reports:

"The condition of this camp is good and the treatment kind." —J. B. Crabb
"The men are in good health have good clothing, shoes, &c." —W. S. Tyson

"No cruelty practiced at this camp." —B. R. Harris
"There has been no abuse of convicts to my knowledge."—W. O. Reese[31]

But the convicts knew a different life and at times had the chance to testify to it. In September 1887 a highly publicized trial resulted from the demand of John B. Gordon, then governor, that Penitentiary Companies two and three show cause why their contracts should not be revoked. And he fired Bingham. The cause of the sensation was a series of exceptionally brutal whippings by Bingham. "I visited . . . the convict camp on the line of the Georgia Midland railroad, known as Bingham's camp, and carefully examined the convicts that had been so brutally whipped just one week before," the physician Dr. Westmoreland wrote to Governor Gordon on 26 August 1887. "Hardy Mobley I found very severely whipped, not only had the skin been denuded from both buttock [sic] . . . but on one side the contusion or braising beneath the skin was very severe."[32]

Gordon appointed Hoke Smith—who as governor twenty years later would preside over the abolition of leasing in Georgia—as a special prosecutor for the case. Smith presented ten allegations, all of them supported by documentary and oral evidence, that show the extent to which the lease had miscarried. The most serious, besides those concerning brutality, were that most of the original lessees had vacated the leases, leaving them to parties unlisted in the original contracts, that they sublet prisoners in direct violation of the statute, and that they worked the convicts in areas other than the mines, roads, and brickyards that their contracts stipulated. The arrogant confidence of the lessees at this high point of Georgia convict leasing is evident in the response of James W. English to Smith's questioning of him on the witness stand. When Smith asked English how much money his company had on hand, the latter replied: "As you have no claims, I don't think it any of your business." English's confidence was not misplaced. Though the trial left Atlanta buzzing, its results were minimal. The two companies were convicted of minor offenses, and Gordon fined them the negligible sum of $2,500.[33]

The short-lived mutiny at Dade in 1886 proved to be prophetic. The following year at the nearby Rising Fawn camp, the whipping boss, Captain Connor, was stabbed by Jim Holt, a convict whom Connor was whipping. The action precipitated another fleeting uprising, which quickly subsided when a guard shot and killed William Jackson, a black convict and alleged ringleader.[34]

During the next few years the camps were relatively quiet. But during the summer of 1891 and the spring of 1892 Brown's mining enterprises once again became scenes of mutiny and violence. At six o'clock on the morning of 22 June 1891, Capt. J. M. Moreland, assistant warden at the Dade coal mines, and Jesse Rankin, the twenty-two-year-old night guard, sent the convicts to the mines. But seven of them remained behind to request fresh overalls, claiming that theirs were still soaked from the previous day's work. These seven were engaged in a desperate conspiracy to escape by any means necessary. They were mostly white men: Jack Landsdowne and his son, S. H. Landsdowne; Sam Green, who was serving a thirty-five-year sentence for burglary; Wilson Palmer; John Rutherford, a black burglar with a reputation for escapes; Abe Wayman; and George Ward.

As the convicts confronted Moreland and Rankin, Wilson Palmer suddenly drew a gun he had somehow managed to obtain and shot Moreland in the face. Young Rankin turned and ran. The seven prisoners then rushed for Moreland's office, secured a shotgun, and barricaded the door. In the ensuing gun battle, Rankin and another guard named Pat Rowland were killed. Of the prisoners, Palmer, Sam Green, George Ward, and Jack Landsdowne failed to survive the shootout. The incident ended the day it began, but six men had lost their lives. Remarkably, Moreland survived.[35]

And on Good Friday, 15 April 1892, the men who mined coal and built a railroad from Chicamauga to the coal mines in Walker County, the men at Penitentiary Camp number nine, refused to go to work. They were upset at the replacement of the camp's superintendent, a relatively amiable alcoholic who had shown up drunk once too often. Governor Northen, mindful of the violence of the previous summer, acted immediately, telegraphing the sheriff of Walker County to suppress the mutiny, and it quickly collapsed.[36]

In 1894 the principal keeper reported for the second straight year that a greater number of convicts had been processed than at any other time in Georgia's history. The population had swelled to 2,328, 740 of whom were between the ages of ten and twenty.[37] Convicts were scattered in fifteen camps around the state, where they worked on plantations and in sawmills, coal mines, and brickyards. The two largest camps were coal mining operations—Cole City, operated by Dade, and Crawfish Springs, operated by Chattahoochee Brick. The third largest was the Chattahoochee Camp in Fulton County, where the convicts manufactured bricks. After mining, sawmills were the most frequent users of leased labor; some 720 convicts worked in eight sawmills in 1893.[38]

Nearly 130 convicts, almost half of whom were women, worked on plantations. The women (there were 62 of them) were sublet by the prominent planter James Monroe Smith to a Colonel Maddox in Elbert County. The remaining 65 male convicts worked on Smith's plantation, Smithonia, in neighboring Oglethorpe County. Smith, however, ran camps in twelve counties from Ware (in the southeast near Brunswick) to Walker (close to the Tennessee border). Most were on his own land. He also subleased misdemeanants from the county, although this was illegal. Smith self-consciously perpetuated the old paternalistic planter ethic. He knew his convicts by name. Occasionally he would appear among his workers (not all of them were convicts), and, it was reported, they would flock around him as he passed out small change. In 1886 Smith was singled out by the principal keeper for negligence in caring for his charges. Flu, pneumonia, dysentery, and diarrhea were rampant at Smithonia, he noted, blaming the diet for the outbreaks.[39] But Smith seems to have corrected these faults, and generally his camp enjoyed a reputation for good conditions. After 1897, when subleasing was legal, Smith never again used state convicts on his farm; instead he worked his land with misdemeanants from the county and sublet the state convicts whom he had leased. His profit from this venture came to $7,200 per year.[40]

In 1897, as the twenty-year lease was drawing to a close, the principal physician characterized the lease as "a veritable slavery."[41] Sentencing data show that reality and rhetoric were drawing ever closer. There were 2,235 convicts in 1897; 56 died and 70 had escaped. Of these 2,235, 399 were lifers. Indeed, the sentence of life had become the most frequent single sentence. The median sentence of the remaining prisoners was 7.4 years.[42]

But by the end of the 1890s criticism and doubt had begun to emanate from business as well as from humanitarian sources. The years of the twenty-year lease had been ones of erratic economic change. In the first half of the decade, the revolt of the farmers against the Bourbon Democrats had included demands for the cessation of leasing.[43] The depression of 1893 provoked some reassessment on the part of lessees whose product inventories were escalating. Still, at three cents a day, it was certainly worth maintaining a labor reserve, even in hard times.

But in the two years just prior to the expiration of the leases, the economic and political situation made an about-face. The Populists were defeated in the 1896 elections, and the nation was enjoying a new prosperity as the grip of the 1893 depression slackened. In December 1897, then, the legislature chose to continue leasing—but with some important changes. The most important were to restrict the lease period to five years and to permit subleasing. Bids would be made on a per-convict basis; they averaged $100 per year.[44] In 1904 the final extension of the policy brought in average bids of $225.52.[45] Now Georgia was beginning to realize revenue. Some $338,000 was anticipated from the 1904 leases, the *Outlook* reported.[46]

A brief review of the price structure puts these later bids in perspective. The first convicts had been let in 1868 at a per capita, per year rate of $25. The next year they went to Grant, Alexander and Company for the sanctimonious promise of good treatment. In 1871 the rate was $50. In 1874 most were leased at the rate of $11, though the average was a little higher. The next lease was the twenty-year arrangement during which prices per head fluctuated. In 1880 a convict cost a lessee $21.08; in 1897, $11.21. After 1899 real prices are difficult to calculate because of the practice of subleasing. What is certain is their steady and very sharp rise. With legal subleasing the practice was more susceptible to market forces, which intensified the pressure to pay close to the going rate for free labor. In 1907 the Prison Commission finally reported that it had just approved a sublease for approximately the rate of free labor: $570 per convict.[47] When the estimated $100 upkeep costs are factored in, the total cost to a lessee was more than two dollars per day, which was the prevailing free-wage rate.

If convicts were worth maintaining at three cents per day during downturns of the business cycle, at two dollars they had to be kept laboring at all times. And another of their advantages, their sheer presence in the labor market, also became a liability at going rates during slack times, for lessees had to feed, clothe, and guard these unproductive workers, who were thus transformed from a productive asset to a drain.

This situation is precisely the one faced by Georgia's lessees as lease prices escalated. The Panic of 1907 and ensuing depression hit Georgia hard. In 1908 the Prison Commission reported that many enterprises that used convict labor faced bleak prospects. Many a sawmill, brickyard, and turpentine still were closed down.[48]

By this time, too, Brown's mines had ceased to produce. As productivity declined, Brown's son, Julius, said he no longer found working convicts to be profitable. To end his family's generation-long connection with the state's prisoners, Julius Brown simply refused to pay the trivial sum of $750—a fine levied on his company for mismanagement. Thus he got rid of the burden of his convicts; they were simply dispersed between the other two companies, while he washed his hands of the matter. The company also declined to pay its fees to the state on the grounds that the original party to the contract, Joseph E. Brown, had died. Although that particular evasion was unsuccessful, it hardly mattered to the state, the convicts, or the company. By the early twentieth century the mines, a local historian says, "were no longer major enterprises in the area."[49]

The facts that yet another searing investigation in 1908 revealed horrendous abuses and that public outcries about cruel practices culminated in an editorial campaign by the *Atlanta Georgian* fade before the stark reality of escalation in the cost of leases. The skittish legislature was still wary about losing revenue; as the *Columbus Enquirer Sun* reported: "The state treasury has just lost a quarter of a million dollars through prohibition, and the complete abolition of the lease system would take as much or more annually from the state treasury. Some of the legislators are coming to the conclusion that while morality is a very good thing, it don't go very well with a low tax rate."[50] But the total package of morality—prohibition, disfranchisement, and abolition—that Gov. Hoke Smith put forward was a program whose time had come. In August 1908 the legislature complied with Governor Smith's request and terminated leasing with the expiration of the existing contracts, in April of 1909.[51]

Five

ALABAMA
Her Most Indefensible Shame

I

The convict lease in Georgia, for all its inefficiency, corruption, and cruelty, exemplified the practice in an undiluted form. It was leasing's ultima Thule, in E. C. Wines's image.[1] Alabama's lease history is notable more because of its enormous quantity than its unmixed quality. First of all, Alabama was where leasing lasted the longest, by far. Alabama was one of two Southern states (the other was Louisiana) that initiated a convict lease as a durable policy before the Civil War, and continued it long after other states had found different outlets for convict labor. When it began, James K. Polk had just maneuvered Congress into annexing the Republic of Texas; when it ended, Herbert Hoover and Al Smith were battling for the White House. Second, it was first in revenue. Alabama was the most successful of all states in negotiating contracts for amounts that were virtually the same as free-wage rates; and, what is equally important when one examines leasing elsewhere, it succeeded in actually collecting the moneys due from those contracts.

For most of the half-century prior to the Great Depression, an enormous conglomerate, the Tennessee Coal, Iron, and Railroad Company, leased Alabama's convicts. But the practice of leasing convicts had an ancient lineage there, and it would display a tenacious continuity.

In line with the nation's most advanced penological practices, Alabama legislators had established a penitentiary in 1839, constructed it in 1840, and discovered it to be badly in debt by 1845. So on 4 February 1846 they elected to lease the penitentiary for a term of six years to J. G. Graham. Evidently they just wanted to wash their hands of the whole convict problem, for Graham took control of all the prisoners at no cost whatsoever, while for its part the state paid nothing for either upkeep or security. Graham simply took the profit from the convicts' labor and was named warden; all other offices except those of physician and inspector were abolished. In the six years of the Graham lease, the inspector issued only one report, in 1850–1851. In this, the first official inspection report of leased prisoners in any Southern state, the inspector urged the abandonment of the system.[2]

It was a futile recommendation. As state officials began to realize that a free lease was a form of tax expenditure, they decided to continue leasing, but for a price. A physician named M. G. Moore and his partner, F. Jordan, were awarded the second six-year lease, in 1852, on terms of $650 per year. However, they never honored their contract's stipulation to pay their fee.

The next lease, in 1858, was likewise a tale of unfulfilled expectations. Dr. Ambrose Burrows agreed to somewhat more costly terms: $1,550 per year for six years. But a convict abruptly suspended the lease by murdering Burrows in 1862. After the convict was executed in the prison yard in full view of the assembled prison population, the state finally assumed control of its prisoners. The years from 1862 to 1866 were the only extended period of full state administration between 1846 and 1928. Those convicts not pardoned to join the Confederate army manufactured articles for the state, under the watchful eye of the warden—Dr. M. G. Moore.

After the Civil War, prison corruption showed as much persistence as any other aspect of Alabama's political life. Strictly on his own executive authority, the first post–Civil War governor, Robert M. Patton, leased the state's 374 convicts to the predatory firm of Smith and McMillen, again for six years. Smith and McMillen, as it turned out, was a dummy firm controlled by the Alabama and Chattanooga Railroad, whose president after 1869 was Robert M. Patton.[3] Although the new governor affirmed in 1869 that the lease was not intended to be permanent, it would be another sixty years before this temporary expedient was discontinued.[4]

The terms of the contract that turned the state's convicts over to Smith and McMillen were simple, yet astounding: the company paid the state five dollars, and the state lent the lessees $15,000. The loan was never repaid. The lone inspection report issued during that entire period gave a convict population of 360, 282 of whom were black.[5] Such figures should be viewed with skepticism, however. In fact, Thomas Peters, Sam Tate, and A. K. Shephard were secret partners of the Smith and McMillen firm, which sublet the convicts for forced labor through-out the state. As was soon evident, it is highly unlikely that Smith and McMillen kept precise records.[6]

When the penitentiary with its 175 convicts was turned over to the state for a brief period in June of 1872, the state confronted an emer-gency almost identical to the one it had faced a decade earlier, for the penitentiary was in a state of near total dilapidation. The roof leaked constantly, rotting the wood floors below. Doors were splintered, win-dows shattered, and engines, machinery, and tools smashed. Equipment valued at $20,000 when Smith and McMillen took control were appraised at $500 in 1881.[7] The state had to step in again.

In another unhappy example of historical continuity, the unscrupu-lous Dr. M. G. Moore—the miscreant who had reneged on his contract in the 1850s—was promptly named warden, presumably because of his experience in the field. Perhaps predictably, both he and his successor, Larkin Willis, proved to be dedicated embezzlers. Moore disbursed $11,000 between June 1872 and March 1873 but left vouchers explaining only $4,700; while Willis left $7,800 in vouchers but spent $30,000. Moore submitted no reports, but in 1873 there appeared in the *State Documents* a short notice that the Penitentiary Board had acquired a farm. This would prove to be an unsatisfactory purchase; the farm, on the Tallapoosa River near Montgomery, was poorly situated on land prone to flooding, and the state tried in various ways to cancel its obligation. The prison popu-lation in 1873 comprised just 219 convicts, 185 of them black. Forty-seven of them would die that year working in mines and on railroads.[8]

Leasing, reinstituted as an informal expedient by a rash, frightened, and destitute board, then began to expand, slowly but steadily. In the next few years prisoners were dispersed all over the state, some at work on state projects, some on the farm, some leased to private individuals. In 1875 Gov. George Houston expressed an ambivalence about leasing that would typify official reactions throughout its history. The $50,000 purchase price for the state prison farm was to have been paid with 8 percent state bonds, Houston explained, but he instead furnished the seller, Thomas Williams, with one hundred convicts for eight years and canceled the bonds. At the same time, however, Houston expressed his dissatisfaction at judges' having discretionary power to send convicts to counties, because he wanted them delivered to the penitentiary where the state could take direct advantage of their labor; he complained that Alabama had spent over $100,000 in 1874 on food, clothing, and upkeep for convicts, many of whom were in county jails.[9]

But, as Houston soon learned, the leasing contracts brought in more revenue than could be collected from the direct use of the convicts' labor by the state. By 1876 eleven lessees were working 520 convicts, and the penitentiary reported a profit of $14,307.40. Never again would prisons be anything but a source of immense revenue to the state. Indeed, Alabama consistently ranked first among all states in revenue from convict labor, and by 1883 at least 10 percent of the state's annual revenue derived from this source.[10]

As early as 1878 the superintendent, Col. J. G. Bass, expressed "pardonable pride [for] our financial success": his department showed a surplus of almost $20,000, half of which came from completing the Wetumpka branch of the Southern and Northern Alabama Railroad. Bass went on somewhat pompously to declare his "pleasure . . . that the contract system of working convicts outside the walls is now becoming efficient and effective, and, in a large majority of cases, under the mild and humane treatment sought to be practiced towards the inmates of this prison, . . . gives hopeful promise in many cases of the reformation of the convict, the great end aimed at by the law." But 60 out of 540 convicts under this mild and humane regime would die in 1880—a fact that was revealed only because of a new law tightening reporting requirements. (By way of contrast, the prison death rate in nonleasing states in 1883–1884 was 1.5 percent.)[11]

J. G. Bass emerges in his reports as a very industrious official—and not just because the law required him to explain what he was doing. As old contracts expired, Bass made new ones at about eight dollars per month. Contracts could be complicated, because the 1879 law resuscitated the old practice from slavery times of classifying convicts as "full," "half," or "dead" hands, and different rates were demanded for each.

Correspondence between Bass and one of the major early lessees, which is now collected in the Alabama Department of Archives and History, illustrates the sometimes precarious position that a convict superintendent faced. On the one hand, the state's interest lay in farming out as many prisoners as possible and in collecting the full amount of the hire contract; for these purposes, Bass had every incentive to establish and maintain good relations with the lessees. On the other hand, he was required to look to the convicts' welfare. It could be a tightwire act for someone with more diplomatic skill than Bass. On 30 November 1876 he wrote firmly to Gaius Whitfield, a lessee near Demopolis: "For Several Months past I have had many reports by citizens of your county of the harsh treatment of your convicts by your Supt. Mr Bush," and made it clear he expected the mistreatment to cease. The admonition appears to have had little effect, however, because a year and a half later the Board of Inspectors resolved that "the convicts [at Whitfield's] are overworked and not allowed sufficient time to rest." "We fear that your superintendent Mr. Bush is not doing his duty as he should," Bass advised the planter. At other times he cajoled and flattered the lessee—as when he wrote to thank Whitfield "as a contractor—*and as Gentlemen* [sic]," for his zeal in recapturing two escaped prisoners; or again, when in December 1876 he had to ask Whitfield for $600 of the fees he owed, so that Governor Houston might have funds on hand to pay interest on the state debt due the following month.[12]

A major preoccupation of superintendent and lessee alike was the size and composition of the labor supply. "I shall do all I can the coming spring to furnish you all the hands you need—Dont trouble yourself about new papers at present," Bass assured Whitfield in January 1877. But he was unable to meet the demand when spring came. "Do not rely on us for more hands. as it will be impossible to furnish you. are getting but few," he wrote in May. By fall, however, Bass was sanguine again: "I hope to furnish you some hands from our fall Courts . . . all you may need for the next Crop." But then, come spring, he had to make his seasonal apology. "The receipt of convicts this Spring has been very light and I fear we will not be able to supply you with anymore." "We will not be able to supply them—Col Williams's has to be kept up and he is now in the grass & wanting hands badly." The racial composition of the work squads was also of concern. Contracts called for black convicts, who were always seen throughout the South as the preferred race for agricultural labor—although it was quickly apparent that, in the event of a shortage, white convicts would do. "If you will agree to take 4 or 5 white men," Bass wrote in the fall of 1878, "I can let you have some 12 or 13 men. I am asking all contractors to take—say 6 to 10 white men, each—then all will work well."[13]

But the position of warden was a political prize, and despite Bass's diligence and diplomacy, when Rufus Cobb was elected governor in 1880 a new man, John H. Bankhead, was appointed to the job. Bankhead, an ambitious political striver, would later serve as a congressman and a senator and make a reputation as an advocate of good roads through convict labor.

Meanwhile a four-man legislative committee investigated allegations of mistreatment. As a rule, the committee found, the convicts were well treated and not overworked—when due allowance was made for whippings and water punishments. The worst feature of the system, the fastidious committee found, was the absence of racial segregation. "This we condemn," they opined in the report's strongest language.[14]

Bankhead himself would be investigated by the House in 1883. Under questioning, he admitted spending up to two-thirds of his time in the House lobby trying to have removal power withdrawn from the governor's hands, so that the warden could be dismissed by impeachment only.[15] However, Bankhead did have enough integrity to visit as many places as he could in his first weeks in office. "He found [the convict camps] totally unfit for use, without ventilation, without adequate water supplies, crowded to excess, filthy beyond description, and infested with vermin," Governor Cobb related.[16]

The legislature responded with a bill that followed the example of Georgia, which had established in 1881 a policy of restricting the power to impose physical punishment. In Georgia the designated "whipping bosses," as they were soon known, quickly became notorious. Alabama's 1883 statute charged that "no corporal punishment of any kind" be administered unless it followed specific procedures—procedures that the law deferentially left to the wardens to establish; and it directed that only designated agents of the warden could inflict such punishment. The law also established a task system in the mines. Finally, it gave the governor the power to cancel contracts and fire wardens.[17] Bankhead had clearly lost his campaign for independence and extended employment.

Toward the end of the 1880s the unsettled nature of convict labor policies agitated the legislature. In 1884 an attempt to sell the prison farm had misfired, and a small portion of it was being leased. By 1886, 559 convicts were dispersed at six locations across the state, from "the Walls" (the penitentiary at Wetumpka) to the Pratt Coal and Coke Company just northwest of Birmingham. The state had netted more than $68,000 from leasing in the previous two years. The reactionary Bourbon governor Edward O'Neal had taken to heart the advice of a friend who had written during his 1882 campaign that "rigid economy should be his sole commit[ment]."[18]

II

The first period of convict leasing in Alabama came to an end in 1886, after forty years of drift and uncertainty. The second period would likewise be one of forty years, from 1888 to 1928. These four decades, however, are characterized by far higher levels of efficiency and organization. They are the years of the TCI lease, when virtually all convicts came under the almost complete control of the Tennessee Coal, Iron, and Railroad Company. Halfway through this period, the TCI became a part of United States Steel, the world's first billion-dollar corporation.

That symbol of sectional reconciliation, Rutherford B. Hayes, whose ascendancy to the presidency in 1877 marked the end of the era of Reconstruction, served in his later years as president of the National Prison Association, an organization whose membership rolls boasted some of the greatest reform figures of the late nineteenth century. Addressing the 1888 convention of the NPA, Hayes expressed the near universal sentiment of non-Southern delegates when he called for the termination of convict leasing. Two nights after Hayes's speech, R. H. Dawson, the president of the Alabama Board of Inspectors of Convicts, rose to address the same group. Dawson was an earnest and intelligent public official, but one detects a note of sanctimonious hypocrisy on this night as he solemnly agreed with President Hayes. "The President told us, the other night, that the lease system must go. So it must, because it is wrong," he declared. "The lease system must go, as slavery went, and as the dram-shop is bound to go."[19]

Nevertheless, 1888, the year of Hayes's prophecy and Dawson's nervous assent, was the year that the old contracts ended, and the TCI took all able-bodied convicts for ten years to mine coal. Most Alabamians undoubtedly agreed with the *Montgomery Advertiser* that the contract was a "new departure." The TCI promised to construct a new prison and a schoolhouse. As the contract was being finalized, convict inspector Dawson observed: "there never was as much pains taken before in settling this business."[20]

"Able-bodied" meant "first-, second-, and third-class" hands—a system, the governor contended, that was established to be sure the convicts were not overworked. For first-class convicts the state received $18.50 per month; those in the second class fetched $13.50, those in the third $9. Since the prevailing wage for free miners who produced as much as a first-class convict at that time was between $45 and $50 per month, the TCI's competitive advantage in labor costs during the period of this leasing contract can be calculated as about $30 a month per hand less rock-bottom maintenance costs times the number of convicts who could displace free miners. The TCI made extensive use of the services of John H. Bankhead, by then a congressman, in the lease negotiations. Those services almost certainly included passing on inside information to the TCI from state prison officials. "Some bidders seemed to know more about the basis than others," the coal operator Henry De Bardeleben testified. Bankhead received a secret payoff of $1,200 for his assistance.[21]

Hence, in the year when both the president of the National Prison Association and the president of the Alabama Convict Inspection Board agreed that leasing was wrong and would have to disappear, Alabama embarked on its second forty-year era of this morally shameful and fiscally brilliant policy. Alabama's net revenue from the first two years of the TCI lease amounted to $163,534.14. Two years later the governor echoed the ambivalence that people continued to feel in Alabama and the South about this unsettling policy. "It was the financial condition which induced the state to adopt the lease system, as it is known, for it is not contended in any respectable quarter that it is best calculated to serve the purpose for which punishment is inflicted," he told the legislature.[22]

In the late nineteenth century, then, most Alabama convicts worked twelve hours a day in wet, suffocating coal shafts far below ground. When they returned to the surface in the evening air, they retired to a two-story frame miners' shack that had a rough-hewn table, benches, and a stove in the center and bunks along the wall. There they took their meals and, two to a bunk, their rest. Roused up at 5:00, and given twenty minutes to dress and eat, they would then descend to the pits for another day. To be a convict in Alabama from the 1870s to 1928 meant in most instances to be a miner.

Convict miners in Alabama, mostly but not entirely black men (1,496 out of 1,710 in 1896, a typical year), were assigned specific "tasks" or quotas that they had to fulfill. A first-class hand had to send four tons per day to the surface, a second-class hand three tons, a third-class hand two, and a fourth-class or "dead" hand one. Such classifications were determined by a monthly physical examination. Kingpins called "check-runners," also convicts, supervised the production tasks.[23]

The consequences for not making the task were often grisly. "Records show an immense amount of whipping is done," a legislative investigating committee reported in 1889. "Nearly all the whipping is for failure to get task, or for getting slate or rock in the coal."[24] In the 1930s an elderly retired guard recalled: "Convicts would be punished for not getting their tasks. The warden and the deputy warden would do the whippin'. . . . The whipping was done with a two ply strap as wide as your three fingers, tied to a staff. The convicts were face down with their pants off. They were whipped on the hips and legs five to twelve lashes."[25] Another old guard interviewed for the Alabama Writers' Project in 1938 remembered "whoop[ing] niggers just to have fun. . . . I've seen niggers with their rumps lookin' like a piece of raw beef."[26] The miners sang about it:

> The foreman he was bank boss,
> And he knows the rule,
> If you don't get your task,
> He's sure to report you.
> And when he does report you,
> The warden with a squall,
> Bend your knees
> Across that door piece fall.[27]

III

The conscientious R. H. Dawson served as convict inspector from 1883 to 1897, thus bridging the periods before and after the TCI lease. His diary, scribbled in pencil in a pocket account book, provides a valuable firsthand perspective on the convict camps in the two periods. Judging from his diary, the effects of the TCI lease were vastly to simplify the inspection process by concentrating the scattered convicts, and to improve somewhat the conditions in which they had to labor. Unquestionably, TCI conditions were usually awful and sometimes murderously so, yet the new lease did provide the state with some leverage, and TCI officials did take steps to rectify illegal conditions when such conditions were specifically pointed out to them.

Dawson's life in the middle 1880s was an incessant round of arduous inspection trips to farms and mines. In the mines especially, Dawson found conditions that were disgraceful. Of his first visit to the Pratt mines, he recorded, "Went into mine . . .—the best arrangements at this place in the state—so they claim—I cannot agree—Filthy—crowded—lice." On the farms conditions varied from deadly to comfortable. At McCurdy's farm on 6 March 1883 Dawson was "not satisfied—clothing dirty—persons of men same—doubt they have enough food." One week later, by contrast, he returned from the Pollard place "entirely satisfied ... Plenty of good food—comfortable lodging—Negroes satisfied—no complaint."[28]

Treatment and general conditions varied in both time and place. About a month after his first visit to McCurdy's atrocious farm, he found "a great contrast since my first visit"; while of Pollard's at the same time he judged "This place going down hill." "Ordered Stevens to prepare hospital and privies forthwith—also to supply table utensils, and give the men more meat."[29]

In the mines Dawson faced a continual struggle for the establishment and maintenance of minimal standards of sanitation, nourishment, and discipline. At Spring Hill in May 1883, for instance: "things in bad order . . . Everything filthy . . . convicts ragged—many barefooted—very heavily ironed." In October he declared himself "more than ever disgusted with mines." But the TCI lease of 1888, by concentrating the prisoners, made inspections easier and remedies for bad conditions more readily implemented. By 1891 he remarked of one mine examination: "Made a close inspection of [Prattville] No 2. I never saw the convicts in such good fix." And the next year: "Went to Pratt mines [on 27 August]. Remained until 29 [August] —Everything doing very well."[30]

On 31 December 1890, obviously feeling that his tireless labors had improved conditions for Alabama's forgotten prisoners, Dawson permitted a unique note of pious introspection to penetrate his pages. "So ends the year 1890," he wrote. "I hope with better results than any previous one. Although I have worked very hard, and had much trouble—still I feel that I am better understood than before, and have a better position among thinking people. May God give me strength to work on, and make the convict system something of which the people need not be ashamed."[31]

IV

Punctuating the history of Alabama's second forty years of leasing are a series of horrific mining disasters, culminating in the explosion at Banner Mine in 1911, which killed 122 convict and 6 free miners. By that time, as two leading Alabama historians have explained, the state had long since successfully used the threat and the reality of convict labor to crush Alabama's emerging union movement. In 1911 TCI president George Crawford frankly asserted the chief tenet of the political economy of convict mining: "The chief inducement for the hiring of convicts," he said, "was the certainty of a supply of coal for our manufacturing operations in the contingency of labor troubles."[32] Such limpid candor affords us a glimpse of theoretical insight into the exigencies of the labor market as perceived by the South's ruling circles. As will be clear when other states are examined, it was this attribute of *reliability* (which is also in a sense exploitability) for which lessees were willing to pay—even pay a premium. In later years when they had to pay the same as the going rate for free labor they still continued to lease convicts whose productivity was agreed by persons familiar with the occupation to be lower than that of free miners.

An explosion at the Pratt Mine killed ten men, nine of them convicts, in June of 1891. A legislative committee had visited the mine in 1889 and found it well ventilated. Their disapproval was reserved for the inadequate pumping system: "Some of the men are required at times to work in water from ankle to knee deep," they noted. However, Mr. Hooper, the mine inspector in 1891, claimed that gas had been building up for some time in the mine. "This is a dangerous and unfit place to work convicts," he judged. But the revenues for both the state and the TCI continued to swell. Net income from convict hires in 1892 was just under $80,000—an increase of more than fivefold in fifteen years.[33]

But even the seemingly hermetic world of Alabama prisons could not remain immune from the crises of the 1890s. The revolt of the farmers, the great industrial strikes of Homestead and Pullman, and the crash and depression of 1893—all converged in a violent, racially charged miners strike in 1894, in which the issues were not simply the 10 percent wage cut imposed by the TCI on its nonconvict miners, but the demand of free miners and their champions for the removal of convicts from the mines.

This laudable objective had actually become official state policy, according to legislation passed in 1893. The law passed on 14 February of that year set forth a vision of a new kind of prison system. The three-man board of inspectors was supplanted by one consisting of one man from each of the state's nine congressional districts. Pursuant to the law the state purchased and constructed with convict labor a cotton mill at Speigner to employ the labor of women and boys. The law required that "The labor and instruction of the convicts of the first or better grade shall be directed with reference to fitting the convict to maintain himself by honest industry after his discharge from imprisonment as the main object of such labor and training." It also directed that all convicts should be under the immediate supervision of a state employee, and called for the removal of all convicts from the mines by 1 January 1895. Section 48 reads like a fantasy to those who know that convict leasing would not be eliminated in Alabama for thirty-five years:

> Upon the termination of the contract with the Tennessee Coal, Iron and Railroad Company . . . said contract shall not be renewed or extended, and all of the convicts worked under said contract at its termination shall be transferred to the penitentiary. . . . It is the true intent and meaning of this act, that the convicts now worked under contract in any of the coal mines of this State shall be removed therefrom as rapidly as practicable, by the first day of January, 1895.

There was, however, one all-important contingency clause attached to these commendable aspirations: they were to be achieved "if it can be done without detriment to the financial interests of the state."[34]

There is little reason to doubt the sincerity of the legislature's reforming intent. Indeed, Alabama's record of struggles for social justice and the amelioration of suffering stands among the most consistent and poignant in Southern history. One of the most remarkable reform figures in Southern history, Julia Tutwiler—"the angel of the stockades" as she was dubbed in the sentimental idiom of the day (more prosaically R. H. Dawson called her the "Female Howard of the South")—probably had a more effective career in bringing about concrete reforms than any of her Southern counterparts. An early student of Southern prisons, Hilda Jane Zimmerman, has argued that Alabama was the only state where the reformers had any impact.[35] The towering irony of Alabama's legacy stems from the fact that it was the state in which leasing was at once among the most brutal and long-lasting, on the one hand, and the object of the most effective ameliorative reforms, such as the establishment of schools and churches to serve the prisoners, on the other.

Probably most important of such ameliorative reforms was the provision in 1887 for schoolrooms to be constructed at the stockades and instruction given to the convicts by qualified teachers, who were paid twenty-five dollars a month. Dawson rightly called it "Miss Julia Tutwiler's Reformatory Bill." Even as the schoolrooms were under construction the assertive Tutwiler immediately began to badger Dawson to hire more teachers and increase their salaries. Frustrated, Dawson responded: "Dear Miss Julia: . . . every person seems to misunderstand me about this convict business. You write as if you thought I had the power or authority to hire more teachers than the contractors will furnish" or to pay them more than the statute provided for. Nonetheless, he found it prudent to solicit an opinion from the attorney general on the matter before conclusively denying her request. The salaries would stay where the legislation had fixed them, and the schools were always short of teachers.[36]

However authentic the reform intentions behind the 1893 legislation may have been, the statute was written in the subjunctive mode: *if* the state's finances would not be jeopardized, the convicts could be removed. In that same year, however, the nineteenth century's own Great Depression struck, and with tremendous force. Panic swept Wall Street when U.S. Treasury reserves fell below the level that the great investment houses considered to be safe. When Alabama miners struck in the spring of 1894 to protest a 10 percent wage cut, Henry DeBardeleben, the Andrew Carnegie of Birmingham, responded by importing "blacklegs"—African American scab labor. The strike lasted until August but was broken by Reuben Kolb's loss in the 1894 election—he had called for the complete removal of convicts from the mines—by the violence of the miners, and probably by the victory of the railroads in the great Pullman Strike of that same year.[37] To abandon the lease, under these circumstances, just seemed too bold an action. Gov. William C. Oates reported a deficit in the state budget of nearly a quarter of a million dollars in 1895. The TCI lease "cannot yet be dispensed with," he concluded. Oates's successor, Joseph Johnston, concurred: "The state should have steadily in view the necessity for getting entirely rid of the lease system." But, given the concerns about "the present condition of our treasury . . . We are constrained to proceed carefully." This display of fiscal caution, however, only poorly masked a determination to proceed with leasing, and indeed has all the earmarks of being a bargaining tactic brought on by the impending termination of the TCI lease, scheduled to expire on 31 December 1897.[38]

So of course the lease was renewed, and Alabama tied its fortunes to those of the TCI. Early in the twentieth century, the state managed to achieve a near-equilibrium between convict and free-miner wage rates, a remarkable achievement brought about not only by the depressing effect of the presence of hundreds of convict miners on nonconvict miners' wages, but also by the virtual destruction of the nascent miners' union, the United Mine Workers of Alabama, in the previous decade. By

1903 Alabama was receiving a per-ton "wage" essentially the same as that of free miners.[39]

But reform legislator Robert Moulthrop was incorrect when in 1911 he thundered: "There is but one argument in favor of working the convicts in the death-dealing coal mine, and the malaria- breeding district where the new saw mill is established, and that is the revenue derived from the lease system."[40] For state revenue was by no means the only reason to lease convicts. Many a Birmingham industrialist nurtured warm feelings toward leasing because of the comparative advantage it conferred in depressing labor costs. And a careful historian of black coal miners succinctly adds a third necessary though not sufficient reason for the continued grip of leasing on the state—a political reason: leasing, he writes, "constituted the quid pro quo of a compromise between the two major wings within the state Democratic party: the conservative planters of the black belt and 'progressive' industrial promoters of the Birmingham mineral district."[41] Thus it was in Alabama as in Georgia, Florida, Mississippi—indeed in every state where leasing's roots took a tenacious hold—that the policy endured because it served a complex combination of interwoven political, economic, and social interests.

In 1898 Alabama obtained 73 percent of its total revenue of $378,120.48 from the hire of its convicts. The state spent $45 on bedding that year. In 1901–1906 the state's total budget surplus increased by a factor of ten over that of the previous five-year period. Of course, the surplus represented more than the hiring of convicts, but the governor reported that "about as many [convicts] as are physically able to be put in the mines are getting out coal by the ton." Colonies of former convicts had begun to grow up around the mines. One-third of the free miners at Coalburg were former prisoners as early as 1889.[42] The convict lease seemed insuperable.

From 1906 to 1910 revenues rose still more, from $1.2 to $1.7 million. In 1915 receipts of the Convict Department constituted one-sixth of the state's total income (although some of that revenue came from the cotton mill at Speigner and from the prison farms, not from leasing entirely). The state had been receiving approximately the going rate for free labor since at least 1903, but, as indicated above, there were other forces keeping the convicts in the mines. In the face of these numbers the continuous attacks on the practice were almost pathetic. Julia Tutwiler died of cancer in 1916, having done much to ameliorate but little to end the system. When a delegate to the American Prison Association (as the

NPA had been renamed) in 1917 condemned Alabama's lease as "her unholiest and most indefensible shame," few lessees trembled.[43]

Of course, not all the funds received by the convict department found their way into the state treasury. In 1911 the department's director, James Oakley, was arrested for having embezzled $100,000 of the state's money. After a three-year judicial comedy of errors, in which three Oakley confederates were convicted of jury tampering, Oakley himself got off scot-free.[44]

The year after Oakley's trial, a legislative investigating committee made its conclusions plain: "The convict lease system of Alabama is a relic of barbarism, a species of human slavery, a crime against humanity." Four years later a committee on convicts and highways resolved: "The convict lease system in the State of Alabama is a relic of barbarism, it is a form of human slavery, it is next to impossible for the average citizen unfamiliar with the conditions to grasp or comprehend the horrors attendant with such a system." Thus it was that, over the years, there had even developed a conventional stock of rhetorical devices to describe the policy—leasing's inventory of platitudinous phrases. One can find the same terms used over and over again in other states where convicts were leased.[45]

The legislature again seemed on the verge of abolishing leasing in 1915. In a speech to Alabama legislators, a former attorney general of Georgia admonished them to consider "the humane side" before all other considerations when it debated convict policy. The proposal to remove the prisoners from the mines, however, suffered from a glaring weakness: it did not contain a provision for any alternatives.[46]

For a compilation of terrible scenes and appalling examples of overwork and of efforts to squeeze every ounce of human labor out of abused bodies, the 1919 report on convicts and highways is particularly illuminating. Prisoners spoke of killings deep in the woods at half-forgotten turpentine camps:

> I have seen them killed in the woods at their work. I saw a guard shoot a boy by the name of "Nelse." He was dipping and I was bunching. The guard had beat him so and I told them to bring him over there and I would dip a keg for him, and he said he could not do any more that he had done give out. He was a boy about seventeen or eighteen years old and he had been running from one tree to another until he had given out and when they shot him he had set his bucket down and was standing by the side of a tree.

113

The report sometimes reveals scenes of almost Dantesque moral deterioration:

> We found at one of the turpentine camps some eighteen or twenty miles from Tuscaloosa located in a dense forest of several thousand acres almost completely away from civilization where convicts are being worked under lease from the State, the superintendent of the lessee who has the charge and control of these men after they are released from the stockade in the morning until they are returned at night laying out in the woods in a drunken stupor with a bottle of wild cat liquor in his pocket and the evidence shows that this same superintendent has been using the State's convicts in the manufacture of liquor and transporting the same by the State convicts to the city of Tuscaloosa.[47]

The committee recommended abolition and the redirection of the first- and second-class convicts' labor to roads and highways. Third-class hands, boys, women, and disabled prisoners it recommended for the Speigner mills and the state farm. The statistics for 1919 showed 2,453 convicts in four mining camps, six turpentine, and one lumber camp, as well as in Wetumpka, Speigner, and the farm.[48]

Once more, the legislature decided to act. All contracts were terminated on 31 December 1919 and new ones entered on 1 January. Based on the price of free labor, 85.5 cents per ton, the new contracts were for $93.12 1/2 per month for first-class men, and $83.12 1/2, $73, and $63 for second, third, and fourth class respectively. The contracts were supposed to last just three years, during which time a new prison would be constructed, and at the end of the contracts leasing would come to an end. The new, nine-hundred-man prison was completed in October of 1922.[49]

But once again abolition, even abolition legislation, proved to be a failure. A 1921 law extended the 1 January 1923 termination date yet one more year.[50] But then in January 1923 the new governor, William Brandon, told the legislature:

> I believe in time the lease system should be abolished and prisoners should be taken from the mines. This can only be done when the State has otherwise made provisions for the convicts where they will not be a liability on the state. I am not convinced that such a time has arrived and would therefore recommend that the time be extended for taking the prisoners out of the mines until such time that the Governor and the convict Board determine that it could be done without liability to the State.[51]

114

So the legislature extended the date for abolition still further—until 1 January 1927. As one historian has pointed out, however, "the legislative action tended to remedy only in name existing conditions. The state, instead of hiring convicts to the mines, leased the mines and worked the convicts in them."[52]

Then, in 1924, the horrifying story of the death of a convict named James Knox brought national attention to the system once more. Knox, whose death certificate, signed by a company doctor, gave suicide as the cause of death, apparently died of fright while undergoing a water punishment. The attorney general's report on the case was graphic:

> James Knox died in a laundering vat, located in the yard of the prison near the hospital, where he was placed by two negroes. . . . It seems most likely that James Knox died as a result of heart failure, which probably was caused by a combination of unusual exertion and fear. . . . After death it seems that a poison was injected artificially into his stomach in order to simulate accidental death or suicide.[53]

The diagnosis of heart failure helps confirm that Knox's death was in effect the result of torture. Decades earlier in a remarkable memoir a Florida convict boss had provided this description of "watering": "The prisoner was strapped down, a funnel forced into his mouth and water poured in. The effect was to enormously distend the stomach, producing not only great agony but a sense of impending death, due to pressure on the heart."[54] This ancient form of punishment had found its way along the intricate byways of Southern penal practice to become as widespread there as it was little known outside. Although Knox's warden and four of his sergeants were indicted, none was convicted on the charge.

The Knox case came uncomfortably close in its horrific details to a Florida scandal that had caused a nationwide sensation only three years earlier. An adventuresome, middle-class North Dakota youth, Martin Tabert, had been caught up in the web of sheriffs, labor contractors, and lessees when he hopped a freight in Jacksonville. Convicted of vagrancy, Tabert ended up in an obscure Florida lumber camp, where he was flogged to death by a sadistic whipping boss, who then had the company doctor certify death from malaria. The similarities between the Knox and Tabert cases were not lost on Alabama politicians, who always displayed a sensitivity to outside opinion, and never tired of invoking "the honor of the state."

115

Finally governor Bibb Graves, who had been elected on an antilease platform, announced a plan to remove convicts from the mines at a rate of one hundred per month beginning in February 1927. In a manner that was long familiar to the rest of the South, Alabama began to construct with convict labor a prison farm. At the same time, some eighteen convict road camps were being built, funded by a new tax on gasoline. The alternatives were thus in place, and on 1 July 1928 the last convict miners emerged from the mile-long shaft near Birmingham, singing not "The foreman he was bank boss" but "Swing Low, Sweet Chariot."[55]

Six

A HELL IN ARKANSAS

I

But Alabama and Georgia, at the midpoints of their respective leasing histories (in 1887 and 1886), were not the worst places where one could be sentenced. According to George Washington Cable, writing in 1883, that distinction belonged to Arkansas and her neighbors, Mississippi and Louisiana. If Georgia, with its twenty-year lease, most clearly displayed the prototypical features of convict leasing, Arkansas most sharply represented the element of public irresponsibility that leasing both encouraged and fed on. As Cable said, Arkansas, along with Mississippi and Louisiana, was where "undoubtedly the lessees are more slackly held to account [than in other states], as they more completely usurp the State's relation to its convicts than elsewhere."[1]

As in every Southern state, the early history of leasing in Arkansas mirrored both political and economic developments. The dilapidated Arkansas prison had been taken over by federal forces when they entered Little Rock in September 1863. In 1867, ignoring the warnings of the financially cautious governor, the legislature mandated the construction of a new penitentiary but contracted the prisoners out to a firm known as Hodges, Peay, and Ayliff, strictly as a temporary measure. In these early days, it was management, rather than labor, which seemed to be at a premium; consequently it was the state which paid the businessmen, rather than vice-versa. For the next six years, Arkansas paid its lessees thirty-five cents per convict per day. When Peay and Ayliff abandoned the company, George Weeks stepped in, and Hodges and Weeks retained the lease until April 1869. Then, under new legislation, a prominent Republican, Asa Hodges (not the Hodges from the earlier firm), took it over. The state obligingly purchased the machinery in the penitentiary for him from the previous contractors.

However, an investigating committee of the Arkansas House concluded in 1871 that Hodges's contract was illegal under the 1869 statute, which had called for "the best possible terms for the State, consistent with the proper and humane treatment of the prisoners." Its findings pointed to corruption at every level. The state had acquired the prison's machinery for Hodges "at the extravagant sum" of $8,845.40. But its actual value, the committee learned, was closer to $3,000. Convicts had been set to work on Weeks's plantation, and forty of them escaped in 1869 and 1870. The committee recommended the formation of a penitentiary board and the working of convicts inside the penitentiary exclusively. Understandably, they were silent about how this latter objective could be accomplished, for while there was enough machinery to occupy eighty prisoners, the population was already over two hundred.[2]

Arkansas's early leasing history can serve to typify the uncertainty and half-measures by which leasing was adopted in many Southern states. The Reconstruction-era legislature wavered on the question of leasing partly out of a reluctance to privatize what was traditionally a state function, and partly in light of the penitentiary's already conspicuous racial composition (according to the earliest extant data [1872], 134 out of 230 prisoners were black). This reluctance, however, was itself complicated by the lure of corruption. It was not until 1873 that something resembling the penitentiary practices in the rest of the South was cobbled together from the shards of the Reconstruction prison system.[3]

The 1871 investigation produced the first of many reforms. New legislation established the South's only elective office of penitentiary superintendent. Until such time as the new superintendent could assume his office, the legislature conferred the appointment on the Speaker of its House, C. W. Tankersley. Tankersley infuriated the laboring population of Little Rock by working convicts on public property in clear violation of a city ordinance, but he did manage to repair large portions of the dilapidated prison.[4]

The convicts' twenty-two guards were all blacks. This was at a time when, as Eric Foner writes, "to those accustomed to experiencing the law as little more than an instrument of oppression . . . it seemed particularly important that the machinery of Southern law enforcement now fell into Republican hands." Little Rock had a black police chief and black city councilmen in those years, and Arkansas's black state superintendent of education was one of four such officeholders in the South.[5]

In November 1872 the new superintendent, George S. Scott, leased the penitentiary for twenty years to Dr. Peter Brugman "on condition that he keep said convicts without expense to the state." But, significantly, others were bidding for the convicts' labor, some offering as much as $1,000 per month. With 230 convicts in the penitentiary, the $1,000 bid amounted to seventeen cents per convict per day.[6]

But Scott in fact had exceeded his authority under the statute, and the lease was canceled. Throughout the early months of 1873, as Reconstruction itself staggered to its end in Arkansas, convict leasing began to take on the appearance of a reasonable solution to a stubborn and expensive problem. The expenses of the prison from April 1871 to December 1872 amounted to some $343,000, while the convicts' labor brought in only $41,440.92—$15,000 of which went to Asa Hodges. The cost of maintaining a convict had actually risen to about $70 per month, considerably more than the wage of a free laborer. "Let the penitentiary be released for a term of years to some responsible party," argued an exasperated Little Rock editor. "Repeal the infamous law."[7]

Repealed it was, and pursuant to another reform measure the prisoners were leased for ten years to John M. Peck, who "offered to furnish everything and hold the state harmless." The hold-harmless clause left the state free "of all responsibility on account of the clothing, guarding, feeding, or subsistence" or medical treatment of the prisoners. "The state shall not be at any expense whatever," it stressed. To mollify the Little Rock workers it prohibited convict labor in the city limits and imposed a ten-hour day.[8] Thus it was that, in 1873, in the midst of the misleadingly labeled "Brooks-Baxter War" between the supporters of two politicians both of whom claimed the governor's office—a struggle which symbolized the prolonged death throes of Arkansas Reconstruction—convict leasing began in earnest in Arkansas.

This lease is a turning point because, for the first time, the state did not pay the lessee for the service of taking the convicts off its hands. Yet a full-blown system, one of material benefit to both contracting parties, was still a decade away, for the state's only advantage from this contract lay in its freedom from expense or responsibility. Convicts' labor was not yet a major source of *public* revenue for Arkansas.

John Peck had a secret partner, Col. Zebulon Ward. In 1875 Ward bought Peck's share in the lease, which he would retain until 1883. The Ward lease, then, coincided with Redemption, and indeed was an element of it.

Ward's political acumen was akin to that of Georgia's Joseph E.

Brown. Like Brown he had a habit of treating legislators to lavish dinners. He was a man of simpler tastes than Brown's, however, with a great fondness for barbecue. The penitentiary physician of those years, interviewed by an enterprising graduate student in 1930, remembered Ward's mounting great feasts of barbecued Southdown mutton at every legislative session.[9]

The payoffs to Ward were tangible. In 1875, the year of his buyout, the newly "Redeemed" or Democratic legislature passed one of the South's infamous criminal laws directed at the poor and blacks. It made the theft of any property valued at two dollars or more punishable by one to five years in prison. As a consequence, between 1876 and 1882 the prison population swelled by 50 percent, from 400 to 600. The law was almost exactly contemporaneous with Mississippi's more famous "pig law," which classified the theft of any cattle or swine as grand larceny with a maximum term of five years in the penitentiary. In 1881 the Arkansas law was amended to raise the threshold for larceny to a value of ten dollars; the prison population fell slightly for the next several years, then remained fairly level until 1890.[10]

Some 200 of these prisoners remained in the walled penitentiary in Little Rock, and in 1876 the legislature authorized a penitentiary expansion. The construction contract went to Zeb Ward, whose obvious competitive advantage—not having to pay wages to his labor force—deprived the bidding of suspense.

It was not, however, until the expiration of Ward's lease in 1883 that the complete lease system already in full flower in the rest of the South was established in Arkansas. As had happened in Alabama, Mississippi, and South Carolina, leasing reached a turning point in Arkansas when that state signed a lease requiring the lessees to pay the state for the labor they received, rather than having the state pay the lessee for relieving it of the convict dilemma. Under the 1883 system, lessees paid the state for the first time. In the two years after May 1884 the prison paid $52,084.54 into the state treasury.[11]

II

George Washington Cable presented his famous indictment of the convict lease in a speech before the National Conference of Charities and Corrections at Louisville on 26 September 1883. Two months later, returning from an exhilarating evening of dinner and conversation at

Boston's exclusive St. Botolph Club with a splendid company that included Francis Parkman, Charles Francis Adams Jr., and Matthew Arnold, Cable wrote his wife Louise: "Help me to remember that pleasing as all this is, it's not the *main thing*. No, no. I read the proof of my prisons article today. Ah! there's where I feel glad. I'm proud of that piece of work! And surely I am much mistaken if it don't make the land *ring* next February [when it was scheduled for publication in *Century Magazine*]."[12]

But Cable's hopes would prove to be sadly misplaced. And even as the article appeared, the full picture of leasing in Arkansas remained shadowy. It would be another four years before the gruesome conditions at Coal Hill, for instance, were brought to light.

In March 1888 Arkansas's penitentiary physician uncovered the corpse of a murdered convict deep in a mine near the grimy settlement of Coal Hill on the Arkansas River. Frank Colbert had been shot by his pit boss because of what he knew: Coal Hill was a graveyard. Adjacent to a railroad switch near the town was a stockade measuring approximately forty by eighteen feet and ventilated by three small windows, where about sixty convicts were housed. There they died by the dozens of scurvy, malaria, overwork, and murder. They were carried to a secret burial ground some seven hundred yards from the stockade and interred in pine boxes under sixteen inches of marshy earth. The graveyard, containing sixty to seventy such graves, resembled "a rooting place for hogs."[13] Evidence of Coal Hill conditions was beginning to leak out, and Colbert was killed to keep him from testifying.

Coal Hill's warden, J. A. Gafford, was a heavy-drinking sadist who, it was revealed, liked to force convicts to fight for his diversion. One strapping prisoner, Mat Bailey, actually killed a slight, scrawny fellow convict, Mose Harvey, in such an entertainment. Investigators sent by the Penitentiary Board had to threaten and bluff in order to get into the Coal Hill camp, where they found the body of Harvey as well as that of Charles Williams, who had been whipped to death. His recently buried corpse had no flesh on its back. An autopsy on Harvey found a broken spinal cord, crushed genitals, and eyes hanging out of their sockets.[14]

The camp at Coal Hill may have been, as the *Arkansas Gazette* put it, "A Hell in Arkansas," but it was not one for which any actual person would have to take responsibility. Neither the board nor the lessees at that time, the Arkansas Industrial Company, were brought to justice. (Gafford eventually received a five-year sentence, which he served in privileged comfort inside the penitentiary.)[15]

Few states have sketchier prison records than Arkansas. One reason is that the state did not even have a penitentiary inspector until 1889. Glimmers of leasing's reason for being can be perceived in various state reports, however. A few months after the Coal Hill story broke the secretary of state noted that the penitentiary posted a surplus of $1,172.96— a paltry sum by any standard, let alone by Alabama's—but at least a surplus.[16]

But the real justification was somewhat more subtle: it was that alternative arrangements were not yet fiscally conceivable. State officials literally seem to have been incapable of imagining any other means of convict management. For example, the inspector, John Carroll, who had been appointed on 18 April 1889, wrote in 1890 that, although Coal Hill was infamous for its brutality, that was "no reason that working them in the coal mines should be condemned," since "they have been just as badly abused out on farms, railroad construction, and other places under this system as at Coal Hill." One might glimpse a hint of irony behind this remarkable judgment, but on balance it is difficult to attribute such an intent to a report of an Arkansas penitentiary inspector in 1890. Certainly Carroll wanted to see leasing eliminated; he could not forbear to announce in his first report that he and the Penitentiary Board "will welcome the day when this system is abandoned in our State."[17] But substitute systems did not spring to mind. The legislation in effect at the time of the Coal Hill revelations, in fact, was a reformation of the system that Cable had described in 1883.

The Arkansas lease was then in the hands of the convict labor entrepreneur Col. Zebulon Ward. Ward had been a member of the Kentucky legislature in 1861–1863 and warden of the Kentucky penitentiary. He also leased prisoners in Tennessee before moving to Arkansas to take control of the state's prisoners in 1873. Ward's arrogance led him to overreach. "I am the sole lessee, and work all the convicts," he wrote in response to an inquiry from Cable, "and of course the business of the prison is my private business."[18]

His mistreatment of convicts was widely known in the state. Federal prisoners sentenced to short terms in Arkansas by a district judge were frequently alleged to request longer sentences in hopes of being dispatched to a different institution. Zebulon Ward left many matters in the hands of his equally arrogant son, Will, another hard-drinking flogger. When typhoid-pneumonia broke out among the convicts on a railroad construction site in 1880, resulting in "a dreadful mortality" of about one in five prisoners, the legislature decided to seek other bids. By that time Ward's fortune was secure anyway.[19] It was this "reformed" system that produced Coal Hill.

III

The office of inspector had expired with Reconstruction in 1875. As late as 1887 Gov. Simon P. Hughes called for the creation of this key office, and when the Coal Hill atrocities were uncovered the state did not even have a functionary charged with this most basic duty of state administration. The only penitentiary officials were a physician and a chaplain, both of whom were paid by the lessees. The shortcomings of these arrangements would be apparent soon enough. As the *Arkansas Gazette* reported, "The public were given to understand that the mining camp was a miniature Paradise on earth, while convicts were being murdered for shirking their tasks, and tied to stakes with chains and beaten to death."[20]

The 1883 lease went to two Helena, Arkansas, plantation owners, J. P. Townshend and L. A. Fitzpatrick. Shortly afterward they were joined by Met L. Jones; the three incorporated themselves as the Arkansas Industrial Company to work the convicts. They paid a monthly rate of $3.75 per convict in addition to the salaries of the physician and chaplain.[21] With the lessees enjoying complete autonomy in the disposition of the convicts, and with not a single state official vested with responsibility for the prisoners' welfare, the 1883 Arkansas lease possesses a Weberian "ideal-typical" status somewhat analogous to Georgia's.

Townshend and Fitzpatrick, paying $3.75 per month into the state's coffers for each prisoner, lost no time in subleasing a hundred of them for $12.50 each. The fact that their subleasing contract was for a period of ten years gives some indication of the size of the profits to be secured—or, in financial terms, of the size of the gap between the costs of monitoring and subsistence for convict workers, on the one hand, and their productivity, on the other. The prisoners found themselves on the plantation of C. M. Neel (or Neal). Neel, seeking to cut his management costs in order to secure still greater gains, provided arms to convict trusties and used them as guards—apparently a common practice among sublessees, and one that would later be refined and perfected by the cost-conscious overseers of Mississippi's nearby Parchman prison.

When Jones joined forces with Townshend and Fitzpatrick, however, the three sued Neel to recover the one hundred laborers and consolidate their holdings. (It was probably the only habeas corpus petition in Southern history that was filed by lessees.) The Arkansas Supreme Court agreed with Townshend and Fitzpatrick. "All the duties required by law to convicts in the penitentiary, are to be performed by the lessee of the penitentiary," the Court ruled, "and he cannot surrender their custody and control by hiring them out to another person." Neel, enraged by the decision, simply allowed many of his prisoners to escape rather than return them.[22]

The Supreme Court's decision in *Arkansas Industrial Company* v. *Neel* does not, as it may seem at first glance, prohibit subleasing, but merely holds the lessee accountable for the ultimate disposition of the prisoners. In fact the company was an enthusiastic practitioner of the sublease, and its profits from this enterprise were substantial.

In 1888 the secretary of state reported a population of 558 convicts, 75 of whom were inside the prison; the rest were leased to farms and brickyards.[23] But exactly where they were all located and under what conditions no one knew, because although the Penitentiary Board inspected the walled penitentiary in Little Rock four times a year, the law lacked a provision for the inspection of the scattered camps until 1889.

John Carroll's appointment as inspector in April of that year seemed at first to be a step toward abolition, for the conscientious former United States marshal immediately set off on a tour of camps. He provided the first public statistics about how many convicts were engaged in what enterprises, and where. The Penitentiary Board reinforced the new sense of responsibility by prohibiting deputy wardens from inflicting physical punishment—although this reform had to be abandoned one year later after lessees complained about not being able to wrest labor out of convicts whom they could not punish on the spot.

Besides reporting an astonishing 192 escapes since the 1883 lease was instituted, Carroll's 1890 accounting showed some 690 convicts sublet to eight plantations and one railroad construction contractor, J. C. Pace, who worked 75 in Toltec, just east of Little Rock. Ninety prisoners remained inside the penitentiary. Between 1883 and 1890, Carroll reported, the lessees paid the state an average of $25,854 annually.[24]

Translating these aggregate figures into per-capita rates displays more graphically the true extent of the contract's profitability. The Arkansas Industrial Company paid $28,894 for 690 convicts in 1890. That year's leasing contract, therefore, cost the company about twelve and a half cents per workday for each prisoner. The amounts the lessees received from their respective subleasing contracts are not available, but if the $12.50-per-month figure that Townshend and Fitzpatrick had secured from the Neel plantation can be taken as a benchmark, it would indicate that they continued to realize about $9 per convict per month. This amount, in turn, when retranslated into an aggregate figure, adds up to between $70,000 and $75,000 per year for the exertions involved in drawing up the contracts. For their part, the sublessees were paying about fifty cents per convict per workday, with perhaps half that amount in monitoring and subsistence expenses: still an amount well below the wage rate for free labor.

Some confirmation for these calculations comes from the memoir of a woman whose father was a convict gang foreman for an Arkansas railroad in the early twentieth century. Marion M. Noble remembered leased railroad workers available at fifty cents a day. They slept in converted boxcars at night, she recalled, and their diet consisted of one quart of beans, one cup of sorghum, and three six-inch squares of cornbread daily.[25]

The prisoners, then, continued to endure a fetid world of mud, vermin, disease, violence, and toil on plantations and in railroad construction camps. An appalled legislative committee in 1881 expressed the paradoxes of convict leasing in the stilted language that was already becoming conventional in denouncing it: "Although your committee is satisfied the contract system is a cruel, barbarous and inhuman one, and is totally at variance with the civilization of this age," its members reasoned, "yet taking into consideration the present embarrassed condition of the state, they forbear to make any recommendation."[26] A decade later Inspector Carroll condemned Arkansas's system in exactly the same terms, calling it "cruel, barbarous, inhuman and totally at variance with the civilization of this age."[27] By 1892, however, some alternative ideas were beginning to take shape in the reformers' minds.

In the late 1880s calls for the abolition of leasing began to be heard. They came chiefly from the awakening ranks of farmers and laborers who were incensed not only at the denigration of the value of their labor but also by the inhumane conditions symbolized by Coal Hill. In 1888 the Union Labor Party platform, endorsed by the Agricultural Wheel, the Farmers' Alliance, and the Knights of Labor, called for abolition. By 1892 the calls had become even more insistent—and more specific. The

Populist platform of that year advocated a prison farm, with "all surplus labor above the farm . . . used in building State roads."[28]

Something else happened in Arkansas politics between 1888 and
1892, however: the disfranchisement of black and poor white voters.
Blacks had voted in substantially the same proportion as whites in the
gubernatorial election of 1888—some 72 percent of blacks and 78 percent of whites. By 1892, as a consequence of new restrictive laws inaugurated by conservative, mostly black-belt representatives alarmed by
the rise of the Union-Labor coalition, voter turnout declined by a full 20
percent. And by the end of the decade the turnout level fell to 37 percent. "In less than a decade," writes Raymond Arsenault, "a political
system that had approached universal manhood suffrage had been replaced by a highly restrictive system in which only a minority of the
potential electorate took part."[29]

It is therefore worth noting that Inspector Carroll, a Democratic appointee in a highly volatile political atmosphere, substantially agreed
with the Populist platform. "Almost every public meeting that has been
held in our State capital during the last two years has passed a resolution condemning the lease system and praying the Legislature to abolish it," he boldly asserted. He recommended Texas's approach, as he
somewhat erroneously understood it: to place all convicts within the
penitentiary as soon as it can be made self-supporting; and to lease under state control until that time.[30]

The legislature did in fact make an attempt to eliminate the system,
but as was the case in every Southern state except Georgia, the vaunted
"abolition" proved to be completely ineffective, an imaginary solution
to a misconceived problem. Like the Alabama statute with which it was
exactly contemporaneous, the Arkansas law of March 1893 called for
the abolition of the lease system, *provided* that the state could locate
"equally remunerative employment."[31] The effect of this provision was
to nullify the ostensible objective of the bill. For it would prove impossible to meet both of the bill's goals—abolishing the lease and retaining
the same earnings.

The penitentiary commissioners—Governor James Eagle, Attorney
General W. E. Atkinson, and Secretary of State Ben B. Chism, reform
Democrats all—made a point of condemning the lease in 1892. Noting
the prevailing opposition of political parties and labor organizations to
the practice, they added their own attack. The profit from the lease, they
stated, "is *blood money* made through agony and bloody sweat of the

unfortunate convict." But the fact that such opinions reflect the demands of the prevailing political climate, rather than a determination to reform the convict system, is evident from their more sober reflections later in their official report, where they advised that abolition ought not be undertaken too hastily because the expense of doing so would be too burdensome.[32] Indeed, Arkansas convicts would continue to be leased for *two decades* more, until 1912, when a disgusted and exasperated governor, George W. Donaghey, "the bricklayer governor," took the boldest step of any politician in the history of leasing, and finished it once and for all.

The 1893 law did, however, require that the state, rather than the lessees, oversee the prisoners, thus ending the ten-year period of what was earlier in this book called "ideal-typical" leasing. The law employed a sort of ideal-typical legislative evasion—that of putting forward a vision of reform but neglecting to appropriate the funds necessary to make that vision a reality. As many convicts as possible were to be employed inside the penitentiary, the law provided. The remainder could be contracted out, but the state could not abandon its responsibility to guard and maintain them. In the future, convicts could labor outside the prison on timber lands, or perhaps on farms belonging to the state.

On 7 May 1893, then, the Arkansas Industrial Company finally disposed of its capital stock, which consisted of some eight hundred convicts, many of whom did not even have suitable clothes. The buildings inside the penitentiary walls were almost in ruins, and all tools and utensils had to be replaced. No funds were available to buy a farm. So the penitentiary commissioners took what seemed at the time to be the only course of action open to them. Under their authority, the state of Arkansas became a sharecropper.

"Nothing was left us to do the next year [1894] but to cultivate land on the share system," the embarrassed secretary of state wrote in 1896. "The land and stock and feed for the stock and the necessary farming implements were furnished by the land owner, and the labor for making and gathering the crop was furnished by the State, and the crop divided between the two, and in this way most of the convicts have been employed for the past three years." "There is something humiliating in a great State being in the attitude of a share cropper," he added. His recommendation was that the state purchase a prison farm.[33]

While the secretary of state may have felt humiliated, however, he might have reflected that there is no operational distinction between leasing convicts and working them on shares. They are contracted out for money in the first instance or for a share of the yield in the second. Whether the lessee puts forward financial capital in the form of a lease price or physical capital in the form of "the land and stock and feed for the stock and the necessary farming implements," the state in either case is contracting with its citizens to undertake a state function in order to avoid expenditures and to enrich certain strategically placed individuals among them. Attorneys for Mississippi lessees pithily expressed this economic and legal truism in 1905: "The books are full of cases in which contracts have been recognized as leases that provided for another form of recompense than that of a money rent. No particular form of expression is necessary to create a lease. . . . As the old writers express it, 'a lease doth signify a demise or letting of land, etc., unto another for a lesser time than he that doth let hath in it.'" The Mississippi Supreme Court agreed.[34]

Although the legislature did appropriate $31,500 to implement the new law in 1893, that was the last infusion of funds the system would receive. As early as 1894 the penitentiary returned nearly $28,000 to the treasury, and by 1896 it was self-sustaining on the sharecrop system, with no appropriation from Little Rock. Within three years of the "abolition" of leasing, the practice was more widespread, and affected more prisoners, than ever, with some seventeen camps spread across the state. And it would seem that, by requiring the state rather than the lessees to monitor and sustain the prisoners, the law had merely shifted the incentives for financial retrenchment to the state. In the absence of mandated standards for the care and treatment of convicts, the state, just like any firm, engaged in callous cost cutting. In 1898 Arkansas maintained its convicts at a cost of nineteen cents per day, a rate half that of Ohio.[35]

IV

The real beginning of the slow and agonizing death of leasing in Arkansas came with a new law, the Kimbell Act, which mandated the construction of a new state capitol located on the site of the existing penitentiary. Pursuant to this law, the ancient penitentiary was dismantled in 1899. In order to dispose of the displaced convicts the state contracted with the Arkansas Brick Company, whose president, W. W. Dickinson, demanded and received a ten-year contract. In spite of the conspicuous outrage—much of it manufactured—of Jeff Davis, who would take office as governor in 1903, the Arkansas Supreme Court upheld the contract in May 1902. In the meantime, the state had shifted to paying money rents for its farming operations. The convict system was becoming an increasingly expensive proposition for the state. Slowly the decision was reached to move in the direction of state-owned prison farms. In 1901, in what can be seen in retrospect as a historic departure, the penitentiary commissioners purchased a plantation.[36]

Still, the brickyard and the farm could not occupy all of Arkansas's felons, who numbered 727 in 1902—despite a staggering 173 escapes. Convicts were being worked on no fewer than four brickyards and eighteen farms, one of which was owned by Dickinson.[37]

Railroads too began to take more prisoners. In 1912 Governor Donaghey discovered conditions in railroad camps that could have been found a quarter of a century earlier: convicts "were fed mostly on sour pork and beans, and were herded in cars at night, twenty-four or twenty-five men to the car, where they slept amid filth and vermin, . . . the slightest complaint upon the part of any convict brought him a lashing on his back with a leather strap six feet long and four inches wide." As outrageous as these human abuses were the fiscal frauds that seemed immune to change:

> While the convicts work for the railroads, the system in practice is that the railroads will not hire them from the state. All efforts to get them to bid directly for the employment of the convicts have so far failed. But a general contractor hires them. Usually, but one man will make a proposal for their hire and after closing up the deal for all the state has to let, he becomes the distribution agent for their labor.[38]

Donaghey had pleaded with the legislature to abolish leasing in his first message, in 1909, and again in his second, in 1911. The legislature responded by authorizing the penitentiary commissioners to purchase an additional farm to take care of all the additional prisoners and end leasing—but, as in the past, it neglected to appropriate funds for the purchase. Like so many laws passed to eliminate convict leasing in the South, it was window dressing. Nearly twenty years had passed since the legislature had "abolished" leasing, but it endured.[39]

Finally Donaghey had had enough. Lessees and penitentiary officials were deflecting demands for abolition with the argument that the number of prisoners in the state at large was far too great for them all to be taken care of on the state farm, in terms of both labor and accommodations. "To remedy this situation," Donaghey recalled years later, "I computed the acreage of arable land at the farm, estimated the number of convicts required to cultivate it, obtained an abstract of the histories of all the convicts in the penitentiary, and paroled enough of those convicted of minor offenses and who had served one-third of their terms, to reduce the penitentiary population to only the number needed to cultivate the farm."[40]

On 27 December 1912 Donaghey, a lame duck, accomplished through executive action what forty years of protests and duplicitous legislation had failed to do. He pardoned 360 prisoners and broke the back of leasing. The next year the legislature purchased the farm. Leasing in Arkansas ended on 31 December 1913.[41]

Seven

MISSISSIPPI
An Epidemic Death Rate without the Epidemic

I

The second of the three Deep South states that George Washington Cable identified as "the worst" for their leasing practices was Mississippi. While the three states had much in common, they also differed in important ways. For example, the labor of Arkansas's leased convicts was somewhat diversified, with convicts being employed at different times in mining, railroad construction, farming, brick making, and road work, but that of Mississippi convicts was much more concentrated in the service of the state's great planters. In Mississippi (and in Louisiana as well), convict leasing's fortunes were tied to the political power of those planters. Mississippi's role in this story stands out by virtue of its almost purely agricultural economy.

But Mississippi is also significant—as Mississippi so often has had to be—as a kind of symbol of all that is most deeply Southern. When the history of convict leasing first began to be related in the 1940s, not only did prison conditions in Mississippi seem to stand for the outrageous nature of the lease as an institution throughout the region, but also a certain rhetoric of humanitarian outrage that was derived from the Mississippi reformers served to determine the conventional discourse about this peculiarly Southern prison system.

Mississippi's prison history recapitulates the familiar tale of state officials who, politically and financially strained to the breaking point, decided to lease out of desperation. Next began the rapid transformation of the practice from a temporary expedient to an institutionalized addiction, followed by the revelation of horrible conditions and abuse, and, finally, before the mounting of abortive and illusory attempts at abolition, the system was finally eliminated.

131

The story of Mississippi leasing must begin with the leading beneficiary of Mississippi's initial postbellum economic distress. He was one of the state's most prominent citizens and was known as the "Cotton King." Edmund Richardson was both a planter and a factor—the owner of numerous plantations in the Yazoo-Mississippi Delta and a major partner in a New Orleans firm that handled a hundred thousand bales of cotton per year. In 1884 President Chester A. Arthur appointed him to the post of commissioner of the World's Industrial and Cotton Centennial Exposition, which was held in New Orleans and was the greatest exhibition of its time. He had previously received the appointment of commissioner from the cotton states to the magnificent Philadelphia Centennial Exposition in 1876, and he was also vice president of the Atlanta Cotton Exposition of 1881.

In truth, Edmund Richardson was the greatest cotton planter in the world. His fifty plantations totaling over twenty-five thousand acres produced an annual output of twelve thousand bales of cotton, valued at half a million dollars per year. Richardson's wealth derived directly from his leasing of convicts. Indeed, his "appetite for prison labor could hardly be satisfied." As part owner of the Vicksburg, Shreveport & Pacific Railroad, he also used convicts in railroad and levee construction, as well as working them to cultivate and gin cotton on his own lands.[1]

Mississippi's Reconstruction legislature passed its first lease law in October 1866. The law was understood to permit the lease of the prisoners only within the walls of the penitentiary, which William T. Sherman had partially destroyed in 1863 because it housed a munitions factory. But the penitentiary could not hold the burgeoning population, and in February 1867 a joint resolution permitted leasing outside the walls— with the convict's written permission! The plan, not surprisingly, failed to generate a profusion of bids. The prison situation rapidly deteriorated into one of desperation and chaos. Convicts languished in the Jackson stockade, nearly starving, while the destitute state government was forced to issue scrip to such Jackson merchants as were willing to provide subsistence rations to them.[2]

In 1868, when a new constitution that complied with the requirements of Congressional Reconstruction failed to be ratified by the Mississippi electorate, a military government was appointed to replace the existing civil authorities. The new military commander, Gen. Alvan C. Gillem, promptly made a contract with Richardson to dispense with the convict problem. Like the early prison labor contracts in such states as

Alabama and Arkansas, where the penitentiary was seen as an enormous headache first and a source of revenue only later, this contract actually paid the lessee. Richardson received not only the labor of the convicts for three years, but also $18,000 annually for the expenses associated with their care. Then for good measure the state tacked on a $12,000 annual bonus to cover the convicts' transportation costs. Mississippi's penitentiary report shows a prison population of only 241 convicts in December 1870—indicating that the lessee's remuneration was calculated as a per-capita maintenance cost of $75 per year. The sum, about twenty cents per day, accords with the amounts being spent on convict upkeep in other Southern states at about that time.[3]

Civilian government was restored to Mississippi in 1870. The first civilian governor, James Lusk Alcorn, objected to the Richardson contract immediately. By relinquishing convict control, he insisted, the state degraded the entire social fabric. When Richardson's lease expired in 1871, therefore, he had to spend $20,000 to bribe the state's legislators into passing another leasing bill. This one would have allowed him to retain control for fifteen years. Alcorn, while declining to sign the measure, was nevertheless compelled by the absence of an alternative to permit the extension of Richardson's lease for one more year—to March 1872. When Alcorn resigned to enter the United States Senate, on 30 November 1871, his successor, Ridgley C. Powers, vetoed the Richardson bill outright. The lease's effect was to "corrupt morals, degrade industry, pervert justice, and thwart the true objects of punishment," Powers declared. He recommended getting rid of the penitentiary entirely and purchasing a state farm.[4]

But the fact that Powers's negative judgment was directed more toward Edmund Richardson than toward the degrading and corrupting influence of convict leasing per se was shown by the governor's next action. He leased Richardson's convicts to Nathan Bedford Forrest, whose post–Civil War career as a planter, railroad entrepreneur, and manager of convict labor is less well known than his previous one as a Confederate war hero, tactical genius, commander of the troops who massacred surrendering black soldiers at Fort Pillow, and founder of the Ku Klux Klan.

Forrest considered himself an expert convict manager. While retired on President's Island in the Mississippi below Memphis he leased numerous convicts and "established an elaborate system, complete with military-style barracks and heavily regimented working and living schedules." Proud of his organizational and disciplinary abilities, he gruffly chided O. M. Roberts, the governor of Texas, when that state proposed minor restrictions on the use of convict labor. "I have been hiring convicts from Miss. Ala. & Tenn for the last six years, at differant [sic] times," he told Roberts. "I have always been allowed to discipline and manage the convicts as my judgement dictated, with the right of Inspectors to make any changes as they might think proper, after a full consultation in regard to the same. I dont [sic]think any man would lease unless he had half the rope."⁵ At the time of the 1872 lease, Forrest was engaged in the construction of the Selma, Marion, and Memphis Railroad, a speculative venture that ended in financial disaster and went into receivership in 1875.

In May 1872 the state altered this contract, awarding it for three years to a construction company associated with the railroad. The owners of this firm were W. P. Dunnavant and Nathan Bedford Forrest's son, William M. Forrest. The lessees took over all the convicts and the state's equipment inside the prison, and paid all expenses except the salaries of the board, superintendent, clerk, physician, and chaplain. This agreement is, perhaps, the pivotal contract in the history of Mississippi leasing. It represents a reversal of the earlier leases in two important ways. First of all, it relieved the state of all expenses, including transportation. Section 10 of the contract reads: "It is further expressly understood and declared to be the intent and meaning of this contract, that the State of Mississippi is to be relieved of all expense of any kind, character, or description whatever, pertaining to said Penitentiary . . . but that all expense of said Penitentiary, or pertaining or relating thereto, is hereby assumed by the lessees." In the second place, the convicts' labor would now *cost* the lessees $8,000 per year. Based on the 1872 population of 331 prisoners, the lessees' expenditure amounted to about $2 a month for each convict.⁶

According to Mississippi historian William C. Harris, the convicts' condition was generally good and they were cared for by a competent railroad doctor. The penitentiary records, however, reveal 41 deaths in just seven months, out of a population of only 212. Such figures may, however, be explained as much by the state of nineteenth-century medical care as by mistreatment. In any case, the concerned superintendent, C. W. Loomis, asked for the removal of all the convicts to the prison as soon as possible.⁷

The convict physician S. V. D. Taylor wrote in December: "On the first day of June 1872, I took charge as Physician, of the Mississippi convicts, who were employed as laborers on the Selma, Marion, and Memphis Railroad, and found forty men in the Hospital, most of them dangerously ill." Twenty died of malaria and pneumonia between 1 June and 30 November along the Tombigbee River, where the railroad was being constructed between Columbus and Okolona.[8]

In Mississippi, as in so many Southern states, the middle 1870s were years in which, after a time of wavering, convict leasing became a firmly fixed policy. In 1872, when Dunnavant and Forrest received their three-year lease, the legislature had intended a shift of prison policy away from leasing and toward prison farms; the 1872 lease was seen as a makeshift.[9] But two factors—the expenses this strategy entailed and the swelling demand for fiscal retrenchment—led to the policy's being abandoned by 1875, just before the Dunnavant and Forrest lease expired. Then, in 1876, the legislature passed a statute that became notorious as the "Pig Law." It classified the theft of any cattle or swine as grand larceny.[10]

The historian Vernon Lane Wharton considered this single piece of legislation to be the primary factor behind the rise, development, and decline of Mississippi's leasing system. It was this law, Wharton wrote, "which was largely responsible for an increase in the population of the state prison from 272 in 1874 to 1,072 at the end of 1877. It was this law that made the convict lease system a big business enterprise, and it was its repeal in 1887 that reduced the number of convicts from 966 to 484 in fourteen months and paved the way for the abolition of that system."[11]

Wharton's analysis of the Pig Law's effect had serious flaws, however, and unfortunately it acquired widespread and somewhat uncritical acceptance. For instance, both Fletcher M. Green and C. Vann Woodward cited Wharton, referred to his figures, and paraphrased his conclusion that the lease became a big business as a result of the law; while William Banks Taylor, in an admirable recent history of Mississippi prisons, also refers to Wharton while making recurrent references to "the convict-generating Pig law" and "the felon-generating Pig law." But the fact is that, Pig Law or no, Mississippi's prison population began to decline after 1877—the year of Wharton's most sensational figure—and continued to do so steadily until 1889, except for small increases in 1884 and 1885. In addition, Wharton's numbers do not conform with Mississippi's official figures, published in the 1890s in tabular form. The latter show a total population of 375 in 1874 and 1,003 in 1877. This is a striking increase, to be sure, but by 1883 the population was down to 752; and the year the law was repealed, in 1888 (not 1887), it was only 499. Furthermore, statistics show that just *after* the law's repeal, the number of prisoners *increased* dramatically, and at a steady rate, climbing from 472 in 1889 to 990 just six years later. The data support an interpretation opposite to the one Wharton advanced.[12]

Wharton, here as elsewhere, exaggerated the effect of a single factor. It is true that the population of convicts, on average, was larger after 1874 than before, but this was for many reasons besides the Pig Law. First, in 1875, against the opposition of the declining number of black legislators, a new law permitted the use of convicts on plantations as well as public works. Second, and perhaps more important, however, was the law's provision for subleasing.[13]

The new lease of 1876 went to Jones S. Hamilton Company. Extending from 1876 to 1880, at a rate of $1.10 per convict per month, with the first 140 convicts delivered free, the contract provided both parties with incentives to raise the convict labor supply. In this respect, the Pig Law can be interpreted, in association with the law of 1875 and lease of 1876, as part of a larger strategy to make forced labor more easily available to the state's leading planters.

Jones Hamilton was in his way just as remarkable as Edmund Richardson, "an almost incredible character who dabbled in Republican and Democratic politics, speculated with race tracks, gas works, railroads, and real estate, and made and spent several fortunes with splendid recklessness." Hamilton was uninterested in using the convicts' labor himself. He was strictly a speculator who derived his income from subleases. Quarrels with former lessees over the possession of the convicts broke out in 1876, and when the dust settled most were subleased . . . to Edmund Richardson.[14]

Subleasing now began in earnest, as the responsible Mississippi officials promised in 1877 that convicts "will hereafter be a source of revenue to the state." Six hundred and two convicts were brought into the camps that year alone, swelling the population to just over 1,000. Nine hundred of them were black. Only 186 lived in the penitentiary; the remainder were working for eleven sublessees on plantations and levees. The sublessees' camps could be found almost entirely in the tier of counties stacked on the east bank of the Mississippi, or on or near the Yazoo: Lee, Washington, Warren, Rankin, Bolivar, Wilkinson, Holmes, Attala, Leflore, Coahoma. A contemporary reformer wrote about the system in another state: "The lessees carried the convicts off, body and soul, though in many a transit the soul took its flight." But her remark was more fitting for Mississippi than elsewhere. That year, 1877, 94 convicts escaped and 50 died, while in the following year 95 died and 7 were listed as killed, and in 1879 the figures showed 77 deaths—and 15 killed.[15]

II

The 1880s in Mississippi, as in the rest of the South, while representing a high tide of convict leasing in terms of revenue, numbers of convicts, and general entrenchment of the system, were also a decade of growing public opposition and disgust—disgust not merely with inhumane conditions but also with the disgraceful corruption of the lessees. In 1879 Mississippi lessees owed $22,216.70 to the state's coffers, and by 1881 the total had nearly doubled. Few lessees, in fact, ever paid the full amount of their contract costs. When Mississippi's contract was drawing to a close, in 1881, the superintendent decided that the penitentiary in Jackson was in dire need of repair and let contracts out to the current lessees to undertake the work. The $9,000 cost of the repair work was credited to what the lessees owed on their lease. The state finally received a total of only $33,944.33 for the entire term of the lease, during which some 900 convicts were worked for three years—a figure of around a dollar a month for each convict.[16]

In 1881 the state contracted with Hamilton and Allen, the successor company to the 1878 lessees. Although the law prohibited convicts with sentences of greater than ten years from working outside the walls, Hamilton and Allen got the attorney general to agree with them that such labor was permissible provided it was undertaken on public works. Every available convict would soon be working on sublessees' camps, mostly in railroad and levee construction. These unfortunate convicts would soon find themselves caught up in some of the worst conditions on record anywhere in the history of leasing, conditions that produced what the 1887 investigating committee called "an epidemic death rate without the epidemic."[17]

And, in fact, the lessees paid exactly nothing for their use of the labor. They received an appropriation of $25,000 for improving the penitentiary equipment; and they contracted for $31,774.04 worth of improvements. The state, Governor Stone reported, actually *owed* Jones Hamilton some $6,000 in 1882![18] This unexpected turnabout might have added fiscal fuel to the fire of the legislature's indignation a few years later. In 1884 lessees paid just $12,100.58, while deducting $27,419.42 in "improvements" from their convict bill. In 1885 they paid nothing. Over the four-year period since the inception of the lease the state had received a total of just $58,121.52.[19]

The widespread dispersal of prisoners to sublessees in the 1880s led to a further decline in treatment and, ultimately, a scathing legislative investigation that led to leasing's being prohibited in Article 10 of the Mississippi constitution of 1890. Throughout the 1880s convicts in Mississippi faced deteriorating conditions. In 1884 prisoners shipped from a Delta plantation to Jackson via Vicksburg were not allowed to march through town—their condition was too horrifying. The news could not be kept from a curious public, however, and it is probable that the sight of the emaciated, half-clothed, frostbitten convicts brought about the first sign of serious public interest in the workings of the state's penal practices.[20] A hard-hitting report by the Mississippi House of Representatives on the lessees' abuses was presented to the legislature, but through some act of villainy that was never explained, the report was not printed in that year's *House Journal*.[21]

In December 1885 Hamilton's assignees transferred their unexpired lease to the Gulf and Ship Island Railroad. In 1886 a new law created a board of control—a board which was conveniently made up of the state's railroad commission.[22] It was the Gulf and Ship Island's camps that provided some of the most sensational and tragic pages of testimony in all the annals of leasing. The lessees completely ignored the welfare of the suffering prisoners, neglected to pay the lease charges, declined to repair the penitentiary, maltreated the prisoners, and refused to fire guards for cruelty even upon the order of the board.

Public antagonism to convict leasing intensified in the latter half of the decade, but the momentum of events still seemed to be moving in the lessees' favor. Indeed, open opposition proved fatal on two dramatic occasions. In May 1887 Jones Hamilton shot and killed Roderick Gambrell, the editor of the *Clinton Sword and Shield*, a belligerent antagonist of leasing, on Capitol Street in Jackson. And almost exactly a year later, only yards away from where the Gambrell killing had occurred, the editor of the *Jackson New Mississippian*, John Martin, was also shot dead. Martin's antagonism to the lessees had been even more intense than Gambrell's, and, as had been the case with Gambrell's, his killer was not convicted.[23]

Perhaps Jones and the lessees had reason to fear Martin. On 11 October 1887 there appeared on the front page of his *New Mississippian* the first sustained, logically argued, empirically substantiated, public attack on Mississippi convict leasing. It was written by a young lawyer named Frank Johnston. Johnston would later serve as attorney general of Mississippi; it was he who, in this story, revealed the curious disappearance of the House report. The information in the article aroused legislator J. H. Jones, who would be appointed the following year as chairman of the investigating committee that issued the most damning single investigative report in Southern history during the entire leasing era. Johnston's article, "The Penitentiary Lease," was picked up and reprinted in a number of other papers in the state and had a discernible impact on public opinion.[24] In a sense it prepared the way for Jones's 1888 report. In its combination of eloquent progressive rhetoric, hard-hitting reportage, and use of telling statistics, it foreshadowed the muckraking journalism of a later generation and deserves to be compared with the attack that George Washington Cable had mounted against leasing in 1883.

Johnston began with rhetorical flourishes that would soon become commonplace in discussions of leasing, portraying it as the "worst form of human slavery" and something "without a parallel in the history of civilized peoples." Then he turned to the three grounds for opposition to it—grounds that would also become familiar: it is in principle wrong to use state convicts for private profit; it leads to abuses; and proper treatment of prisoners is impossible in the absence of government control. Like Cable, he used death-rate statistics to devastating effect. From the penitentiary reports he provided the following mortality percentages among Mississippi's prisoners:

1881	1882	1 883	1884	1885
8.48	15.35	10.81	11.55	9.54

By comparison, he observed, the city of New Orleans endured a 2 percent death rate, a figure that includes infant mortality. And in 1885 penitentiaries reported mortality rates of 1.5 percent in New Hampshire, 1.08 percent in Ohio, and .76 percent in Iowa.

After recounting the horrors of one of the worst camps on the Gulf and Ship Island Railroad, Johnston concluded forcefully, if somewhat inaccurately: "Such is the 'convict camp,' not alone in Mississippi, but in Georgia, Louisiana, Tennessee, and wherever it has an existence. After twenty years of investigations, tinkerings, and patchings, the institution retains all of its original and distinctive features."[25]

In March 1888 W. L. Doss, a newly appointed superintendent, set out to ascertain the treatment of convicts in the Gulf and Ship Island camps. All along the line citizens told him about the terrible way the convicts were being handled. The report of the investigating committee fully confirmed the awful tales. The board of control finally canceled the railroad's lease in December 1888. The state's remuneration from this disastrous contract was a total of $38,333.33 in the railroad's bonds, "the value of which we suppose at present amounts to but little," the board reckoned.[26] In 1890 the Mississippi constitution abolished leasing after the expiration of the lease contract.

But to judge this constitutional provision as somehow symptomatic of an awakening of humanitarian progressivism—as several of its defenders, then and later, would try to do—would be a serious mistake. In Mississippi, as in Georgia and Louisiana, the abolition of leasing was actually a portion of a much larger and extremely retrograde package. Indeed, among students of Southern history the 1890 Mississippi constitution is renowned as the very prototype of reactionary racism. It embodied the so-called Second Mississippi Plan, as a result of which black Mississippians would be effectively barred from even the most trifling participation in public life for three quarters of a century. Before the 1890 constitutional convention met, over 190,000 blacks were registered to vote in Mississippi. By 1892 the number had dwindled to 8,600. No black appeared on any jury list after 1892.

Furthermore, as C. Vann Woodward notes, by the late 1890s (after the collapse of the Populist challenge to the South's social hierarchy) "reaction was in the air" throughout the South; and Mississippi's overall strategy, which would be condoned by the United States Supreme Court in the case of *Williams* v. *Mississippi* in 1898, became the blueprint for the entire region—and even, in some of its larger implications, for an increasingly race-conscious nation. Henry Williams was a black man convicted of murdering a white man and sentenced to be hanged. Blacks had been excluded from both the grand jury that indicted him and the trial jury that convicted him. Williams appealed, contending that in his indictment and trial he had been denied the rights of due process and equal protection under the Fourteenth Amendment. But the Supreme Court unanimously found that the constitution and the laws of Mississippi which established qualifications for voting and jury service "do not on their face discriminate between the races."[27]

Despite the 1890 constitution's prohibition, convict leasing endured. In Mississippi, as in neighboring Arkansas, acreage on the state farms was inadequate to keep large numbers of convicts employed, so leasing continued under the subterfuge that the contracts that were let, which were share contracts between the state and landowners, were contracts of land not of prisoners. But everyone knew that "in effect the old convict lease system remained in vogue."[28]

In 1895 the state had three farms, the Rankin farm and the Oakley and Belmont plantations. It rented land on a per-acre basis from A. G. McLemore, G. T. Darden, and J. C. Hall. And it had straight sharecrop arrangements with seven other landowners. The board cried for more state farm land. "The system of contracting with land owners, for planting operations on the share plan or any other basis, is unsatisfactory, but could not be avoided by the Board under the conditions of the penitentiary," they explained.[29]

In January 1901 the state purchased a massive plantation from the penitentiary warden, J. M. Parchman. As the twentieth century opened convicts in Mississippi were working on four state farms, two rented farms, and nine share farms. The age and sentencing data for that year show very young prisoners serving long terms. Of 910 convicts, 198 were minors and another 299 were between the ages of twenty and twenty-five. The most common sentence was for two-to-five years (245 prisoners); the next most common was five-to-ten (220), and the third was life, the sentence of 198 Mississippi prisoners.[30]

In the fall of 1902, after an acrimonious dispute on the penitentiary board that never became public, J. M. Parchman resigned as warden. At the board's meeting on 7 October 1902, board member J. C. Kincannon made a dramatic charge that Parchman had diverted funds intended for supplies to his own use, and that he had ordered a sergeant at the Levy plantation to Jackson in order to circumvent his being interrogated by the penitentiary investigating committee. The other members of the board appear to have been taken by surprise by these charges, and the group adjourned without considering them. Four days later they reconvened to consider the formal charges, which they investigated for several weeks more. Although the secretary of the board, William McWillie, could discover no entry in the account books for the mules and guns Parchman claimed to have spent the disputed funds for, Parchman nevertheless was able to explain everything: he had traded two mules and purchased two Winchester rifles with the proceeds. The board vindicated him (with a dissenting vote from the exasperated Kincannon) on 3 November. But two weeks later the affronted Parchman resigned his position and submitted a long statement cataloging the injuries he had suffered. He was quickly succeeded by John J. Henry. The leases were unaffected.[31]

Then in 1905 Gov. James K. Vardaman sued for an injunction against lessee H. J. McLaurin. McLaurin, besides being a state senator, former governor, and member of the board of control, was also the governor's bitter political enemy. In his suit Vardaman contended that McLaurin's contract was in fact a lease of convicts, not of land. He got a favorable ruling from chancery court, but McLaurin appealed, and the case went to the state supreme court.[32] In December 1905 the penitentiary board passed a resolution asking the tribunal to rule on the case promptly, insofar as "a large number of able bodied negro convicts lying in idleness, at the expense of the state for an indefinite time, . . . does not accord with the policy of the laws of the state." The court complied with the board's wishes; whether they did so because of the resolution or for more pressing political reasons is not clear. This case, *State* v. *Henry*, is notable not only for the convoluted reasoning that the supreme court's majority used to reach it, but also for the passionate dissenting opinion of Chief Justice Albert H. Whitfield.[33]

In the suit the state attempted to force the transfer of all the prisoners from McLaurin's place to a state farm, arguing that the plain meaning of Article 10 of the 1890 constitution required it: "The legislature may place [convicts] on state farms, not on private farms. They may be employed, under state supervision and the officers and employes [*sic*] of the state, on public works, or public levees, or on state farms, but never on a private farm. The language of the constitution and all its implications plainly mean that, and nothing else."[34]

With intrepid sophistry, however, the court made much of a clause in the constitution concerning the manner in which the prohibition on leasing was to be carried out. That clause reads, in part: "The legislature may place the convicts on a state farm, or farms . . . and may buy farms for that purpose." Because the clause contained the word *may* and not *shall*, Justice Calhoon decided, the state was free to enter into any contract it liked, so long as the prisoners remained under state supervision. "The *prime object* of the state in maintaining a penitentiary, under whatever system adopted, is to properly guard and care for the convicts, and to *lessen the public burden of* . . . caring for them. . . . A farm leased by the

142

state is, therefore, a 'state farm' and not a 'private farm.'" Consequently the McLaurin contract "constitutes a leasing of lands, and not a hiring of convicts."[35]

The chief justice, outvoted, helpless, and angry, dissented vigorously. The foundations for his argument were the relevant legal documents, which made it clear that the complete cessation of leasing in all its forms had been the intent of Article 10. "It is as clear as day, therefore," Whitfield wrote, "whether we look to the face of the constitutional provision or the subsequent statutes or to the journal of the constitutional convention, that the purpose was to abolish the leasing of land and employment thereon of convicts. . . . The makers of the constitution . . . repudiated emphatically, once and forever, the idea that the legislature could, under the constitutional provisions, provide for the working of the convicts in any other manner deemed expedient." As to the labored distinction between *may* and *shall,* he contended: "[The other justices] pivot the whole argument as to the power of the board of control to lease the farm of a private individual upon whether the word 'may' buy farms in sec. 225 of the constitution is permissive or mandatory. This is a complete *non sequitur.* . . . The word 'may' is here plainly mandatory," because the enforcement of the constitution requires it to be so construed.[36]

Given the court's disposition of the case, the eloquence and logical force of Whitfield's dissent were cold comfort to the opponents of convict leasing. Yet the legislature was driven into action by the Vardaman-McLaurin feud, by the knowledge that the state farms were prosperous, and perhaps by the thought that the public had learned more than the legislators might have wished. In 1906 it gave statutory force to the words of the constitution ratified sixteen years before, and in words almost identical to the constitution's. The law prohibited convict labor on privately owned enterprises of any sort and provided that convicts could be employed only on public levees, roads, or state-owned farms. In 1907 Vardaman had the satisfaction of transferring all the prisoners to the Sunflower farm—the name of which was later changed to Parchman. His biographer considers his successful fight to abolish leasing (and other prison reforms) to be "the major progressive achievement of Vardaman's administration." This judgment is undoubtedly correct, but one should remember that the achievement consisted of carrying into execution a constitutional mandate that had been handed down sixteen years before.[37]

Eight

LOUISIANA
The Road to Angola

I

L ouisiana is rivaled only by Florida in the recklessness and unmanageability of its post–Civil War convict system, the frontier character of its justice system, and the rashness of the men who directed it. It is closest to Mississippi and Arkansas, not only, as George Washington Cable observed, in the degree of the state's abdication of its authority over prison management, but also in the close linkage between the prison and the state's planters. As Mark T. Carleton tersely noted in 1971: "The survival of agricultural operations within the penal system into the 1960s suggests that the terms 'convict,' 'slave,' 'Negro,' and 'farm work' have remained unconsciously interchangeable in the mind of institutional Louisiana."[1]

Louisiana, Carleton wrote elsewhere, was "perhaps the most violent state in the South between 1865 and 1900."[2] It was a state in which the agony of Reconstruction was prolonged, and to little productive benefit. The state's penal policy, if such it can be called, was an unsteady mix of fiscal privation and racial retribution. One searches in vain for glimmers of bureaucratic organization, regular records, unambiguous sentences, or clear goals—even the goals of exploitation or profit—in the first years after the Civil War. E. C. Wines, seeking information on Louisiana conditions on behalf of the National Prison Association in 1873, was completely unsuccessful. He could find no report to refer to, nor any mention of prisoners in the governor's message. This was still true in 1880 when he tried again, and in 1883 when George Washington Cable noted that neither Arkansas nor Louisiana had gone to the trouble to print a prison report.[3] Carleton, an assiduous researcher, found that "no

... report of the Board of Control during [the years of the lease] contains any financial information relative to the lessees whatsoever. No reports of any sort, in fact, emerged from the penitentiary in 1873, 1874, 1876, 1877, or during the inclusive period from 1879 to 1889."[4]

In contrast to those in neighboring states, Louisiana officials always knew convicts were a valuable commodity and never made the mistake of paying anyone to take the burdensome problem off their hands. The only indecision occurred when convicts were briefly returned to the penitentiary in January 1867.

The first postwar prisoners had been admitted to the penitentiary on 13 February 1866. "Upon taking possession we found the buildings in a dilapidated condition, some being partially and others entirely destroyed," the Board of Control told Gov. Madison Wells. The prison's cotton factory was completely wrecked. Only the walls and roof were left of the carpenter's shop, the pressroom, and the female prison. So forty-five convicts were furnished to the Baton Rouge, Grosse Tete and Opelousas Railroad for fifty cents a day. "In complying with this request the Board of Control was actuated by a knowledge of the large interest possessed by the State in the stock of that company, and by the fact that we had no work for that number of prisoners to do at that time," the board wrote in words that could have come from almost any Southern state in 1866. The lease was a benefit to both the railroad and the state because of a labor shortage, but the convicts were returned in January 1867, "the supply of freed labor becoming greater."[5]

The next year, 1868, the board tried to wash its hands of the growing convict problem. The prison had 352 convicts (9 died and 15 escaped). The board had received no appropriation. In March it gave the contract for the convicts to John Hugher and Charles Jones. The prison's debt at the time of the lease was $54,231.73.[6]

By law the board was in full control of the management of the penitentiary. It selected the warden, physician, and captain of the guard. When the board sought to exercise its prerogatives, however, the lessees sought an injunction and actually found a judge to rule the contract null and void. Soon a new bill was approved in the legislature giving final authority in all matters save "the health and religious regulations of the convicts" to Hugher and Jones. The board was never thereafter a serious factor in Louisiana convict policy. One of its final acts before relinquishing power was to issue a plaintive appeal to the legislature: "Will not the legislature inquire into the reason why so many are sent to this institution for the term of three and four and six months, upon the most trivial charges? Does there not lurk beneath, the low, mean motive of depriving them of their right of citizenship?" In one case, the entire thirty-eight-man membership of a black social club had been sent en masse to the penitentiary by a white mob after a mock trial.[7]

Hugher and Jones celebrated their judicial victory by selling out to S. L. James, who blithely worked the prisoners without any contract from the state for nearly a year. In 1870 the legislature obligingly substituted the names of James and his partners, Bynum and Buckner, for those of Hugher and Jones and, more important, extended the term of the lease for twenty-one years, making it the longest, by one year, in the history of the practice of leasing convicts. From that date until 1901 prisoners were worked either by James or, after his death in 1894, by his successors under new leases on the plantations he owned, on railroads, and on the endless task of constructing and shoring up levees along the Mississippi. The contract amount was $5,000 the first year, $6,000 the second, and so on until the amount reached $25,000 in the twenty-first year.[8]

James never paid more than two-thirds of this contract amount, which would have averaged $15,000 each year. While detailed figures are certainly hard to come by, one can estimate from those that are available an average annual population during James's lease of 600 to 700. James was therefore paying for convict labor at the rate of about $15 per convict per year over two decades.

Major James did not use all that labor himself, however. He sublet considerable numbers of them. In 1874 the board gathered together enough of its sense of duty to issue a rare report that contained a frank confession of ignorance. "At the time of our appointment to the Board of Control, the penitentiary was under the control of S. L. James and others; but from April 1 until some time in November it was conducted by Messrs. Garig, Bogle and Rosenfeld," they related. However, "since that time the management of the whole concern has been transferred to other parties, so that it is now difficult for the Board to determine who are the legal lessees." The next year they said the information still could not be furnished, although (regardless of the limited value such statistics might have under these circumstances) they did report 53 deaths and 29 escapes from a population of just 449 convicts.[9]

The legislature—particularly its black members in these late Reconstruction years—became exasperated enough in 1875 to pass a law forbidding convict labor outside the penitentiary walls. James simply ignored the law. The district attorney in Baton Rouge that same year sued James for nonpayment of the lease fees. James ignored the suit. Under pressure from the executive branch, the suit was not pursued, and James actually made no payments for six years. In 1881, after extensive negotiations, the disdainful lessee began to compensate the state for the labor of its prisoners. In 1878, immediately after the overthrow of the Reconstruction regime, the legislature repealed the 1875 ban on working prisoners away from the penitentiary.[10]

The demand for prisoners increased in the 1870s, and with it the population, which was 582 in 1876 and 625 in 1878. The state's chief engineer asked for convict help with the levees: "I must recommend that proper acts be passed combining or consolidating the contract of the Levee Company with the lease of the penitentiary, that more levee work can be done than is now possible." While the request was not fulfilled, since James wanted the prisoners on his plantation as well as on the levees, it is clear that the elimination of the lease was out of the question. As Gov. Francis Nicholls, no friend of leasing, pointed out in 1878, the state was getting no revenue from the convicts' labor, but it was not laying out any expenses, either.[11]

Shame and indignation over leasing's waste and corruption sometimes swept through the Louisiana legislature. Indeed, the Democratic Party itself went on record as favoring abolition as early as 1883. At the party's convention in Baton Rouge the delegates adopted a resolution that read in part: "the convict labor of the State should be appropriated and assigned to labor on the public levees, under the direction and control of the State authorities, by such legislation as may be necessary." But such legislation as was necessary would be almost two decades in coming. In the next legislative session, and every subsequent session until 1890, bills to abolish the lease were introduced—and were defeated.[12]

Gov. S. D. McEnery, a staunch supporter of Major James, the lease, and the lottery—he was known as "McLottery" to his numerous enemies—pointed to a troubling reality about convict labor in the mid 1880s, however. After floods in 1882, 1883, and 1884, the governor, with the generous permission of Major James, diverted convicts to build and repair levees. But, as McEnery saw, convicts could only be used by the state for a few months a year on the levees.[13]

McEnery's observation illustrates what Ralph V. Anderson and Robert E. Gallman call "Genovese's rule": the principle that "slavery requires all hands to be occupied at all times." "Those scholars who have referred to slaves as 'capitalized labor' have grasped an important truth," Anderson and Gallman write. "To own a slave was to have access to his entire labor and to be responsible for his full maintenance. Thus a slave was a form of capital; specifically, 'fixed' capital (as opposed to 'circulating' capital, such as inventories)."[14]

While convict labor was not a form of slavery, it did share this characteristic with slavery: that lessees had made a capital investment which, ideally, required constant use in order for the return on that investment to be realized to its maximum extent. "That slavery converted labor into a form of fixed capital helps to account for the planters' tendency to diversify," as well as for the drift toward "labor intensive work routines at certain seasons of the year when labor was in surplus," Anderson and Gallman conclude.[15] But diversification was not characteristic of convict leasing. Convicts were leased to contractors for specific projects, or to planters. Although during much of the history of leasing the strain of Genovese's rule slackened, then—since prices were extremely low—when prices did begin to rise it began to assert its inexorable force. Governor McEnery, for example, wondered in an 1888 address to the legislature about the problem of "supporting them in idleness at periods of the year when they could not be employed in such work."[16]

He was wise to be so concerned, for in spite of the repeated failure of bills for the abolition of the lease during the decade, the James lease would expire in any event in 1891. And when it did, market forces were unleashed.

II

When Governor Nicholls broached the question to the legislature, he knew he was addressing a politically delicate problem. The Democratic Party was on record as favoring abolition, the lessee retained great political clout, abolishing the lease would cost money, and the state had not received much in the way of income from the leasing contract. Consequently he demanded that any new lease be of a much briefer duration. It was an astute maneuver. As Carleton explains:

Neither James nor his critics was likely to be entirely satisfied with a short-term lease, the former because he was accustomed to a contract of

148

twenty-one years' duration and the latter because they were opposed to any further contracts. But each, presumably, could learn to live with such a settlement, James remaining in business for a time and his opponents taking solace from the limited duration of his tenure. The state, meanwhile, would continue to make money and Nicholls himself could avoid the responsibility for terminating an easy source of revenue without having to appear as another McEnery. The governor's proposal contained something for everyone.[17]

Including, it was soon apparent, other potential users of convict labor. The crafty James had become somewhat complacent and was taken by surprise when he found himself in the middle of a bidding war. The first legislative proposal essentially renewed James's current lease for ten years, calling for annual payments of $25,000. But then a new figure entered the scene, one familiar to residents of neighboring Texas: C. G. Ellis, partner with Edward Cunningham in the spurned company that had briefly held the Texas lease. When he learned of the Ellis proposal, also for $25,000, James raised his own bid to $35,000. The offers sailed back and forth, the bids increasing at every turn—$45,000, $50,000, $55,000—until James finally outbribed Ellis and won a $50,000, ten-year contract.[18] During the previous two decades he had paid perhaps one-fifth of that amount annually.

But it would be the last lease contract. In 1892 James's bitter political enemy, Murphy J. Foster, became governor. Foster, the champion of the antilottery forces in the state, was also a rabid white supremacist. Like political reformers in other Southern states at this time, Foster's program combined racism with moralism. The lease, he said, is "vicious and runs counter to the duties and responsibilities of the State and to the enlightened Christian sentiment of the present age." To him, cleaning up the state meant the elimination of the black vote, the lottery, and the convict lease. The lottery and the lease had divided Democrats since Redemption, allowing the few black legislators in the General Assembly to acquire the balance of power. Foster "decided that the lottery, the lease, and the Negro vote would all have to be disposed of. By 1898 they had been—in that order."[19] The abolition of the lease in Louisiana is thus strikingly similar to that in Georgia. It was actually part of a larger strategy that involved the disfranchisement of black voters. As in Georgia and Mississippi, an isolated component of a reactionary strategy dressed itself up in the garb of humanitarian reform. Significantly, the lottery had been the object of an intense bidding war at the same time as the lease.[20]

In 1894 S. L. James died of a hemorrhage on the porch of his plantation at Angola. That same year the General Assembly approved a joint resolution calling for state responsibility for convicts after the current lease expired, in 1901.[21] In 1898 the substance of this resolution became Article 196 of the state's new constitution, a constitution that also disfranchised most of the state's black voters, and many of its white ones as well, by means of property and literacy qualifications. Louisianans at that time had the lowest literacy rate in the United States. In 1898, the year of the new constitution, the National Prison Association met in New Orleans. The delegates who attended the session on "Louisiana's Convicts" would have had no doubt what the future had in store: the consensus was plantation work.[22]

One wonders if the convicts noticed any change. The state owned James's plantation, the penitentiary board was administered by the executor of James's estate, the warden had been James's warden, and one of the plantation managers was James's son.[23]

In both Mississippi and Louisiana, leasing's end was an act that combined political retribution with economic calculation. In both states the abolition of convict leasing was part of a radically undemocratic package of political changes cloaked in the garb of reforms, and it was made possible by the creation of vast state-owned plantations. Convicts had been working on plantations for generations by the time the shift occurred, but they had been privately owned plantations. Some convicts, to be sure, had been diverted from farms to labor on levees and railroads. The shift from these public works to plantations confirmed the purely agricultural solution to the prison labor question that was latent in these states' prison practices from the first.

III

Parchman and Angola—the very names of the immense prison plantations of Mississippi and Louisiana resound in our national popular culture via the songs and stories of African American lore and tradition. They are places of unremitting labor in unbearable heat, of unrequited loneliness, and of the ever- present possibility of a violent resolution of the most insignificant dispute. In the eyes of white Mississippians and Louisianans at the turn of the century, they also represented a fundamental rightness in the order of things, at least in the domain of criminal justice. The long rows of stooped black bodies working in gangs with overseers at the end of each row, the production of huge amounts of cotton, the disciplined organization of large crews of black forced labor in agricultural pursuits—all these aspects of life and work on the prison plantations seemed to them to represent a return to the natural order after decades of floundering. If these huge enterprises reminded people of an ideal form of slavery, it was with reason.

In 1968 the Southern Regional Council issued a report on the prisons of Arkansas, Louisiana, and Mississippi—those same states that, in 1883, Louisiana's George Washington Cable had singled out as the nation's worst. The council found that "the three states put together could not, out of presently available funds and facilities, provide the components of one prison which would meet minimum national standards set forth by the American Correctional Association." The report's description of Angola and Parchman throws light on the enduring qualities of Southern prison management, for the picture it draws had not appreciably changed for seven decades:

> The Louisiana State Penitentiary is located at Angola, West Feliciana Parish, near the Mississippi border, almost fifty miles north of Baton Rouge. Nearly 3,000 of its 20,000 acres are planted in sugar cane, producing, this year, 10,200,000 pounds of sugar and 550,000 gallons of blackstrap molasses.

> Angola Prison, like the African colony for which it is named, is difficult to visit. Its 3,800 inmates are more isolated, perhaps, than any other group of prisoners in America. The prison itself is 22 miles from the highway, and officials have traditionally been loathe [sic] to grant permission for visits from "outsiders."

> More than 260 inmate guards provide the main security for the prison. There are also more than 300 civilian personnel, 200 of whom are correctional officers. . . .

> The lash and the dungeons have been eliminated, but allegations of brutality are still common. Prisoners still fear sexual attack by fellow inmates because of inadequate supervision of sleeping quarters. Inmate guards, armed with weapons, still supervise their fellow inmates.

> There is little or no rehabilitation program at Angola. A budget cut in 1963 resulted in the firing of more than 100 employees, mostly teachers and counselors. These funds have never been restored. . . .

> The legislature consistently in previous years has answered budget pleas with a demand that the penitentiary become self- supporting. Actions of the Board of Institutions suggest the members believe that their chief function is to produce a profit. . . .

The Mississippi State Penitentiary at Parchman, in Sunflower county, is a Delta cotton plantation of more than 21,000 acres, housing more than 2,000 inmates.

Parchman is a self-supporting institution. . . .

Of the 210 armed guards at the penitentiary, 170 are inmates.[24]

The conditions of prison life in Louisiana and Mississippi in the 1960s were a direct inheritance of the era of convict leasing. The professionalization of corrections officials in the decades since has been offset by an immense increase in the population of the prisons they administer, such that the potential benefits of a rational approach are, if not nullified, then seriously diminished.

Nine

TENNESSEE
The Economics of Coercion

I

Tennessee appears at first glance to furnish that indispensable exception which many historians demand in order to show that patterns of historical development are not rigidly determined but rather are subject to the forces of human will and caprice. Its history shows the most anomalies of any of the leasing states. Its lease period was relatively brief—about twenty-five years. Few of its convicts labored on plantations or sawmills or brickyards, and when the lease was abandoned in 1893 not many of them, proportionately, were sent to road camps or prison farms. Humanitarian indignation was almost absent from the acrimonious debates surrounding the proper use of Tennessee convict labor, and the state's prison system by 1900 was closer to that of Northern states than was the system of any of its Southern neighbors.

It is the violent opposition of Tennessee's mining population that explains many a Tennessee anomaly. The role that political pressure, market forces, humanitarianism, good roads agitation, and prison farms played in Mississippi, Arkansas, Texas, and Georgia, violence played in Tennessee. That is why it was the first Southern state to destroy the convict lease.

Tennessee's experiment with convict leasing was a Hobbesian one— and was fittingly nasty, brutish, and short. For in Tennessee, in contrast to other Southern states, leasing was bitterly hated by a significant minority of its own free population, and as a consequence it pitted the state's sovereign authority against the wrath of much of the working population, whose interests were directly endangered by the presence of hundreds of convict workers.

Tennessee's bargain with the huge Tennessee Coal, Iron and Railroad Company, which was the lessee of Alabama's convicts until 1928, provoked massive resistance among the miners of East and Middle Tennessee almost from the start. The opposition culminated in a violent uprising of free miners in 1891 and 1892 that pushed the state to the breaking point. It was, as C. Vann Woodward says, an insurrection "fought on a . . . primitive level, for the most elemental rights, and fought with savage violence."[1]

Tennessee's leasing spanned just a quarter of a century, from 1871 to 1896, a brief stretch in comparison with the duration of leasing in the rest of the South. The midpoint of Tennessee's lease was also a turning point. In the first half of the period, from 1871 to 1883, the state let two contracts to a group of investors who engaged the convicts in the usual kinds of harsh labor: railroad construction, plantation labor, and mining. From 1883 to 1896 the prisoners worked chiefly in mines under the truly remorseless supervision of the TCI. Dominating the first period is the figure of "Major" Thomas O'Conner (or O'Connor), a high-stakes gambler, entrepreneur, and former Confederate prisoner of war who was killed in a gunfight on the streets of Knoxville in 1882. O'Conner stood at the head of a syndicate of bidders who first took over the penitentiary in 1871, and he became the chief stockholder in the TCI upon its formation just prior to the 1883 lease.

II

Like other Southern states, Tennessee in the late 1860s confronted a seemingly insurmountable fiscal wall. In 1869 the situation was so dire that the state comptroller told the governor: "The demands upon the State Treasury at the present time are of such a nature—as is well known to all—as hopeless to bankrupt the state in one month." The penitentiary alone was $50,000 in debt in 1866, the year the directors of the penitentiary leased the labor of the convicts inside the prison to a firm of furniture manufacturers, Ward and Briggs, at forty-three cents per convict daily. But when the lessees' equipment was destroyed by fire in June 1867, they and the state became involved in a ferocious legal wrangle. By mutual consent the lease was canceled in 1869, although a full settlement was not reached until the following year, when the legislature reimbursed Ward and Briggs with an appropriation of $132,000.

Finding themselves unable to lease the penitentiary with its ruined capital equipment and damaged inventory, the directors recommended the prohibition of leasing. Tennessee actually was the first state to do so—for five months. From February through June 1870 legislation was in effect prohibiting the leasing of a convict—without the convict's consent.[2]

Then in 1871 the inspectors signed a lease with Cherry, O'Conner and Company—essentially O'Conner—and Robert F. Looney of Memphis. Looney was a stalking horse for Arthur S. Colyar, one of the New South's great corporate plungers, who had extensive mining interests in the Cumberland Plateau. In late 1869 Colyar had called a secret meeting of mining and railroad magnates in Atlanta. Significantly, the conclave was held at the headquarters of the Western and Atlantic Railroad, whose president was Joseph E. Brown. The participants made arrangements for the partnerships in the Tennessee lease. This meeting was an event worthy of the pens of Samuel Clemens, Charles Dudley Warner, or Henry Demarest Lloyd, but it has received little attention from historians, perhaps because, although it was a classic Gilded Age scene of industrialists in collusion, it took place in the agrarian South.

The lease contract was for $30,000 per year for five years. Again, this was a lease that was made on an aggregate basis, not on the basis of the individual convict. As in Texas, the Tennessee prison experienced irregular and not spectacular growth in population during the period of the leases. Population grew by about 80 percent between 1872 and 1890, from 793 to 1,448, with no increase—in fact, a slight decrease—occurring when the TCI took over in 1883. The average yearly increase was 128, but with extremes of 171 additional prisoners in 1878 and a decrease of 107 in 1886.[3]

The O'Conner contract was typical:"[The lessees] are to take, carry out and fulfill all the contracts and obligations, for which the Penitentiary is bound, and to bear all the expenses thereof, and to have all the profits and emoluments arising therefrom."[4] The state was obligated for only about $6,000 per year in salaries for the superintendent, warden, assistant warden, physician, and chaplain.

Prior to the O'Conner lease, the state itself had conducted an experiment, and it was one in which Colyar had participated. As the inspectors explained in 1870:

It appeared to us that the application of the convict labor to such enterprises as were general, and not merely local in their benefits, were the natural fields to which it should, *as State labor*, be directed. Proposals, there-fore, having been received for the Tennessee and Pacific, Nashville and Chattanooga, and Nashville and North-western Railroad Companies, to hire the convict labor for the building and repairing of their respective roads; and from the State Asylum for the Insane, for draining and other purposes, we concluded to make an experimental test as to its profitable employment outside the Penitentiary, with those interests. The result is, after a few weeks trial a complete and satisfactory demonstration of the fact that convict labor can not only be remuneratively, but *safely* employed in outside work.[5]

It was under this arrangement that the pioneering Colyar had leased 100 prisoners.

The features that inevitably accompanied leasing wherever it was in effect appeared immediately in Tennessee as well. From 1872 to 1874 some 881 convicts entered the system, and 95 escaped from it. In the next two years, as leasing was firmly instituted, 257 escaped. Only three of those escapes came from the penitentiary building itself.[6]

George Washington Cable, speaking with conspicuous and heavy irony, but also rhetorically establishing the groundwork of his argument about the wickedness of leasing under any circumstances, called the Tennessee lease "the system at its best." But what made the Tennessee arrangement "superior," in his estimation, was precisely the fact that nearly half the convicts were working on industrial projects *within* the Nashville prison. The other half were distributed in three mines and on two farms. Convict leasing itself—that is, the contracting out of labor to enterprises outside the prison—he judged to be no better in Tennessee than anywhere else.[7]

The benefits of having the penitentiary, moreover, were dependent on the number of beds within it. The Nashville prison, a model of ad-vanced penology on the Auburn model when it was erected in 1828, contained 112 cells in each of two wings, plus 120 cells in a third wing constructed in 1858. With a total of 344 cells, the penitentiary had a maxi-mum capacity of 688 beds, although that situation provided the prison-ers with only about one-third the amount of air to breathe recommended by proper sanitation: "an air space at night less than the cubic contents of a good-sized grave," Cable observed.[8]

Tennessee was "best," then, only because it was one of the few South-ern states that had a penitentiary building. And Cable's assessment was

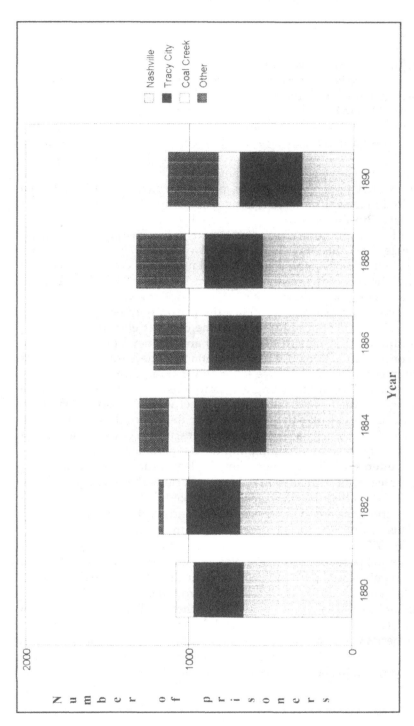

Convict Labor in Tennessee, 1880–90

made just *before* the advent of the TCI.

Most of the leased prisoners in this first venture worked on the Tennessee stretch of the Cincinnati Southern Railroad, a city-owned concern intended to link Cincinnati with Chattanooga. O'Conner had other Cincinnati links at this time, having become a partner in a bridge and tunnel construction company with contracts along the Cincinnati Southern right-of-way. Convicts began work on this difficult and dangerous stretch in the Cumberland Mountains in 1873.[9]

In March 1875 the legislature, perhaps realizing that it had been swindled in the O'Conner and Looney lease, approved a new five-year lease law. But the bids the state received were far below what it had hoped to attract, and it was forced to extend the existing arrangement. Tennessee was able, however, to wrest two improvements in the lease terms: first, the extension was for a fixed number of convicts—800; and second, the cost of the contract rose from $30,000 to $40,727.[10] That figured to a per- convict hire rate of about a dollar a week, plus maintenance and supervisory costs. Since the prison population was 964 in 1874 and only 800 would be leased, the contract effectively removed unproductive prisoners from O'Conner and Looney's purview.

The governor, James Davis Porter, attacked the lease itself in 1877 as being in competition with free labor and making escapes remarkably easy. Porter favored restricting extramural leases to the mines. Such a plan, argued the former Whig, would meet with the opposition of the miners, but, he calculated, there were only about three hundred of them who would be directly affected, and besides, it would lower the costs of coal and iron ore, thus "stimulating the development of our manufacturing interests." Shortly thereafter the legislature authorized a new six-year lease but stipulated that it must guarantee $50,000 per year. The lease in fact netted the state of Tennessee $591,617.02 in its first twelve years—about the amount per year its early advocates had anticipated.[11]

This second lease went again to the firm of Cherry, O'Conner, this time for $55,000. This company had been established in Nashville for the sole purpose of handling subleasing contracts. Cherry, O'Conner immediately leased their prisoners at a rate of $70,500 annually to A. M. Shook, manager of the Tennessee Coal, Iron and Railroad Company's mines at Tracy City, which would from then until 1896 be the largest user of Tennessee convict labor. Shook had bid directly for the contract that Cherry, O'Conner won, and bid a higher figure. His bond, in fact, had been signed by O'Conner. But O'Conner got the lease and then sublet the convicts to Shook for the amount of Shook's bid to the state. Shook,

O'Conner, Cherry, and Looney were all major stockholders in the company.[12]

In 1876 the Cincinnati Southern Railroad had come close to bankruptcy, and work on the Tennessee portion of the line was discontinued, just thirty-nine miles from Chattanooga. O'Conner then leased many of the convicts to a plantation in far western Tennessee on the Mississippi. But he also decided to shift his operations to mining.

The miners' opposition to this decision was instantaneous and hostile. At the first word of the impending use of convict miners, free miners began to combine. "Certain evil disposed persons in the neighborhood of Coal Creek, Anderson County, are forming, or are threatening to organize illegal combinations for the purpose of preventing the owners of the coal mines in that vicinity from employing convict labor in working their own property," the governor wrote the superintendent. "The whole force and power of the State will be used, if necessary in making good this contract."[13] The convicts did finally work the mines, but it took fifty armed guards to place just two hundred prisoners there. It was but a portent of what would happen nearly fifteen years later, when a larger and more unified group of miners confronted larger and more organized forces of the TCI and the state. It is unlikely that the shrewd O'Conner would have let things come to such a pass as they did in 1891 and 1892, but he was shot dead by one of his many enemies before the final lease was signed.

The 1883 lease law stipulated a minimum annual contract price of $100,000, twice the 1877 minimum. All expenses rested on the lessees' shoulders. They were to furnish adequate food, not work the prisoners more than ten hours a day, give them a change of clothing once a week, and (following the example of Georgia's 1876 lease law) transport the convicts directly to the place of work from the place of conviction. The Tennessee Coal, Iron and Railroad Company won the contract with a bid of $101,000. The only two companies to submit bids were the TCI and Cherry, Morrow and Company, both of them successor companies to the previous lessees. The lease was of "penitentiary and property"— the whole thing. The TCI, headquartered at Tracy City, worked 60 percent of the prisoners—some 774 in 1884—there and at branches at Inman and Coal Creek and sublet most of the rest to work in the main prison. Twenty were employed at Spence's farm raising vegetables to supply the main prison; of the rest 20 were in the foundry, 25 in the furniture factory, and some 485 making the sturdy, cheap wagons for which the penitentiary was famed throughout the West and South.[14]

"I am informed," Gov. William Bate fatuously reported early in 1885, that "no honest free laborer, applying for work, has been denied employment by reason of the presence of convict labor." Perhaps not—not immediately, anyway—but a joint investigating committee found in 1893 that the rate for free labor in the Coal Creek area had fallen from $1.25 to fifty cents per ton. In good times both convict and free workers found employment. Otherwise, they found, convict labor was preferred. And, of course, 1893 was not part of the good times. That year, when Tennessee was abolishing convict leasing, the United States entered the worst depression in its history.[15]

In 1884 the new system received 1,129 convicts; 93 escaped, and either 205 or 43 died, depending on whose report, the inspectors' or the surgeon's, one believed. But a minority report from a House investigating committee in 1889 called the system "a horror and a shame upon the state." "These branch prisons," they concluded, "are hell holes of rage, cruelty, despair, and vice."[16] Even allowing for rhetorical exaggeration or for any political capital the committee members may have been trying to accumulate with such charges, the preponderance of the evidence does support their claim.

In November 1889 the National Prison Association held its annual convention in Nashville. After the congress several delegates decided to visit the mines on Cumberland Mountain. They found the whitewash on the stockade still wet. Such a flimsy attempt at concealment is a reminder of the tangible reality behind the word *whitewash* when it is used as a figure of speech. Whitewashing before inspecting visits was common. As Plumber Freeman, a convict at Ellis Camp number two, told inquiring Texas senators in 1902: "I whitewashed these buildings inside and out about a year ago. They have not been whitewashed since till this week. We were told that they wanted us to clean up around here this week."[17]

The tangible reality beneath the whitewash, however, was unrelievedly harsh. Tennessee miners were routinely whipped for not getting their quota, a goal the inexperienced convicts were expected to accomplish after two weeks in the mines. The usual punishment was fifteen licks. The strap was a double, two-foot length of harness leather. It was estimated that half the black prisoners and one-fourth of the whites were infected with venereal diseases. Again allowing for a degree of sensationalism for political or other reasons, an 1893 investigating committee found the conditions appalling: "The bedding was filthy to an extreme degree. . . . The convicts had no night-shirts or change of cloth-ing, but slept two in a bed, close against each other and naked, or in the clothes in which they had worked. . . . the beds were without sheets or pillows and covered with grease, grime and coal dust."[18]

The conditions in the Tennessee mines were equaled by the treat-ment the convicts suffered at the hands of the guards and foremen. "My brother was a guard," recalled Mr. Thompson of Tracy City in 1938. "I used to visit him no tellin' how many a Sundays. I heard 'em beating the convicts. You could hear the strap. . . . I heard 'em holler. Yes, Lord. It was a sight to behold. I saw 'em kill 'em in the mines. The mine boss that is, for not getting their tasks. And maybe they was sick." Mrs. Sarah L. Cleek remembered how "me and a widow woman used to carry pies to the stockade and sell them to the convicts. They were treated cruelly. With my own eyes I saw where they was buried. Their thighs or shank bones were not buried deep enough or something. . . . the bones stuck out of the ground. I could see where the coffins was buried. Nigger Hill, the convict burial ground was called."[19]

Terrible as these conditions and barbaric as this treatment may have been, however, and however widely the accounts about them may have been disseminated, they were not, in Tennessee or anywhere else, what caused the death of this particular form of privatized forced labor. The termination of leasing in Tennessee came to pass because free miners raised the stakes to the point that defending the institution ended up costing Tennessee taxpayers more than the income derived from the leases themselves.

III

It is a somewhat curious feature of the events leading up to aboli-tion in Tennessee that the miners were not in the first instance concerned to end convict labor as such, but were incensed at the mine owners for other reasons and then saw the convict miners as the symbol and cause of those other grievances. On this question there was eventually full agreement between owners and free miners: both saw that the chief rea-son for the presence of the prisoners in the mines of eastern Tennessee was to break the power of the workers.

One TCI official put it this way: "One of the chief reasons which induced the company to take up the system was the great chance it of-fered for overcoming strikes." And Arthur S. Colyar, by then the TCI's

chief counsel, said in 1892 that "For some years after we began the convict labor system we found that we were right in calculating that free
laborers would be loath to enter upon strikes when they saw that the
company was amply provided with convict labor."[20] Whether it was to
break strikes or forestall them, the free miners understood soon enough
the implications of the convicts' presence.

Colyar's statement deserves a brief explication. The key words in it
are "for some years" and "calculating." The company, like the state, made
a decision to lease on the basis of a cost-benefit analysis that, for a time,
proved to have been worth the risk. But by 1892 the price of the lease
outran the income, and both TCI and Tennessee let it go.

The miners, as pointed out earlier, were highly sensitive to the use
of convicts at the outset of O'Conner's lease. Still, free and convict miners coexisted for over a decade in eastern Tennessee, and it was not the
importation of the convicts but the imposition in 1891 of a new contract
by the TCI that ignited a summer of dramatic violence in the coalfields.

One of the miners' grievances concerned payment in scrip, and the
concomitant requirement to use that scrip in company stores in the impoverished villages surrounding the mines. The scrip's actual value varied from place to place, but according to figures provided by Tennessee's
inspector of mines in 1891, it was discounted an average of 15 percent.
More galling was the paucity of alternative places of business in which
to spend it and the insistence of the company that the scrip be circulated
in the company stores. One miner received a letter from a company
manager clearly stating these expectations:

> Dear Sir—
>
> I believe I have twice spoken to you, kindly advising you that it would be
> a good policy for you to come to this office when in need of scrip to buy
> goods from us, and not go elsewhere and buy it; and now I write this note
> to you, saying that hereafter if you don't wish to comply with this re-
> quest, you can work out your six days' notice and come to this office and
> get your pay, and then you can work for the outside parties as well as to
> buy scrip from them, provided they have any thing for you to do, which
> you will find they have not.[21]

A second source of fuel for the coming blaze was the TCI's dismissal
of the miners' choice of a check-weightman—the man, employed by the
miners themselves, who checked, verified, and credited to the appropriate miner far below, the weight of the contents of each coal car. Such

an employee was explicitly permitted by law—but then so was payment in currency.

These grievances certainly inflamed the hard-pressed miners of Anderson County, but it was the decision of the company to close down the mine at Briceville for "repairs" in April 1891 that served as the precipitating event for the ensuing rebellion. For when the mine reopened that summer, it was with a company demand for workers to sign a new "iron-clad" contract that was extremely hostile to miners' interests. It included a no-strike clause and a presumption of right on the company's part in the event of any disputes. The miners balked at this direct affront. When they refused to sign the ironclad contract, the company turned to convict labor entirely, importing forty convicts on 5 July 1891. The miners were then summarily evicted from their company homes.[22]

The next week some three hundred miners, armed with everything from rocks to rifles, entered the prison stockade where the convicts were housed, evicted them in their turn, and placed them in boxcars on the train to Knoxville, some thirty-two miles to the south on the (convict built) Kentucky and Ohio Railroad.

The insurrection had begun fortuitously for the free miners and their families. But the state also had a duty to enforce contracts, and neither side was likely to back down. The convicts were soon returned, escorted by the state militia. Over one hundred troops occupied the convict stockade.

At this point miners from all over the area began to advance on Briceville. Some hailed from as far as Kentucky. All were armed. They came on foot and on mules, and came with the determination to expel the convicts and their nervous keepers. On 20 July some 1,500 free, armed miners surrounded the Briceville stockade and, in negotiations with the militia captain, promised that no company property would be harmed if the stockade would surrender. The prudent militia commander complied. That afternoon not only the well-traveled prisoners but also their guards and some 107 troops were all transported down the K & O line back to Knoxville. Following this success the miners tramped the four miles to Coal Creek, where 120 more convicts were removed in the same fashion.

After this second liberation, Gov. John P. Buchanan, who as an Alliance candidate ostensibly favored the miners' as opposed to the mine owners' objectives in this struggle, nevertheless responded by dispatching to Anderson County fourteen companies of militia—some 600 soldiers—with tents, guns, ammunition, and three days' rations. Meetings, negotiations, and a virtual impasse followed. The convicts were returned to the stockades, the militia departed, and the governor acceded to the miners' demand to call a special session of the legislature to repeal convict leasing.

Alliance politics in Tennessee were always "cautious," "tentative," and "less radical" than elsewhere, one historian says, because of the "relatively prosperous condition of the state's economy." It was the Conservative Alliance legislators that passed a Jim Crow railroad law in 1891 and that sent in the convicts as strikebreakers in 1891 and 1892.[23] In Tennessee, therefore, the pressure against leasing that in other states was applied by dissenting political movements was virtually absent, and political violence, provoked by the deeds of these Alliancemen manqués, rushed in to fill the vacuum.

The promised extra legislative session proved to be an exercise in paralysis. Solemn discussion occurred in abundance—but it was limited to ways to modify the lessees' contract, not to prohibit convict leasing.

Instead of ending leasing, the legislature actually took steps to fortify it, specifically by augmenting the appropriation for the militia and authorizing its use in the event of mob action "whether existing or imminent." The miners then, in A. C. Hutson's words, decided to have "an 'extra session' of their own."[24] The more conservative leaders of the rebellion's first months were ousted in favor of men who were less solicitous of the TCI's property rights. On 31 October and 2 November 1891 almost five hundred convicts were simply liberated by the miners from three stockades, and the stockades were then burned. The major difference between the two phases of the rebellion seems to be that in the second, the miners actually freed the prisoners and destroyed the compounds in which they were confined, instead of leaving company property alone and shipping the prisoners to the authorities by train.

The free miners and the convicts enjoyed a considerable measure of support from the nonmining population of the area, and even from the militia. W. M. Scoggins, a participant, recalled years later how many store owners put merchandise out for convicts to have, some out of fear of robbery, others from sympathy. This memory was corroborated by his wife Mollie, who attested: "I clothed two of the convicts myself so they could get away and so did a number of the neighbors." But most were recaptured because of an $85 bounty offered for their return.[25]

By January 1892 most convicts were back in Coal Creek, and a veritable militia post called "Fort Anderson," complete with trenches and a Gatling gun, was in place to assure compliance with the law. In July of that year, however, the dam of miners' resentment broke completely when the TCI cut its free miners to half-time while continuing 360 convict miners full-time. On 10 August miners burned the convict stockade and shipped the prisoners to Knoxville. On 15 August the pitched battle between miners and militia occurred. The stockade was destroyed. The fighting ended only after some five hundred militia reinforcements arrived. The stockade was rebuilt again, however, and the convicts returned, to stay until 1896.

In his last message to the legislature, in January 1893, the ineffective John Price Buchanan called for the "erection of a *new penitentiary*." It was a recommendation the legislators accepted gratefully. On 25 March 1893 they passed a bill captioned: "to prepare for the abolition of the convict lease system." It also provided for the lease's alternative, a new penitentiary that would eventually be erected at Brushy Mountain. In Tennessee, then, there was a third alternative solution to leasing, besides prison farms and road building: the construction of another penitentiary.

Four years later, with the leases having expired, Governor Turney looked back on the lease as a policy that could not continue. "The state really made no money," he said, "but rather lost by leasing of convicts on account of riots, outbreaks and invasions." P. D. Sims, a Tennessee reformer, explained the calculation this way: instead of having a system that paid $50,000 to $75,000 per year to the state, the taxpayers had to put out an extra $200,000 for the militia. "That was a strong argument among the mass of the voting population. . . . Now came the demand from the people, 'We must cut down this expense; we must abandon the lease system for one that will cost us less money.'"[26]

Yet in Tennessee, as in the other states, there was more to the picture than has been previously recognized. The abandonment of leasing did not occur solely because the cost of defending the institution came to exceed the state's return from the leasing contract. There is always the question of why the TCI was not willing, for example, to import its own militia. That, after all, was what the Carnegie Steel Company did during the contemporaneous Homestead strike near Pittsburgh, when armed steelworkers fought Pinkertons in a gun battle that left thirteen men dead on 6 July 1892.

The fact is that the demand for convict miners was relatively inelastic—and especially so during a depression. The United States entered a severe depression in 1893—the year of the abolition law—which persisted through 1896, when the contracts expired. There were in Tennessee no enormous convict population increases of the sort that occurred in Texas or Georgia. As Figure 2 shows, the number of convicts engaged in mining fluctuated quite a bit, but increased by around 200 during the TCI lease, from 598 to 786 miners at its greatest extent during the final, depression, year of 1893. Moreover, TCI was already using some 1,500 convict miners in its Alabama operations at the same time.[27] Had convict leasing in Tennessee been providing labor to diverse firms engaged in sundry forms of extraction, construction, or farming, as happened elsewhere, the demand for convict labor would have been much more elastic. In any case, it was not just the taxpayers' calculations that were relevant to the abolition of leasing in Tennessee, but those of the TCI, as well.

Ten

TEXAS
Here Come Bud Russel

I

On 3 April 1883 Thomas Goree, the superintendent of Texas's Huntsville Penitentiary, and F. R. Lubbock, the state treasurer, filed into the office of Gov. John Ireland in Austin. As the newly constituted Penitentiary Board, the three men had to decide what to do with Texas's convicts in light of the fact that the legislature had just assumed full control of the convict population—thus ending, as it seemed to many, the iniquity of convict leasing. The board's first act was to rebuff a lease offer, evidently with some indignation. "The Board considered that the recent action of the legislature [in revoking leases] was not only condemnatory of those particular leases but of the lease system," it resolved.[1]

By the end of the following year, that firm conviction had disintegrated. "What shall we do with our surplus labor?" the board plaintively inquired. "Owing to short crops in both 1883 and 1884, the stringency of money matters, and the general decline in both the passenger and freight traffic," the price of a railroad section hand had declined from $1.25 to $1.15 per day, while the number of convicts commanding such rates plummeted from 700 to 60. Because they could not be hired "at prices that would support them," convict boys and "second class negro convict men" had to be set to work on the plantation of Hearne, Rogers, and Hill, near Millican, for a term of three years; and 150 white and Mexican prisoners who had been returned from railroad construction outfits were contracted for one year on two other plantations. Texas, like Arkansas and South Carolina, had become a sharecropper, providing a labor force, guards, and clothing to landowners who in turn furnished land, seed, gin stands, and cotton presses.[2]

Further pressure against truly abolishing the lease came from the parsimonious legislature. "The penitentiary committee of the Legislature has returned to Austin and reports that it will require at least $1,000,000.00" to repair the crumbling Huntsville prison, reported the *Dallas Herald*. Hence it is "impossible for the State to resume control . . . at this time[;] convicts will continue to be leased out."[3] Far from being an accomplished fact, as the Penitentiary Board had presumed in 1883, the abolition of convict leasing in Texas was still thirty years away.

II

As might be expected, one can find in Texas numerous traits of leasing that were also typical of the practice elsewhere—only on a larger scale. Also to be expected, as with any state, were leasing trends and practices peculiar to the state itself. Texas's leasing record is closest in types of labor, and in the twisting course of its road to abolition, to that of its neighbor Arkansas. In the numbers of convicts who were leased it compares with Georgia and Alabama. And in the racial composition of its convict population it is unlike the rest of the South, except for the disproportionate representation of African Americans in the convict camps.

What must strike any observer of convict leasing in state after state is the abortive nature of the efforts to eliminate it, in spite of what seems, publicly at least, to have been a consensus about the corruption, barbarity, and humiliation it fastened upon the state and region. Texas provides one of the clearest examples of this fruitless agitation. The failed abolition of 1883 makes sense only with an understanding of both economics and ideology; with a knowledge, that is, of the labor market and fiscal condition of the state, and of what it was that lawmakers might have sincerely believed they were doing in revoking the 1883 leases. To develop such an understanding, it is necessary to move deeper into the past, to the chaotic and uncertain years immediately following the Civil War.

The problems of prison management in Texas in the late 1860s were typical of the region: the dilapidated prison at Huntsville was overcrowded with prisoners, many of whom were ill, while population pressures continued to mount and the state treasury was virtually empty.

Meanwhile, the political situation in 1865 and 1866 was as dire and confused as the condition of the penitentiary. Under President Andrew

Johnson's "Restoration" plan, Texas had proceeded to fulfill the conditions for readmission to the Union: most of her voters had taken the oath of allegiance, then elected a convention which proceeded to revoke the secession ordinance, abolish slavery, ratify the Thirteenth Amendment, and repudiate the state's war debts. A governor and a state legislature were duly elected, and in August 1866 President Johnson declared the state readmitted to the Union.

But Congress had other plans for Reconstruction, and as soon as it convened in December of 1865 it set about to dismantle Johnson's policies. In March 1867 Congress superseded Johnson's "Restoration," and Texas once more had a provisional government. Between August 1866 and March 1867, however—that is, in the brief interval of the Restoration government—the Texas legislature, in addition to passing the Black Codes, approved "An Act to Provide for the Employment of Convict Labor on Works of Public Utility." The statute's title suggests, first, that prison policy was seen chiefly as a question of labor rather than reformation or even punishment and, second, that such labor was properly directed toward the public benefit rather than private gain. Under this short-lived act, the Board of Public Works leased 250 convicts at a monthly rate of $12.50. They built railroads: the Airline took 100 men, and the Brazos Branch 150. The result would prove to be prophetic of future attempts to lease, but the premonitions were unheeded. Endless squabbles broke out between the contractors and the board, and lessees mistreated their prisoners, while failing or refusing to make their payments. The board refused to renew the lease when it expired in November 1867. The prisoners were shipped back to Huntsville while the politicians debated what to do.[4]

The Reconstruction convention that met in 1868 to draft a new constitution following congressional requirements concluded that, while on the one hand the costs of maintaining the prison were prohibitive, on the other prisoners could become a source of considerable income—an estimated $25,000 per year—if they were to be leased. No further action was taken in the 1860s, but when military Reconstruction ended in 1871 and a new penitentiary superintendent, A. J. Bennett, took office, he lost no time in informing the legislature that an investment of a quarter of a million dollars would be necessary to prevent the penitentiary from becoming a further financial drain—unless inmates were to be leased. The prison had a population of 497 at the end of 1870, with an additional 230 working on a state-funded railroad project and 10 more, probably women, "hired out in the neighborhood." Yet the legislature had not appropriated a cent for the prison in 1870. Expenses, and thus a deficit, had totaled $23,023.02. Bennett took the only action he could under the circumstances: "The managers of the institution . . . fed and clothed all the State's convicts, charging the sum required therefor, to the State, trusting to the sense of justice of the Legislature to refund."[5]

The sense of justice of the 1871 Texas legislature was certainly a thin reed to lean on, but leasing offered a more solid and sensible hope. How practical men could see it as fiscally necessary can be seen in the record of the state's finances. By 1874 the state's indebtedness was $2,248,831.75—and by that time the first prisoners had been leased.[6]

The state's first full lease had been awarded in July of 1871 to Ward, Dewey and Company. The lessees were prominent Republican businessmen from Galveston. A. J. Ward was the director of the Port of Galveston. His partner E. C. Dewey was a codirector with Ward of the Texas Mutual Life Insurance Company. A third partner was Nathan "The Fox" Patton, who had been a member of the Reconstruction convention, serving on the committee that recommended leasing the inmates of the penitentiary.[7]

The company's lease was for a term of fifteen years and gave Ward, Dewey virtually complete control. Under its terms, the company would pay $5,000 per year for the first five years, and $10,000 and $20,000 for the second and third five-year increments. This contract shows how the state factored in an anticipated increase in the prison population, while the company's risk consisted in a wager that the per-convict cost would diminish over time. The contract anticipated Georgia's massive twenty-year lease contract of 1876, by which lessees paid $25,000 per year for the prison population irrespective of that population's size.[8]

Like other apologists for leasing, Ward and Dewey put on a bravura performance before skeptical penologists at a meeting of the National Prison Association. At the New York convention in 1874, when they were already experiencing difficulties, Ward and Dewey made a presentation on "The Texas State Penitentiary." Their primary rationale for leasing convicts may have been profit, they conceded, but a sincere interest in the welfare of the convict was a motivation as well. In particular, they wanted to ensure that the convict was released from their oversight "with a love of labor in him." Goree came closer to the truth many years later when he attributed the cruelty and general mistreatment of that lease to the enormous leeway the businessmen enjoyed. "There was no responsibility," he remembered. "The lessees employed all the guards and sent the convicts where they pleased. There was no inspector and no one to see that the convicts were properly treated."[9]

For the state of Texas and its convicts, the Ward, Dewey lease was a mistake of massive proportions, and it could be seen to be a disaster almost from the start. The rates of escape and death were enormous. Probably 300 escaped in 1876 alone (1,723 convicts were on hand in March of that year), while 109 died from disease, 28 more were killed by guards, and 182 could not be accounted for.[10] That year, Ward and Dewey lost their lease. But as elsewhere in the South, people understood that although leasing had calamitous effects alternative solutions were hard to come by.

A leading historian of Texas prisons, Donald R. Walker, has argued convincingly that the revocation of the Ward, Dewey lease was due chiefly not to the mismanagement so glaringly evident from the available evidence but rather to the fact of the lessees' well-known Republican loyalties. The Texas Constitution of 1869 inaugurated what one careful historian has called "the most hated regime in Texas' history." "Redemption from Radical rule," writes Lawrence Rice, "was underway almost from the beginning of the Davis administration [of 1869]." When Richard Coke was elected governor in 1873, the forces of the Radical Davis administration refused to concede the election, so that when the new legislature arrived in the capitol, they found their seats occupied by unyielding Radical legislators who refused to depart. A circumspect President Grant refused to intervene in Texas's internal affairs and eventually the new legislature was able to inaugurate Coke. As Coke's accession on 15 January 1874 symbolizes the successful Redemption of Texas, so the ejection of the Republican lessees—who were certainly vulnerable on other grounds—was yet another stage in the Redemption process.[11]

One of the last acts of the Republican Reconstruction legislature had been to override Governor Davis's veto of a bill that enabled Ward and Dewey to postpone their lease payments until the end of the lease. In fact, the funds were never paid.

Although at first Ward and Dewey and the new governor seemed to get along well, eventually bad publicity placed the lessees in an awkward position. One year after taking office Coke praised the lessees for their "excellent" management and "humane" discipline. But five months later he was castigating their "inexcusable mismanagement." What had caused this turnabout, in brief, was the dissemination of a Kansas newspaper's report about horribly emaciated United States Army prisoners who were transferred from Huntsville to the Kansas state prison toward the end of 1874. The embarrassing facts forced Coke to appoint one of the prison-investigating committees—dozens existed in the South—whose critical appraisal was a far cry from Coke's earlier, sunny judgment.[12]

Yet another factor in the demise of Ward, Dewey may have been the bitter relations between the inspector and the lessee. Coke appointed the energetic J. K. P. Campbell as inspector of the convict camps. The promulgation of new rules as a consequence of the 1875 investigation became a source of enormous tension between Campbell and Ward in particular. While the rules in general seem reasonable enough, problems of convict management have seldom proven amenable to solution by the application of sensible principles. It was especially difficult to ensure enforcement of the elaborate rules when convicts were scattered about in plantation and construction camps in groups as small as 10 and as large as 150. But for the record, at least, convicts were supposed to receive humane treatment: one hour for breakfast and one and a half hours for dinner, limited hours of work, a change of clothing once a week, soap, and good food—cornbread, beef or bacon, soup, and vegetables.[13]

The root cause of the tension between inspector and lessee lay in the fact that the lessees continued to pay the guards, but according to the new rules the inspector could dismiss them. "By the new rules, the discipline of the prison is virtually taken away from the Lessees, and placed in the hands of the inspector," the Board explained. "This has produced conflict of authority . . . which is very prejudicial to good discipline." In June 1875 Campbell tried to exercise his legitimate authority. At one camp he demanded the discharge of the night sergeant, Veitch. Ward took up the challenge and singled out Veitch for duty. "The very greatest indignity has been offered me, and I am satisfied it is intended as such," a mortified Campbell wrote the board. These are among the strongest terms a nineteenth-century Southern male could use to express the kind of dishonor to which Campbell had been subjected. The two came to hate each other, and subsequently Campbell made certain that the governor was aware of the lease's many shortcomings: scurvy among prisoners at Huntsville and serious financial trouble for the lessees, who mortgaged their land and crops in Walker County and sold other lands.[14]

In truth, however, Ward and Dewey were probably their own worst enemies. Incompetent and greedy they certainly were, but it is doubtful that anyone could have proved capable of meeting the management challenges involved in overseeing a large and rapidly growing population scattered over half the state. By 1876 there were 1,723 convicts. In 1873 the number had been 883; by 1874 it was 1,454. Nine hundred seventy-two had been received between August 1874 and August 1875 alone. There was neither an adequate penitentiary to send them to nor projects sufficiently large to keep them concentrated, as the legislature had intended. Consequently, Ward and Dewey described themselves as "compelled" to disperse the convicts. "The convicts are scattered in detachments, varying from 10 to 150 men . . . on railroads, farms, &c." Some twenty-five such squads were in operation by the end of 1874; each one was worked under the direction of a sergeant selected by the lessees. It became apparent that the lessees had not even managed to provide socks or underwear to the convicts, who wore the same clothing to shreds winter and summer. An indication of the condition of the prisoners at the end of the Ward, Dewey lease is a memorandum from their successors showing the new lessees' purchase of 900 shirts, 1,522 jackets, 954 pairs of pants, 420 hats, and 375 pairs of shoes to issue to the prisoners.[15]

Finally the board made its explicit recommendation to revoke the lease: "It is now the duty of the State to lift [the penitentiary] out of the mire and place it on firm land. The only way it can be accomplished is for the State to assume control of her prison."[16] The legislature complied in August 1876.

III

Governor Coke, who had been elected to the United States Senate, resigned in December. It was left to his successor, Richard B. Hubbard, to make the specific arrangements for the state to gather together the convicts, then lease them again. For, in spite of the state's recent experience, the law did not call for state control; rather it required a temporary lease to be in force while bids for a permanent lease, to commence on 1 January 1878, were obtained and considered. A student of this brief episode comments: "[Governor Hubbard] did not forsee [sic] the extent of the enmity nor the seriousness of the opposition which preceded every step taken in the disengagement of the lessees from their profitable operations." Indeed, it would turn out that the new temporary lessees, Burnet and Kilpatrick, took in none other than A. J. Ward as a secret partner, and tried to conceal the arrangement from the governor. Goree, who as newly appointed superintendent at Huntsville was just beginning a long and honorable career of service, tipped Hubbard off. The governor was livid: "I have been duly *disgusted*—not to say *outraged* by their conduct & am glad the time of opening bids draws near. I don't care how *high* their bid may be—or however solvent their Bond . . . I have now no faith in the men. . . . B & K exacted $1500 per month from the *firm* (B & K & Ward)—as a consideration for letting Ward in. . . . It was signed by *all of em*. It was to go into *their own* (B & Ks) pockets."[17]

Although every scrap of evidence showed the lease to have been brutal, a nuisance, and a political headache, the notion of eliminating the practice never seems to have arisen in the 1870s. The problems lay not, it seemed, in the practice itself but in the lessees who were chosen. The solution was to annul the contracts with the bad lessees and put good ones in their stead. The disastrous failure of the first leases in 1866 and 1867 under the Board of Public Works did not deter the state from awarding the Ward, Dewey contract; the Ward, Dewey debacle did not cause second thoughts about the wily Burnet and Kilpatrick; and Burnet and Kilpatrick's graft brought no one to question awarding yet another lease to Cunningham and Ellis. This last company would lease all of Texas's prisoners from 1878 to 1883. When their contract expired, some began to think that convict leasing itself ought to expire with it.

The Cunningham and Ellis lease—unlike the preceding one, in which Ward and Dewey paid a fixed sum for the convicts en masse—was made on a per-capita basis. They took control of the prisoners at a rate of $3.01 per prisoner per month. With 1,564 convicts when their lease commenced, Cunningham and Ellis were paying substantially the same per month ($4,708) as their predecessors had paid yearly ($5,000). This per-capita provision may be thought to have contributed to the great growth of the prison population during those years—in other words, it might seem to have been in the interest of the state to increase the number of prisoners during the years of the per-capita lease contract in order to increase state revenue. But numbers do not follow utility in such a smooth and regular manner.

Texas had 1,564 convicts when the Cunningham and Ellis lease commenced in 1878 and 2,450 when it ended in 1883, an increase of 56 percent in just five years. But in fact the prison population seemed to grow at a fairly steady rate regardless of the basis for the convict rate—that is, irrespective of whether convicts were hired per capita or whether the whole penitentiary was leased on a fixed charge. The figures, then, are not easy to interpret. In the years of the Ward, Dewey lease, when the company paid a fixed rate for the penitentiary, the convict population actually grew at a faster rate than it did under Cunningham and Ellis— almost 23 percent annually, or an average of 200 prisoners. From 1878 to 1883, however, the average annual rate of increase was about 9 percent, or 177 prisoners.[18] But such high rates as these could hardly continue indefinitely. The system itself could only absorb so many.

Moreover, the demand for convict labor fluctuated. Shortly after the 1883 lease ended, the penitentiary board was in a quandary: "What shall we do with our surplus labor?" Goree had asked. Yet just two years later he faced the opposite problem. "The demand for labor of all kinds in Texas is greater than the supply," he advised the governor.[19] That oscillation, indeed, is probably why leasing did not end in 1883.

IV

Cunningham and Ellis were sugar planters, eventually among the greatest in the world. In their plantation at Sugar Land, "a scabrous shanty town-plus-tent city" known as "The Hell-Hole of the Brazos," both convicts and free laborers lived—the convicts being engaged in cane cutting and the free men in processing. Decades later, black Texas prisoners sang

> "Here come Bud Russel." "How in the world do you know?"
> Well he know him by his wagon and the chains he wo'.
> Big pistol on his shoulder, big knife in his hand:
> He's comin' to carry you back to Sugarland.[20]

Few connections have been more thoroughly documented in the historical literature than that between sugar and forced labor. From its first appearance in the historical record sugar cane was cultivated by slaves. In the middle of the ninth century there occurred a revolt among slaves in the Tigris-Euphrates delta who worked on sugar plantations fundamentally similar to those of the eighteenth-century Caribbean. Because the production of granular sugar is an operation that demands close coordination of the two stages of cane cultivation and sugar processing, it has led to a peculiar fusion of field and factory, demanding, in Sidney Mintz's words, "careful scheduling at the top, and the application of iron discipline at the base." Mintz and other historians of sugar and slavery have demonstrated the intimate bonds between "sugar cane, sugar making, African slave labor, and the plantation form in the Americas"; these links in turn further disclose why, after slave emancipation in the nineteenth century, planters throughout the Western Hemisphere "sought to re-create pre-emancipation conditions—to replace the discipline of slavery with the discipline of hunger."[21] The Texas prison lease— and, later, the purchase by the state itself of a massive sugar plantation—demonstrate the enduring truth of this linkage.

The prisoners working the cane fields, not surprisingly, were an entirely black labor force. Texas had the lowest proportion of blacks among its prison population of any Southern state—only about half. In 1880, for instance, there were 782 white, 119 Mexican, and 866 black convicts were received; in 1882, 710 were white, 128 Mexican, and 812 black. But farm labor was assigned almost exclusively to black prisoners. The railroads generally "hire fifty or sixty men and make provisions for a large car for cooking, for guards, etc. . . . For this labor we employ the surplus white labor. The negroes generally go to the farms," Goree told the National Prison Association in 1897. Share farm contracts called for black laborers explicitly. "Negro convicts . . . are much better adapted to field labors, and we have placed them on the farms in larger numbers for this reason," the superintendent explained in 1910. Nor was this emblematic of a regional prejudice only. In 1906 the great New England prison reformer Frederick Wines singled out Louisiana's decision to work prisoners on a huge state plantation as especially enlightened: "It is difficult to conceive of a more ideal method of dealing with prisoners, especially Negro prisoners, than this."[22]

About 700 convicts were set to cutting cane for Cunningham and Ellis. The company began to sublease the rest immediately, and the state quickly learned it had almost no control over the prisoners. Cunningham and Ellis entered into subleasing contracts on 1 January 1878, the very day the lease came into effect. In the contracts the lessees passed the entirety of their obligations—for feeding, clothing, guarding, and constructing quarters—to the sublessees. The subleasing rate was $125 per convict per year, while Cunningham and Ellis themselves had to pay the state just $36.12 ($3.01 per month). These subleasing arrangements alone, involving just over half of the convicts, netted Cunningham and

Ellis over $90,000 in 1880. The other half of the convict population worked the lessees' own properties. It was an enormously profitable operation.[23]

Yet, as Governor Hubbard proudly noted in his final message, "More actual cash goes into the treasury under this lease in one year than has been paid into it from the establishment of the penitentiary to the making of this lease." Hubbard's assertion was undocumented and probably wrong, but the state did begin to realize considerable gains: some $136,321.65 in the first twenty- two months of the contract alone.[24]

Hubbard lost the 1878 election, partly as a result of allegations that he had mishandled the lease transition. He was succeeded by one of the legends of Redeemer budget retrenchment, Oran Roberts, who had been president of the secession convention in 1861. "It may be doubted," Roberts said in his inaugural address, "whether our plan of leasing and working the convicts outside of the penitentiary is favorable to reform any more than whipping and hanging," but nonetheless he could see no alternative to it. That same year he vetoed the state's education appropriation as an economy measure, while in 1882 he would propose the complete exemption of all manufacturing capital from taxation for ten years.[25]

While far from being a reformer, Roberts did want to bring some order to the system. When demands arose for an investigation of a convict camp at Mineola, some eighty miles east of Dallas, where (mostly white) convicts cutting wood for the Texas and Pacific Railroad were being badly mistreated, Roberts complied quickly, and the eventual result was a new law somewhat limiting the lessees' freedom of action— the first glimmer of an end to the system.[26]

Although conditions at Mineola were certainly atrocious, the clamor for investigation originated from local hostility to convict labor—a factor less at issue near Sugarland, where the convicts were black—as much as from humane considerations. Eighteen convicts had died at Mineola in four months. D. M. Short, Goree's deputy whom Goree placed in charge of the investigation, found himself "irresistibly forced to the conclusion that much of the mortality was produced by harsh treatment and neglect."[27]

But Texas, it seemed, was beginning to reap real benefits: $186,190.97 in *net* proceeds as early as November 1880. Yet convict camps were more dispersed than ever. There were no fewer than fifty-one such squads engaged in plantation labor, woodcutting, and railroad construction that year. Cunningham and Ellis were using 1,044 on their own properties while subleasing 1,113. Some 256 prisoners died between 1878 and 1880, and 366 escaped. These numbers seem astonishingly large. No doubt the fear in countless rural communities about dozens of desperate escapees abroad in the land, as well as the stories of abuse and violence brought home by former guards and former prisoners, contributed to swelling public antipathy to leasing. Indeed, "The reports of nearly all the penitentiaries where convicts are worked outside the walls show fearful death rates," a troubled Goree wrote. "No one will deny that the system is an evil," he admitted. "It can only be defended on two grounds: necessity, and because it is a source of revenue."[28] It began to appear early in the 1880s, though, that the grip of the first of those enabling conditions—necessity—was weakening somewhat. Perhaps, some began to think, it would be possible for the state itself to reap the rewards of convict labor, now that Cunningham and Ellis had proven that such labor could be profitable. When the lessees inquired in December 1881 about the possibility of a lease extension, they were rebuffed.

Governor Roberts had already explained his own solution to the problem at a special session of the legislature early in 1881. If prisoners, he argued, could be worked "in large bodies on farms, they can be taken care of better, and will be more healthy, there will be fewer escapes, and fewer of them will be wounded and killed in the effort to prevent escapes; they can be made equally as profitable to the State in that way."[29] The other side of the coin would be to have as many prisoners as possible inside the penitentiaries at Huntsville and Rusk. The whole scheme, then, would involve many more—mostly white—prisoners inside engaged in industrial labor or outside nonfarm work, while large squads of mostly black prisoners worked a state farm. In 1882 Texas took the first step toward the realization of that overall strategy.

After refusing the continuation of Cunningham and Ellis's lease—significantly remarking that such a step would be "impolitic"—the board advertised for bids for convicts inside the penitentiary walls. The theory was simple. "Outside labor can be operated without any investment of capital, and it is the most profitable," the board explained. "The policy of the State is to increase the inside force at the expense of the outside." Thus the strategy should be one "of contracting the outside labor directly from the State, and try to lease the Penitentiaries."[30]

However elegant it may have been in theory, however, the effort was a dismal failure in practice. The board received no satisfactory bids for months—and for reasons explained in their own theory. The long-term strategy was for the state to take advantage of labor with no expenditure of capital, while at the same time leasing the labor that *did* require capital expenditure to make it productive. But no business firm would take the bait. Why should they bid for cheap labor if, in order to use it, significant outlays for capital would be required? Finally, the board actually invited specific firms to place bids—including Cunningham and Ellis, a sure sign of their desperation.

But then a shell of scandal exploded over the exposed legislature. An Austin newspaper revealed that the lessees had avoided the "vulgar and ungentlemanly" method of directly bribing key legislators, opting instead to arrange for them to win at poker. The ostentatiously indignant solons thereupon refused to ratify the leases, and shortly thereafter voted to end leasing altogether, with the state taking control of the prisoners. The net receipts from the five years of the Cunningham and Ellis lease came to more than $367,000.[31]

It was at this point that Goree, Lubbock, and Ireland felt the tightening ring of the economic depression that began in 1883. They entered into sharecropping contracts in 1884, as well as other leases. Even Cunningham and Ellis received a couple of hundred convicts for their sugar plantation.[32]

But in 1885 the state purchased a plantation of its own, one where "outside labor" could be used with profit. This was the 2,450-acre Harlem Farm (later known as the Jester Farm, after reforming governor Beaufort Jester). The plantation, near Richmond in Fort Bend County, was in fact contiguous to Sugar Land. The first convicts to be shipped there were taken from the Hearne, Rodgers, and Hill farms that had received the original group of "boys and second class negro men" the year before.

The population continued its inexorable growth: 2,539 convicts in 1884, 2,859 in 1886. Five hundred nine convicts escaped between 1882 and 1886, and 427 died. In 1894 there were over 4,000 prisoners: 1,593 whites, 1,956 blacks, and 572 Mexicans. The system was "a mammoth concern," noted the harried new superintendent, L. A. Whatley, who was clearly no Goree. "A great many prisoners have to be daily transferred from one camp to another to keep contracts up to an agreed number; discharges here to-day and there to-morrow; receipts of men on every hand; the sick to look after. . . ." Still, Whatley could comfort himself with the fiction that what Texas was doing was not technically leasing. "Our present system of prison management is so much better, when compared with the lease and other systems, that every taxpayer and citizen has cause to be congratulated." On the one hand, Whatley could congratulate his superiors on having abolished leasing in 1883, while on the other he fretted about the problems associated with "keep[ing] contracts up to an agreed number"![33]

Beginning in 1886, eighty-five convicts were dispatched to the Oatmanville quarry, in an area still known as "Convict Hill" near suburban Austin. Soon an additional three hundred were working at nearby Granite Mountain. Texas, like Arkansas, was constructing a new capitol with convict labor. The contractors for the project were faced with a loss if they could not obtain such labor. Their only alternative, they told Governor Ireland, was to purchase stone from out of state. The patriotic governor insisted on Texas material only, and, in light of the state's depressed financial condition and the specter of "surplus labor" in the prisons, he was able to divert these otherwise unproductive prisoners to production for the public benefit. The lease rate was sixty-five cents per day for each convict.[34]

But the work on the state capitol was a stopgap. Something permanent had to be undertaken. Yet with no large-scale alternative arrangement, leasing continued for decades more. The way out, for Texas, would prove to be the prison plantation. In 1899 the state bought a second sugar plantation, the 5,500-acre Clemens farm, also located on the Brazos. Nine years later the purchase of the Imperial and Ramsey farms added another 13,000 acres, and a tract adjoining Harlem added 975 acres to that operation. All these properties were nearly contiguous and located in the fertile "Sugar Bowl" region southwest of Houston. By 1910 the state of Texas owned over 20,000 acres of prime sugar property. The 1908 crop alone paid for the Ramsey farm, the tract adjoining Harlem, and half of the Imperial estate—some $225,000.[35]

An important stage in the transition from convict leasing was completed with these purchases. The situation now began to conform to the picture Governor Roberts had envisioned in 1881. Texas was in a position to be working convicts in large numbers on huge plantations, with the state capturing the gains that Cunningham and Ellis had been able to secure in 1881. As the penitentiary officials correctly noted in 1910, "The progress made in the last four years toward the abolition of the lease system has been achieved wholly through the acquisition of plantations."[36]

But the conceiving and even the installation of alternates, while necessary, is not sufficient to explain the demise of Texas leasing. Two other factors present at the end of the Texas system were political and economic. Politically the system was the object of withering public attack in a series of influential newspaper articles in 1908 and 1909, attacks which led as usual to another investigation, revealing the usual horrors. Three somewhat unlikely confederates combined to mount this attack: a young, idealistic progressive journalist for the *San Antonio Express*, George Waverly Briggs; a hardened veteran journalist for the *Dallas-Galveston News*, Tom Finty Jr.; and Jake Hodges, the devout, earnest chaplain at Huntsville, whose humanitarian interest in his charges had thoroughly alienated him from prison officials.[37] But the two newspapers kept the issue in the public eye during an election year, and Oscar Colquitt, campaigning for governor that year, made the elimination of leasing the centerpiece of his campaign. His victory led to a special session which ended the contracting out of prison labor to private citizens.

The economic factor has not been noted in the few commentaries about the cessation of convict leasing, but it was at least as important as the political pressure and the public outrage, both of which had been there all along—and almost as important as having alternatives in place and ready to be implemented. In a manner that parallels Georgia's almost exactly, and at precisely the same time, the cost of convict labor in Texas rose steadily in the early twentieth century, until it just reached that of free labor. Sugar workers in 1882 commanded $15 per month for the state; by 1904 the rate was $21—and first- class hands only were being leased. In the next few years the price was bid much higher, so that by 1908 (the year of abolition in Georgia), 833 prisoners were working for the Texas Turpentine Company at $45.[38] As had been the case in Georgia that same year, the price of a convict had tipped the scales balancing free and forced labor. Forty-five dollars per month plus the estimated $8 in maintenance and monitoring costs comes to just under $2 per workday—again, the price of free labor.

So in Texas as elsewhere it was not just the muckraking journalists, nor the politicians with a finger on the pulse of public feeling, nor even the gradual construction of alternative methods of wringing wealth from convicts' muscles that would converge to bring about the end of convict leasing; it was also an economic environment in which convict labor was losing its advantage to lessees, who were coming ever closer to paying labor costs that were the same as free wage labor rates. When faced with the alternative of hiring free workers who could be laid off in slack times, or leasing equally expensive convicts who had to be maintained even if the bottom fell out of the labor market, Texas businessmen proved receptive to the logic of state control. Leasing was abandoned in Texas at exactly the same time that it was in Arkansas: at the expiration of the contracts then in force, on 31 December 1913.

Eleven

FLORIDA
Leasing on the Frontier

Florida was as remote and marginal as any portion of the eastern half of United States during the early years of convict leasing. Before the Civil War the state had fewer people than the city of New Orleans, and even in 1870 the population of the entire state was under 190,000.[1] Florida's sparse population and frontier circumstances impart a singularly untamed flavor to its leasing story. Of course, convict leasing seems a wild and barbaric practice wherever it appeared, but Florida's experience with it had an especially intense, violent quality.

People did move to Florida in ever greater numbers in the nineteenth century, but not fast enough to satisfy anxious employers there, whose complaints of labor shortage were a constant refrain during those decades. Operators of lumberyards and turpentine forests in particular sought labor wherever they could. In 1906, for example, the Georgia-Florida Sawmill Association passed a resolution calling on those states' legislatures to "make the vagrancy laws of Georgia and Florida more effective."[2] Florida's legislature complied by expanding the law's definition of vagrancy to encompass all but the state's most staid bourgeois inhabitants. The new definition encompassed:

> rogues and vagabonds, idle or dissolute persons who go about begging, common gamblers, persons who use juggling or unlawful games or plays, common pipers and fiddlers, common drunkards, common nightwalkers, thieves, pilferers, traders in stolen property, lewd, wanton and lascivious persons in speech or behavior, keepers of gambling places, common railers and brawlers, persons who neglect their calling or employment and misspend what they earn, . . . idle and disorderly persons including therein those who neglect all lawful business and habitually spend their time by frequenting houses of ill fame, gaming houses or tippling shops, persons [who are] able to work but are habitually idle and live upon the earnings

183

of their wives or minor children, and all able bodied male persons over eighteen years of age who are without means of support.[3]

Vagrancy was a widespread "offense" in the South throughout the late nineteenth and early twentieth centuries, one that frequently led to outright peonage, but in Florida it was most pervasive.[4]

From Reconstruction onward, then, Florida was a labor-hungry state. And from the beginning of its postbellum history Florida's employers understood that the key to production would lie in the ability to concentrate and control black labor. Two complementary ideas converged in the middle of the 1860s to reinforce this understanding: first, that (in the words of a white Floridian in 1865) "There is now nothing between me and the nigger but the dollar—the almighty dollar"; and second, that blacks would not work without compulsion.[5] These convictions, almost universal among whites, combined with the complete absence of a prison tradition to create a situation in which state officials had virtually to invent a system of punishments through forced labor.

Florida was one of the few states in the nation that had not constructed a penitentiary prior to the Civil War. Late in the summer of 1868, however, Gov. Harrison Reed traveled to Washington, D.C., and received from Secretary of War John Schofield the federal arsenal at Chattahoochee for use as a penitentiary. The structure, it was estimated, would accommodate 300 prisoners. That fall the legislature arranged to offset the new prison's expenses with the returns of the labor of its prisoners. The money received from the labor "either within or without the prison enclosures," a new law provided, was to be directed to a special fund for prison costs. This provision was immediately construed to permit the leasing of the prisoners. The law, which was a part of the state's postwar Black Code, also stipulated that the prison was to be "conducted as a military establishment," which was why the penitentiary came under the jurisdiction of the adjutant general for the next twenty-two years.[6]

Florida officials, therefore, attempted to overcome the state's prewar penitentiary shortcomings, not by taxing its citizens and planning and constructing a penitentiary building, but by short-circuiting that whole process and entering the penitentiary era at a stroke. This feeble attempt to follow Northern penological development would probably have failed anyway; within a year fifty of the Chattahoochee prison's ninety-four convicts were already being leased. Governor Reed thought it would be advisable to allow them to be worked for ten rather than eight hours per day, as they had been.[7]

In 1868 a hulking, probably alcoholic former U.S. Army quarter-master and failed farmer named Malachi Martin decided to try politics, a field that was certainly wide open in postwar Florida. From May to November of that year Martin served as an agent of the Freedmen's Bureau, whose major policy, its leading Florida historian asserts, was "forcing blacks to contract to work for whites." Then in November Martin was named first "commanding officer" of the new military-style penitentiary. Soon the disenchanted governor tried to remove him, probably because of his drinking and his use of convicts to construct a new house for himself. Unfortunately the governor had overlooked the fact that he had already appointed Martin's intended successor to another position. Since the governor's main object was to provide a job for Martin's rival rather than to deal effectively with the problems of the penitentiary, Martin was permitted to remain at his post, where he would continue to direct Florida's penitentiary affairs until 1877.[8]

Florida's leasing, like South Carolina's, was desultory before 1877—before the restoration of Democratic rule in the aftermath of the Hayes-Tilden Compromise of 1877 ending Reconstruction. But as soon as the Republicans were out, the lease was in. A sweeping 1877 law eradicated the prison whose roots were so shallow, and made the lease the exclusive form of convict management. In spite of the Redeemers' enthusiasm for leased convict labor, however, it must be recalled that leasing was not introduced by them but merely continued and amplified.[9]

Martin, an industrious cultivator of the scuppernong grape, had used the prisoners in his own vineyards to his great profit. Yet there was not enough labor in the vineyards to keep all the prisoners occupied, and small squads began to be leased out, mainly to railroads. In 1870 N. W. Haines took 15 at $1.25 per day; two years later many went to the Jacksonville, Pensacola, and Mobile Railroad. As in Tennessee, North Carolina, Georgia, and to some extent Texas, then, the earliest years of convict leasing in Florida were mainly ones of railroad construction. Records are sketchy in these first years, but it is noteworthy that as late as 1876 there were only 107 convicts in the state. It is evident that in Florida before 1877 leasing was but a makeshift "system" that showed no particular pattern—except for the usual cruelties.[10]

After 1877, though, convict leasing did begin to show some signs of being a system, as the state inaugurated a bidding procedure and required regular reports. As in Georgia, and more briefly in Arkansas, Florida in 1877 relinquished all responsibility for all convicts to an allegedly omnicompetent lessee. The 1877 statute eliminated Malachi Martin's position entirely, allowing the adjutant general to contract directly for the convicts' labor, supervision, and subsistence. And it fastened leasing even more securely on the state by changing the old arsenal-turned-prison at Chattahoochee into an insane asylum, thus depriving the criminal justice system of any alternative to hiring the prisoners out.

In the two years preceding the end of Republican rule, Florida had paid over $60,000 for its uncoordinated efforts to manage prisoners. In a typical example of corruption, the adjutant general, John Varnum, had taken 72 convicts to work on the St. Johns, Lake Eustis and Gulf Railroad in Sumter and Orange counties—wilderness locations in central Florida. "Dozens of those who went into the tropical marshes and palmetto jungles of Lake Eustace," J. C. Powell wrote in 1891, "went to certain death. . . . Rude huts were built of whatever material came to hand, and in the periods of heavy rain it was no unusual thing for the convicts to awake in the morning half submerged in mud and slime. . . . There was no food at all. In this extremity, the convicts were driven to live as the wild beasts."[11] Powell's account is a sensational one, and he undoubtedly exaggerates on occasion, but generally it is authentic. State officials admitted, when they turned over the care of the prisoners to new lessees, that the St. Johns convicts endured horrible conditions.

Florida, like Arkansas, thus began leasing by gratefully paying a lessee for the service of removing an unwanted expense. The state paid two lessees, H. A. Wyse and G. A. Chairs, to take the convicts and pay all maintenance costs. After a few months on the St. Johns Railroad, the tattered prisoners were conveyed to Wyse pursuant to the new legislation; he put some to use on his turpentine farm at Live Oak, a desolate pine woods area about halfway between Jacksonville and Tallahassee. The rest went to Chairs's farm near the capital city.[12] (Powell, writing from memory, referred to G. A. Chairs as "Green Cheers" in his memoir.[13])

Chairs was to Florida what E. C. Ward was to Texas or Thomas O'Conner to Tennessee: a lessee who, at the outset of the state's decision to relinquish control of its prisoners, completely betrayed his responsibility for custody of the men and women (there were three or four female convicts) entrusted to him and a lessee the lesson of whose utter disregard for the convicts' health and well-being was lost on the part of the state. At Chairs's farm convicts known only by their numbers lived in the lower story of the farmhouse, where conditions were appalling; Chairs and his family inhabited the upper floor. The state made no attempt to inquire about the convicts' condition, and Chairs kept no records. In 1879 the prisoners mutinied but were betrayed by another convict. The upshot was a pitched battle between prisoners and a posse that left several dead. Word began to filter out about these events, and Chairs lost his lease. When the reassigned convicts straggled into H. A. Wyse's turpentine farm some weeks later, "some of them were clad in the filthy remnants of the very clothing they had worn at the time they received their original sentence in court."[14]

When the 1879 bids came in under the terms of the 1877 law, two of them called for payment by the state, in keeping with the practice that had been established earlier. But the canny Wyse offered to pay all expenses for the entire prison plus a nominal sum of $100. The state, rather than being relieved of an expense, could now foresee a future stream of actual profits. Then, from 1880 to 1882, the East Florida Railway Company took the convicts for all expenses and $15 annually for each prisoner. Such terms, said Gov. William Bloxham, would be "much better for the tax- payers of the State." So they would prove to be, as the state earned $6,705 on this contract.[15]

Wyse, the original 1877 lessee, had contracted with New York merchants named Charles Dutton and Ruff Jones, dealers in turpentine, rosin, and naval stores. Dutton, who had apparently been impressed with the Florida operation, bid on and won the contract for 1883–1884 with an offer to pay all expenses plus $9,200. Then in 1884 Dutton seized the opportunity presented by a downward slope in the business cycle. As discussed earlier, in 1883 and 1884 economic distress affected convict labor markets elsewhere in the South. In Texas, Thomas Goree was asking, "What shall we do with our surplus labor?"; while Tennessee awarded the labor of hundreds of convict miners to the TCI for just $55,000. When Florida received no proposals for its convicts in the 1884 round of bids, then, the adjutant general finally accepted the offer of a man named Henry Wood, an agent for Dutton. According to the arrangement, Wood would take the convicts and the state would pay *him* $8,500. Since he had paid the state $9,200 in 1883 and then collected $8,500 from the state in 1884, Dutton enjoyed the labor of all of Florida's convicts for three years for a net payment of $700. After 1885 Dutton took all the prisoners to his turpentine works in Suwanee County on a four-year lease.[16]

The prison population, which had been small, now began to grow. From 1877 to 1881 there were never more than 163 convicts, and an average of only 124. The East Florida Railway, lessees in 1880–1882, worked an average of 139 convicts. But with Dutton on the scene, prison camps would begin to swell. Florida had 208 prisoners in January 1883, 291 two years later, and 339 in 1888. The following year saw a decline, but it was the result of the yellow fever epidemic's having prevented the holding of regular court sessions and was only a temporary and slight dip. There were 530 convicts in 1895 and 1,071 by 1904.[17] There can be little doubt that part of the growth can be attributed to the assiduous enterprise of the labor agents whom Dutton hired to pay the fines of vagrants and transport them to the stockades.[18]

Florida too went through a charade of abolition. A new constitution of 1885 evidently pointed toward the Texas-Arkansas-Mississippi solution of prison farms by requiring the establishment of a penitentiary and removing it from the purview of the adjutant general—an embarrassing anachronism dating from Reconstruction—placing it instead under the direction of the commissioner of agriculture. Unfortunately for this scheme, there was no such commissioner, as there was no such bureau, until 1890. Much more important to the destiny of Florida's prison laborers was the discovery of phosphate in 1881. In Florida, as in industry.[19]

Many of them would be sublet for such labor. Subleasing was a particularly prominent feature of Florida leasing. It tended to accompany rapid population growth (or rapid population growth accompanied it) throughout the South. In Florida both extensive subleasing and work in phosphate mining began with the 1890 lease awarded to E. B. Bailey. Bailey's first contract was on a per- convict basis: at the outset it was $1.25 monthly—the same rate, when annualized, as that paid by the East Florida Railroad a decade earlier. However, the state raised the rate for the second year by 50 percent to $1.87 1/2 per month: an annual rate of $22.50 apiece and the current per capita price in Georgia. Since there were only about 320 prisoners in 1890, however, the actual revenues from leasing remained small, and the population figures do not begin to match the large numbers of Florida's neighbors to the north and west. Nevertheless, Florida's prison population as a percentage of its total inhabitants would exceed that of any Southern state by the turn of the twentieth century. By that time the prices commanded by convict labor had also escalated enormously and edged close to the wage rate of free workers.[20]

E. B. Bailey's bid was viewed with favor partly because he proposed to have the convicts laboring on his Jefferson County plantation, and such labor would remove the prisoners from the terrible, dangerous conditions of the turpentine camps. Not surprising, then, the convicts were gladdened by the prospect of leaving the piney woods to work on Bailey's plantation. "The news of the change of lease was received with rejoicing by the prisoners at the turpentine camps," Captain Powell recalled. "They were eager to exchange the hack and dipper for the plow and hoe."[21] But then in the spring of 1891 Bailey purchased three hundred acres of phosphate land for $10,000, and by the next year the focus of his—or his convicts'—efforts had shifted from farming to phosphate. Nevertheless, his phosphate beds could absorb fewer than half of the prisoners, so he sublet 180. For this venture he received $12,000—or $66.67 per convict per year for prisoners whom he had leased from the state at a rate of $22.50. In this subleasing transaction, therefore, Bailey tripled his investment in convict workers while simultaneously recovering the entire cost of his investment in the land.[22]

It was phosphate, not farming or turpentine, that increased the price of convict labor, and by doing so it fixed the parasitic practice even more firmly on the lifeblood of Florida's commerce, politics, and society. After the Bailey 1890 venture had proved so successful, the state began to see real possibilities for revenue. While as recently as 1885 Florida had to pay Charles Dutton to take the convicts off its hands, by 1894 it was driving a very different bargain. After much haggling, Bailey received control of one-third of the prisoners, but the lease cost him and the other lessees, with whom he certainly colluded, $21,000. The prisoners were grouped in thirds, with equal shares going to Bailey, the West brothers—J. W., E. E., and W. S. West—and T. G. and J. A. Cranford. By then there were 530 convicts, over 90 percent of whom were black. Eighteen died, but only 24 escaped that year.[23]

The 1894 contract represents a departure of the same historic significance for Florida as the 1883 leases did for Arkansas or Tennessee, for in that year the state abandoned the nuisance of calculating per-capita rates and turned over the prisoners to the three lessees for a set price. At the inception of this new sort of contract the price of $21,000 for the 530 prisoners represented a total annual outlay of about $40 each; by 1899, because the number of prisoners had risen, the per capita price had been discounted to $30.

But Florida's 1894 departure also has some salient differences from other states' policies. Unlike the disastrous Georgia multi-year lease that was approaching its end in the mid 1890s, Florida's leases were maintained on an annual basis. One reason for this contrast lies in the general economic climate in which the contracts were drawn up. Georgia entered its two-decade lease in 1879 (pursuant to 1877 legislation), and by the early 1890s both the state and the lessees had reason to question the wisdom of such a protracted commitment. The restricted duration of the Florida lease also shows caution on both sides, as both state and lessee factored the current economic uncertainty into the terms of the contract. Indeed, the period of lump-sum payments would last only eight years, to 1902. After that, contracts reverted to a per-capita basis.

During the two decades after Reconstruction, Florida did not have an inspector of convict camps, delaying on this matter even longer than Arkansas, which had no such official until 1889. Bailey, the Wests, and the Cranfords held the leases from 1894 through 1897, when the legislature finally provided for an inspector, whose salary of $125 per month was derived from the lease income.

The evidence, while somewhat elusive, makes it clear that at the end of the 1890s the convicts' labor was worth much more than the $21,000 price of the annual contract—a mere $30 or $40 per prisoner. Moreover, some state officials were resentfully aware of the disparity between the state's proceeds and the profits of the lessees. In 1901, for example, the state's convict population was 800, but only some 293 were under the lessees' direct custody. The other 507 were scattered in nine sublessee camps in crews ranging from 30 to 163 convicts in size. Most of these camps' locations cannot be found on modern maps. They were wilderness points whose names were sometimes those of the sublessees: Dutton, Thompson, Waller. Most were located in the still-remote region between Ocala and Tampa near the Withlacoochee River and the present-day Withlacoochee National Forest.

Convicts were becoming cheaper by the year under the fixed- price contract as the population grew. In 1901 Gov. William Jennings observed: "The lessees pay the State about $26.40 per capita per annum, the sub-lessees pay the lessees amounts ranging from $90 to $180 per capita per annum. The $180 contracts being for picked men." In 1893 Marion Phosphate Company had paid E. B. Bailey a dollar a day for each of 100 prisoners. Consequently, the governor estimated, "the labor of the State prisoners are [sic] reasonably worth upward of $130 per capita per annum, without pick or choice, net to the State."[24]

In 1899 a House committee recommended a lease price of at least $50,000. That year's penitentiary report noted the increased demand in phosphates and naval stores and concluded that Florida "should receive a much higher consideration for the labor of convicts than has heretofore been given." That year's contract went to four lessees—A. L. West, R. J. Knight, S. L. Varnadoe, and W. N. Camp—but for the usual $21,000 total.[25]

The state had provided for an inspector in 1897, and it was not long before knowledge of terrible treatment and conditions came to light. Camp's prisoners worked a phosphate mine in Citrus County, which investigators found to be a deadly environment. Eight of the camp's 80 prisoners died in 1899. A House committee reported: "We found a system of cruelty and inhumanity practiced at this camp, that it would be hard to realize unless it could be seen and heard direct." One former prisoner, S. P. Horne, testified before the legislature about a convict whipped until his skin was literally beaten off his back. Thomas Allen, a foreman, Horne said, "would beat sick men that died two days later, some would be so badly beaten that they could not lay on their back for weeks. . . . It would take me two weeks to write it all up."[26]

Still, pressure continued for driving a harder bargain for the disposition of this kind of labor. Behind such pressure lay a recognition of the value of the natural resources the convicts were extracting from Florida's land, and especially of phosphates, which in the 1890s overtook turpentine and naval stores in importance. Indeed the relative value of these two commodities was reversed in that decade. Although the revenue of both industries was rising, in 1900 the total value of turpentine production in the United States was less than $1 million, while phosphate's value was $2 million in 1888, $5 million in 1900, and $7 million by 1903. The production capacity of phosphate fertilizer plants was 336,000 tons in 1900, but 1,447,000 by 1920. Meanwhile the value of turpentine and pitch, as measured by export value, fluctuated wildly. In 1904 exports were worth $32,253. In 1905 that amount increased to $74,938, but that was a peak not to be reached again before World War I. The Panic of 1907 sent prices plummeting, and in 1909 exports were valued at just $31,809. By 1903 some 800 Florida convicts were digging phosphate, while only about 300 were in the turpentine woods.[27]

Florida's legislature passed a reform statute in 1899. The new law, in Governor Jennings's candid words, represented a recognition that "the present system of leasing the convicts deprives the State of thousands of dollars, as the lessees invariably pool their bid and secure them at a nominal sum and sub-lease them at a big profit [and that] if the lease system is to be continued that under proper management same can be done in such a way that the State will receive a proper remuneration for the services of the convicts, and that they will receive better and more civilized treatment." The law provided for a supervisor of state convicts, and R. F. Rogers was appointed to the difficult position. Five hundred seven were scattered in seven camps mining phosphate, and 190 had been dispatched to five log prisons in the piney woods.[28]

Following the provisions of the 1899 statute, a committee whose responsibility was to recommend future prison policy made a report in 1901. The consequence, in an irony that fades in intensity the more one knows about the history of convict labor, was to usher in the high point of Florida leasing. After 1901 more convicts were leased, and at higher rates, than ever before.

One immediate result of the new policy was to abandon the lump-sum payment and return to a per-capita rate. Beginning on 1 January 1902 the Florida Naval Stores and Commission Company received all convicts at $150 apiece for four years. When this contract expired, Florida was at last on the way to the revenue goal some of its public officials had long sought—a million- dollar convict lease. All 1,200 of its convicts went to C. H. Barnes and Company of Jacksonville for four years at an annual rate of $207.70 each. For the Sunshine State, then, somewhat longer leases were the price of greater total revenues. Florida took a middle position between very long-term contracts at very low per-capita rates, of the sort that Georgia had made, and short-term leases of the aggregate prison population. The 1906 lease raised twelve times as much revenue as the lease of 1900.[29]

But if Florida did well under the new policy, C. H. Barnes did better still. Barnes subleased convicts to a dealer in the Convict Belt around Ocala, S. A. Rawls, who in turn subleased them again to turpentine and phosphate operators. Rawls's own profit from this venture in 1906 alone was about $100,000. The sub-sub-lessees paid about ninety cents per day for them. With Barnes paying about fifty-seven cents per day and the direct exploiters of the convicts' labor paying ninety cents, the size of the demand in this particular labor market is evident. Writing of the gap between the lessees' and operators' prices, a muckraking journalist wrote in 1907, "The difference is the graft."[30] But graft, while certainly important, was not the whole story. More important was the demand for difficult and hazardous labor to extract valuable natural resources. The sublease was not illegal, and of course the state still did not have a penitentiary.

Unlike other states then, Florida still lacked alternatives to leasing in 1908, the year that Georgia eliminated it. Yet slight stirrings toward abolition could be discerned by sensitive observers. In 1910 voters in a referendum in Hillsborough County, in the vicinity of Tampa, decided against continuing the system of hiring convicts. In 1911 the state purchased 16,000 acres in Bradford County for a prison farm. Two years later Gov. Park Trammell recommended an end to the lease, although in context the reference to abolition was more an oratorical effect than a policy recommendation.[31]

By 1913 it was well-worn oratory to boot. Public opinion in Florida, insofar as it bestirred itself at all about the question of a few hundred mostly black convicts doing forced labor, seems to have opposed the convict lease starting in about the 1890s. A considerable portion of the citizens of Ocala, for instance, threatened to storm the stockade and free the convicts in 1896, and word often seeped out about the conditions and treatment the prisoners endured. J. C. Powell's *The American Siberia*, published in 1891, provided a stinging denunciation of Florida's convict policies, and newspaper reports and legislative investigations periodically unveiled the horrors awaiting people unfortunate enough to be convicted in the state. When a sixteen-year-old convict at Dutton's camp died from a whipping, the autopsy report read "Death from torture." One of the most horrifying and inhuman episodes in fifty years of inhumanity occurred in October 1905 in Washington County, far out on the Panhandle south of the Alabama line, when a fire at the camp of the Aycock Brothers Lumber Company destroyed the log prison. The convicts, chained inside with their "log chains" running down the center of the building, were unable to escape. They screamed for rescue while inebriated guards cursed them.[32]

The lease did have its defenders. After all, when the Barnes lease ran out in 1910, the contract went to the Florida Pine Company, which took the prisoners for $281.60 apiece, producing revenue of $316,000 per year for the four years of its duration. Gov. Albert Gilchrist, in speeches reminiscent of Henry Holcomb Tucker's performance in Atlanta nearly a quarter of a century before, told the National Prison Association in 1909 and 1911 that Florida had a humane, sanitary, and healthful method of convict management. "In the lease, every little detail which may go for the betterment of the prisoner, is specified," he correctly noted. Citing the numerous humane provisions of the lease contract concerning lodging, clothing, and medical care, Gilchrist mounted what was essentially the last-ditch defense of the system that was being replaced throughout the South in favor of farms, road building, and penitentiaries—though that these alternatives resulted in the overall improvement of conditions is an arguable proposition.[33]

But Gilchrist's feeble defense fades beside the exertions of Florida's penitentiary physician Dr. R. S. Blitch, who was also the penitentiary supervisor—and a state senator. From 1903 on, Dr. Blitch exonerated Florida's convict management in several forums, from the National Prison Association to the floor of the Florida legislature. In 1904 approximately three hundred prisoners were sent to turpentine farms and about eight hundred to phosphate mines. Blitch contended that the turpentine and phosphate camps were perfectly adequate to the state's and convicts' needs. Although there was occasional cruelty, Blitch sometimes admitted, it came at the county, not the state, level. Short-term county convicts were also being leased. In 1902, for instance, D. W. Monroe of Columbia County was paying $10.50 per month, and in 1905 children under twelve years old fetched $15 in Marion County.[34]

In January 1903 the state opened Marion Farms in the county where employers could rent children for $15. Marion Farms was a hospital for aged and infirm prisoners, and Dr. Blitch was its director. Its operator, however, was the lessee, the Florida Naval Stores Company. Some idea of why the company ran the hospital comes from the report of a 1903 legislative committee of which Blitch was a prominent member: "It is estimated that at least 90 per cent. of those who shall from time to time be placed in the hospital, will be permanently cured and returned to the lessees," they explained. The Florida Naval Stores Company sublet nearly two-thirds of its prisoners. In consequence there were some twenty-eight prisons in rural and wilderness Florida that year, an increase of sixteen over 1901. While Dutton Phosphate had 150 prisoners, most camps had only 30 to 40. Addressing the NPA in Massachusetts as its token Southern officer in 1904, Blitch defended the prisoners' living conditions: "In the matter of construction for sleeping purposes they have a long hall and an aisle running through the centre of it and each prisoner has his own little bed and just opposite each bed is a window and the ventilation is good all around and we think we have the best ventilation."[35]

Blitch's defense was in part a response to Fred Cubberly's recent revelations about the conditions of Florida's peculiar labor system. In 1903 Cubberly, a young federal prosecutor, uncovered and began to publicize the vicious network of peonage that provided labor for many enterprises in Florida's turpentine, railroad, and phosphate industries. Most Southern states had contract-labor laws rendering a worker who left his employer prior to the expiration of his contract liable to criminal prosecution. Such laws were vigorously enforced by employers and sheriffs in both Florida and Georgia. Often, however, they ignored the niceties of state boundaries, of extradition procedures, and of due process in any form. Generally what would occur was that a sheriff, or sometimes agents of the employer, would simply round up alleged debtors at gunpoint and compel them to enter, or return to, the labor gangs. Apparently Florida's law simply codified what had been the longstanding conventions of the industry. "It has been the universal custom and practice of the turpentine men in Georgia and Florida to go and take negroes whenever they wanted to in this way," confessed the sheriff of Levy County, just west of Marion Farms. Cubberly's crusade led to a landmark case, *Clyatt* v. *United States,* which upheld the long- forgotten federal peonage statute of 1867.[36]

S. M. Clyatt was a prominent turpentine farmer from Tifton, Georgia, not far from the Florida line. In 1901 he pursued two men who had left his employ, Mose Ridley and Will Gordon. He found them working in the Florida camp of J. R. Deen, a naval stores operator, had the sheriff arrest them, and brought them back to Tifton in irons. It was Deen who complained to Cubberly about Clyatt's high-handedness. After a thorough investigation, Cubberly decided to prosecute the first peonage case ever tried in the federal courts.

The case reached the United States Supreme Court, where the constitutionality of the peonage statute was upheld. But in a bizarre turn of the case, Clyatt was awarded a new trial. The prosecution, Justice Brewer wrote for the majority, had charged in its indictment that Gordon and Ridley had been "returned" to a condition of peonage, but it had failed to prove that peonage had been their condition before they were apprehended. That they were in fact peons the court considered proven, but not the specific charge in the indictment that they had been returned to such a state. Justice Harlan refused to accept such casuistry and dissented vigorously: "The opinion of the court concedes that there was abundant testimony to show that the accused, with another, went from Georgia to Florida to arrest the two negroes, Gordon and Ridley, and take them, against their will, back to Georgia to work out a debt. And they were taken to Georgia by force. . . . [I]t is going very far to hold in a case like this, disclosing barbarities of the worst kind against these negroes, that the trial court erred in sending the case to the jury."[37]

The legal significance of *Clyatt* v. *United States* resides in the fact that the old statute against peonage passed constitutional review. But the workings of justice in this specific instance were less clear-cut. S. M. Clyatt never stood for his second trial, because the two men whom he had held in thrall, Ridley and Gordon, had disappeared, never to be heard from again.[38]

Peonage, of course, was but one strand of oppression that was woven into a dense fabric of racial and class exploitation. As the pioneer black educator, feminist, and civil rights leader Mary Church Terrell noted in 1907, "the connection between disfranchisement and peonage is intimate and close." Now that the white South had seen how easy it was to disfranchise, she argued, it saw that it could also violate the laws against peonage with impunity.[39]

Even more closely connected to peonage was the convict lease itself. Peons and convicts were housed together and were not distinguished in the treatment they received. In order truly to eradicate the one system, the other would have to be destroyed as well. Unfortunately, that would not happen for another twenty years after Cubberly's courageous efforts. The legislature came close in 1911, however, when an abolition bill passed both houses only to be vetoed by leasing's champion, Governor Gilchrist; the legislature failed by a single vote to override the veto. In 1915 a visitor to the turpentine camps found conditions that were little changed from the days of Captain Powell a quarter of a century earlier.[40]

However, Florida did begin work on a penitentiary during World War I, and this institution, along with the burgeoning demand for working convicts on roads, helped to nudge leasing toward its demise. Death would come slowly, however. In 1919 the Carlton-Igou Bill abolished the state lease and created a roadworking force under the highway department. Nevertheless, leasing of county convicts in the awful turpentine and phosphate camps continued. Cubberly uncovered clear and widespread evidence of peonage by the Putnam Lumber Company as late as 1921. One camp, Shamrock, typifies the conditions that were later shown to be widespread—and that, significantly, duplicate those in the sugar-producing areas of Florida and Texas. Workers at Shamrock were housed in locked compounds guarded by armed men. No visitors were permitted. The camp boss operated with complete autonomy, except for the ardent assistance of the judge of Dixie County.[41]

196

The sensational case of the death of young Martin Tabert, probably the most famous cause célèbre of the history of leasing, focused a dazzling and exceedingly uncomfortable spotlight on Florida in 1923. When the story was publicized in the *New York World*, its author won a Pulitzer Prize, and Florida ended county leasing, although forced labor continued in other forms. Sheriff J. R. Jones of Leon County ran a racket. Railroad brakemen would wire him the number of men who were riding the rails into Tallahassee. The men were arrested on arrival and sentenced to $25 fines payable in two days, or to ninety days at the Putnam Lumber Company Turpentine Camp. The sheriff received $20 a head for his pains. He pocketed $3 of it while his confederates up and down the line split the rest. Martin Tabert, a North Dakota adventurer off to see the country, was swept up in this net, and died because of it. The camp boss at that time, Walter Higginbotham, whipped the malarial Tabert to death while holding him down with his boot. A fellow convict, John Gardner, later recalled how "Martin's back was all scabs and cuts from his shoulders to his knees."[42]

Back in North Dakota, Tabert's family was staggered and bewildered at the tragic turn of events, and they refused to believe that Martin had died from malaria, as the death certificate warranted. They turned to an attorney, Gudmunder Grimson, for help. When Grimson was unable to secure cooperation from Florida officials, he contacted the *New York World*, which launched a press campaign. Higginbotham was convicted at a sensational trial, but not before two key prosecution witnesses were murdered before they could testify. Higginbotham's conviction was eventually overturned on appeal. He was later transferred to the Shamrock camp by Putnam Lumber—where he killed another man.

The committee established by the legislature to investigate the charges concerned itself with the policy of leasing more broadly, and in May 1923 abolition was recommended. The legislature heeded the suggestion, and leasing ended that year. There may be a trace of irony, however tragic, in the fact that a system of black forced labor would come to an end because of the hideous murder of a white convict. Horrible as Martin Tabert's end was, it undoubtedly had analogues in the deaths of numerous black convicts in the cruel half century of Florida leasing.

Twelve

THE CAROLINAS
Paradigms for Abolition

I

By 1873 South Carolina was so poor that John Dennis, the super intendent of the penitentiary, was forced to lease the state's convicts in order to feed them. He was not supposed to do so, but when he arrived at the site of the penitentiary in Columbia he "found everything about the Institution in a very dilapidated condition." The prison had accumulated an enormous debt—some $102,000 by October of that year, the amount having doubled just since April—and merchants were unwilling to advance the state even six months' credit. The 300 prisoners lacked clothing, shoes, hats, and even blankets. Scurvy broke out among them that spring. Thus "It has at times been compulsory upon me to hire out the convicts, in order to earn their subsistence," confessed the clearly overwhelmed superintendent. Convict leasing in South Carolina began as an administrative exigency undertaken piecemeal so that its convicts could eat.[1]

South Carolina's leasing history has its dreadful chapters: In 1880, for instance, 94 of the state's 590 convicts died, while in the two previous years 153 had died and 82 escaped. Perhaps if the convicts were property, the superintendent correctly theorized in 1879, "then the contractors, having more interest in their lives and services, would look after them with greater zeal, and not leave them . . . to the ignorance, inattention, or inhumanity of irresponsible hirelings." In August 1887 the Penitentiary Board had to cancel the lease of the contractors building the Blackville and Newberry Railroad on account of the mistreatment of the 100 convicts under their care. The men were returned to the penitentiary in a wretched condition, but were soon re-leased to the construction firm of Rice and Coleman on a different stretch of track.[2]

Generally speaking, however, it must be acknowledged that South Carolina escaped some of the outrages found in Arkansas, Florida, Alabama, and Georgia. Probably the principal cause of South Carolina's relative success in this respect was the state's persistence in building a penitentiary during Reconstruction. Although the project was a classic source of corruption and jobbery which ended up costing half a million dollars, the completed structure provided an institutional alternative to the devolution of criminal punishments to the private sector.[3]

The post–Civil War prison histories of North Carolina and South Carolina share several common features. Most notable is the fact that the Carolinas, which, with Florida, were the only states in the South that had neglected to construct penitentiaries in the decades preceding the war, were the only two to press forward with plans for penitentiary construction, often in the face of enormous fiscal and political difficulties, in the Reconstruction years immediately afterward. Although during the antebellum years the penitentiary had become, in Edward L. Ayers's term, "a Southern institution," it was always one whose life was precariously supported. "The South was American enough to build penitentiaries," Ayers wrote, "but Southern enough to remain skeptical of its own handiwork."[4]

One reason for the decision in favor of postbellum penitentiaries in the Carolinas was that, before Reconstruction came to its sad end, a political climate was created in those two states in which social services would have a short-lived opportunity to succeed in receiving appropriations. This willingness to finance public services is itself a remarkable feature of Reconstruction throughout the South, but in the Palmetto State especially it represents a genuine turnabout.

If Boston was the Athens of antebellum America, South Carolina was its Sparta. No state had been more self-consciously archaic, localistic, hostile to institutions, or resolutely antimodern. And clearly, the fact that no penitentiary had been built there was due to these characteristics. As Michael Hindus has argued, South Carolina's "immobility" on this score was due "to a certain view of society and the groups that comprise it. This view excised from reality those groups that were most likely to benefit from, stimulate, or require social legislation." Yet that same state's legislature appropriated funds for a penitentiary in its very first Reconstruction session. That this decision represents the ascendancy of some of the groups likely to benefit from social legislation—and hence represents too a new and more expansive vision of who comprised "society"—seems more convincing than Ayers's contention that the penitentiary, as a Southern institution, "had established a tradition in the region, had developed its own inertia." The institution's "inertia" had always been retarded in South Carolina by the friction of the state's hostility to public expenditures. It was the changed political climate that lubricated the path of the penitentiary in South Carolina. Of course this first session occurred, as one South Carolina reformer delicately put it in 1916, "before Reconstruction had interfered with control by the white people"—that is, before Radical Reconstruction, which began in 1868. But what deserves emphasis is the persistence with which, through all the subsequent vicissitudes of Reconstruction, the project was pursued.[5]

The Tarheel State had evinced a comparable immunity to the lures of Northern philanthropy. Although demands for a penitentiary had agitated the legislature repeatedly in the antebellum years—some twenty-three proposals had been introduced into the legislature before 1846—no administration had been successful in convincing the citizenry to pass a referendum for the purpose. Nevertheless, North Carolina's Reconstruction constitution of 1868 restricted the punishment for crimes to death, fines, or imprisonment, thus in effect mandating a prison. Even when the constitution was modified in 1876 to permit leasing ("labor for the public and the farming out thereof"), the pertinent clause also required that the punishment of convicts could be meted out by state officials only, not by lessees or their hired camp bosses.[6] One consequence of this restriction was that North Carolina never admitted to being a "leasing" state. In truth, convict labor in North Carolina was always a hybrid. "The labor system [of North Carolina] is quite *sui generis*," E. C. Wines wrote in 1879. "The labor is neither leased, nor contracted, nor managed by the prison. . . . [Many convicts] would seem to be given to railroads in the State without any cash returns whatsoever."[7]

Of course, it can hardly be maintained that the Reconstruction politicians of the Carolinas were all cynosures of classical republican virtue. A prominent historian of South Carolina blacks during Reconstruction, Thomas C. Holt, emphasizes that ample evidence exists to support the two stereotypes of Reconstruction in South Carolina—namely black domination and blacks' manipulation by whites. And surely, he adds, Reconstruction's ultimate failure must also be attributed to "the considerable social and cultural distance between many of these [black] legislators and their constituents."[8] But the fact remains that these two were the only Southern states before the Progressive Era that sought to address the vexatious and complex questions of crime and punishment without recourse to complete privatization.

II

In North Carolina, more than any other state in the nation, criminal justice functions had always devolved to the counties. After the Civil War the legislature began to move in the direction of concentrating penal affairs at the state level. Much of the force for this drive came from the hard-pressed counties themselves, who were required by an 1866 law to establish houses of correction that many of them felt they could not afford. What eventually emerged from the North Carolina experience was a composite—in effect a dual system of both county and state incarceration. The Mecklenburg Road Law of 1880 illustrates this meshing of state and county obligations that are separately apportioned elsewhere. It made available to county commissioners for road work any prisoners sentenced to the penitentiary who were not required to be kept there. Although this law was soon repealed, its provisions reap-

The prison at Raleigh, 1880s. Julian Ralph, "Charleston and the Carolinas," *Harper's New Monthly Magazine,* vol 90, issue 536 (January 1895), p. 222

peared in several other laws of the 1880s, and in 1889 lawmakers both codified and extended the principle. In fact, North Carolina's prison system would not be consolidated at the state level until 1933.[9] The campaign for state-level responsibility dates from Reconstruction.

The North Carolina penitentiary was ultimately constructed near the capital city, Raleigh—but only after what Dan T. Carter calls "a comedy of fraud and errors" that, among other things, fully confirms the worst stereotypes of carpetbagger misrule. A New York operator named Milton Smith Littlefield persuaded the Tarheel legislature to construct a prison near some worthless land he happened to own on the Deep River, accessible only by a railroad whose bonds he held in abundance. By the time the penitentiary committee realized its blunder it was too late; it was forced to sell the land and purchase the new site near Raleigh. The penitentiary's construction costs were far in excess of appropriations. And like the Virginia penitentiary on which it was partly modeled, which had been constructed in 1796 and designed by one of the great figures in the history of American architecture, Benjamin Latrobe, it lacked facilities for heating; convicts sentenced there suffered from frostbite. The first prisoners, 121 in number, arrived in 1870, when the structure was still being raised. In the next few years the population would increase faster than the cells in the prison could be constructed, and by February 1872 the first prisoners began to be "farmed out."[10]

Because of the swelling size of North Carolina's prison population, a law of 1872 permitted leasing. Given the condition of the state and its prison, however, it is remarkable that leasing did not begin earlier. In 1871 the state's debt stood at $34,887,464.45. The prison housed 389 convicts, 264 of whom were completely illiterate and 108 of whom were in their teens. By 1874 the numbers had swelled to 455. Of the 214 sentenced to prison in the latter year, 190 were black. Between 1870 and 1874 some 960 persons were sent to Raleigh. In the summer of 1874 dysentery became epidemic in the prison: 186 prisoners suffered from it, and 7 of them died. But even under such conditions the 1872 law showed the same circumspection that typified the first tentative steps toward leasing elsewhere, forbidding the lease of those doing time for murder, manslaughter, rape, attempted rape, or arson.[11]

Events just to the south revealed even more hostility to leasing. In November 1869, at almost exactly the same time as the arrival of the first North Carolina prisoners at the unfinished Raleigh penitentiary, Gen. Carlos Stolbrand, the official in charge of South Carolina's penitentiary affairs, counted 295 convicts in the unfinished prison at Columbia. Somewhat prophetically he suggested that the state acquire a farm for the use of the convicts' labor, and stressed the importance of ridding the state of the expense of maintaining its convicts as soon as possible.[12] The unsettled condition of the next few years can be illustrated by the statistics of 1870, when some 280 prisoners were sent to the penitentiary, and 205 (of the total population) were pardoned. Thirty-four of the new prisoners were white, 8 were women, and fully one-third were teenagers. Most had short sentences: 69 percent had two years or less, and fewer than 9 percent faced more than ten years. By way of contrast, as convict leasing was getting under way in Georgia that year, 24 percent had one-to-two-year sentences, and 19 percent were sentenced to serve more than ten years. (The 1870 Georgia statistics themselves show conditions that were mild compared to one and two decades later.)[13]

But in 1874, after the expiration of Dennis's emergency sharecropping contracts, the South Carolina legislature forbade convict leasing altogether. It was the only state to do so, with the exception of a five-month period in Tennessee in 1870. And in the next session, when Gov. Daniel Chamberlain sought to make the practice legal once again, the lawmakers staunchly resisted. Chamberlain's effort was part of a government-spending slash that portended the end of Reconstruction, with its dramatic political and fiscal commitment to the public welfare. The penitentiary's budget was reduced from $40,000 to $20,000; while the appropriation for the University of South Carolina, which was mostly black in the early 1870s, was cut by over 30 percent, to $30,000. Chamberlain wanted to get rid of the professors entirely and replace them with Northern women. Given the university's clientele, "we only want a good high school," he reasoned. The defeat of the leasing bill may have been "one of the few entirely pro-labor accomplishments in nine years of Republican rule," but another way to look at it is as the only successful suppression of convict leasing during the Gilded Age. Convict leasing in South Carolina, with the exception of the 1873 sharecrop contracts, would be a creature of Redemption.[14]

Yet Carlos Stolbrand and John Dennis had evidently defrauded the state of thousands of dollars. The sources of these allegations are themselves far from unsullied, since they come from the reports of the first Redeemer government of Wade Hampton in 1877. However, their author, Theodore Parmele, was a comparatively capable and diligent administrator. And it would certainly appear that his allegations should not be dismissed altogether, for the documents of the time give considerable support to the accusations. In 1871 one can already detect Stolbrand equivocating on the huge expenses that were being run up. "The supplies for the support of the convicts have necessarily been purchased on credit, which, coupled with the uncertainty of the time of payment, have considerably advanced the cost price," he explained. And the penitentiary building itself was proceeding slowly and expensively; Stolbrand estimated that it would cost the staggering sum of $1,000 per cell. But he and the directors felt it was essential that construction proceed. Again and again they called for prison workshops inside the walls, the purchase of a farm, and the separation of female prisoners (a baby was born in the prison in 1871).[15]

An investigative commission specifically charged in 1877 that in 1871 Stolbrand had doctored the books, robbing the state of $3,576.65 for textile machinery that never appeared in the prison. Stolbrand failed to keep any prison account books before 1875, but Parmele estimated that Stolbrand pilfered some $33,000 during his years of service. As to his successor, Dennis, under his administration there were "frauds and irregularities not surpassed in any other department of public service," Parmele charged. So it seems to have gone, but it should be kept in mind that accusations of this sort seemed to follow almost every change of administration in the South during these years. Texas's Reconstruction governor, Elisha Pease, for example, bitterly castigated the preceding prison administrators when he took office in 1866. But as a seasoned Texas historian remarks about Pease's tirade: "Pease's comments regarding the management of the prison under his predecessor were virtually identical to those made by each incoming administration throughout the period of [the convict lease]. All existing problems were blamed on previous administrators, while boasts were made that the new management was correcting many of the inherited difficulties."[16] His remark could be expanded to cover the rest of the region's prison politics.

Superintendent John Dennis, faced with the overwhelming problems of caring for hundreds of prisoners for whom no proper accommodation could be made, could not be counted among the opponents of leasing. In 1874 he recommended legislation permitting him to lease, citing Georgia as a model. The next year Parmele arrived on the scene—and the scene was a disaster. There were no records, the guards were incompetent and demoralized, and the buildings themselves were in a shambles from a tornado. There were 322 convicts, 50 of whom were under twenty years of age. Yet at the legislative session held during his first year in the position, the legislature refused to condone the leasing of the state's prisoners.[17]

It was the last stand of Reconstruction. When Wade Hampton and the Democrats triumphantly ousted the Republicans, symbolically not only ending Reconstruction in South Carolina but bringing to a close a period in the nation's history as well, he called a special session of the legislature. "The penal, charitable, and educational institutions of the State," said this model of Redeemer retrenchment, "should be made self-supporting as far as possible. . . . With proper legislation the labor of the convicts in the penitentiary could be made profitable." The law permitting leasing was passed the day before the special session ended. When Hampton called the legislature together, there were about 400 blacks and 30 whites in the prison. However one might choose to interpret such statistics, wrote a prominent historian of black South Carolina, "It is certain that the majority of Negro prisoners had been placed there by juries which were predominantly Negro and by judges, prosecutors, and officers of the law who depended on Negro votes for their support." But that era had come to a close in 1877. South Carolina was about to experience its second political turnabout in ten years.[18]

III

The dysentery that had struck the North Carolina penitentiary in 1874 to such devastating effect returned the following year, accompanied by typhoid and erysipelas. In August 1875 typhoid dysentery again reached epidemic levels. This time 71 of the state's 794 convicts died in another of the medical disasters of Southern prison history.[19]

In addition to the inadequacy of the facilities for housing prisoners was the financial plight of the prison itself: it was over $20,000 in debt by 1875. In North Carolina, as elsewhere, then, convict leasing seemed increasingly sensible, even inevitable, as the 1870s progressed. The legislature that year, 1875, provided that all convicts except those needed to complete the construction of the penitentiary could be leased.[20] Both the law and the Redeemer constitution of the following year required the state to guard and maintain the prison population. North Carolina then entered on a truly "hybrid" system, as E. C. Wines had called it. All leases went to railroads. Some 332 convicts went to the state-owned Western North Carolina Railroad. Another 50 went to the North Carolina and Georgia line; they paid expenses but no compensation to the state. And the Spartanburg and Asheville Railroad paid $62.40 for each of 200 convicts for two years. In April 1880 the state would sell the Western North Carolina to W. J. Best of New York, who promptly unloaded the dubious holding to the Richmond Terminal group. Under the agreement, North Carolina supplied at least 500 convicts, for which the railroad paid $125 apiece annually.[21] North Carolina's convict leasing was thus entirely given over to railroad construction, and the majority of its first leased convicts worked on a publicly owned line.

Meanwhile South Carolina embarked on its own lease experiment.[22] Predictably, it was circumscribed in extent and number. Only about one-half of the 560 prisoners were let. A shoe manufacturer, Charles Mayhew, took 20 inside the walls, for $9.60 per month apiece, to be paid in merchandise; and the Greenwood and Augusta Railroad took 100 at $3 each. The rest continued to labor on prison construction.

In a double irony, John Dennis, the Radical Republican appointee, favored convict leasing, while the Redeemer Theodore Parmele opposed it. Foremost among the reasons for Parmele's antagonism was the large number of escapes that leasing facilitated: some 73 as early as 1877. Indeed, as soon as leasing was instituted, the familiar trends asserted themselves: high escape rates, mistreatment, and population growth. The convict population would nearly double in the coming decade. Meanwhile, in January 1877, prior to the leasing legislation that took effect in June, Parmele had dealt with the terrible overcrowding problem in the prison by slipping some 150 convicts through an apparent loophole and sending them to the plantation of John Seegers. Like the first lessees in many states, Seegers paid South Carolina nothing; he undertook only to maintain and guard the prisoners. He seems to have kept the first part of that bargain at least; but some 34 of his 150 convicts escaped.[23] His contract was broken.

In the same manner, North Carolina immediately tallied staggering death and escape totals, although given the mortality crisis within the penitentiary the lease camps' death rates were not appreciably different from that in the penitentiary, as they were elsewhere: a 9 percent death rate, for example (22 out of 254), on the Western North Carolina Railroad, and 21 of 152 prisoners on the Spartanburg and Asheville. In the penitentiary itself, meanwhile, 106 deaths were recorded in 1875–1876. Almost as disturbing, perhaps, were the numbers of escaped prisoners: 14 of the 254 sent to the Western North Carolina; 22 from the Spartanburg and Asheville, and 25 from the Insane Asylum—half of the leased convicts who had been sent there as construction hands.[24]

But the demand for railroad construction in the years after Reconstruction was strong, and North Carolina concentrated more of its convict labor in that sector than any other state. In 1877 the 200 Spartanburg and Asheville convicts were transferred to the Western North Carolina, and the Chester and Lenoir took 150. Then in 1880, 245 went to the Cape Fear and Yadkin Valley Railroad, 55 were sent to the State University line, and 67 went to the Oxford and Henderson. From then until 1891, 65 percent, on yearly average, of North Carolina's prisoners would be laboring as railroad construction hands.[25]

IV

The Columbia penitentiary was also a site of great suffering. Like the Raleigh prison, it was unheated. Prisoners there, like those at Raleigh, died in great numbers in the 1870s. The physician reported rampant tuberculosis and dysentery. Consequently over one-sixth of all South Carolina's prisoners died in 1878, including 39 of the 62 convicts sent to the Greenwood and Augusta Railroad.[26]

Camp number five of the Greenwood and Augusta, located in an isolated portion of Edgefield County, became the site of South Carolina's worst leasing scandal the following year, when the physician found ill and dying prisoners lying on vermin-infested shelves in a log pen, and other convicts in stockade hovels so filthy that the odor was "sickening to the uttermost extent." All but nine of the convicts who were actually laboring at the work site were suffering from scurvy. The new prison superintendent, T. J. Lipscomb, who had succeeded Parmele in January 1878, was prompted to investigate the reports himself, and he ordered the return of twenty-six desperately ill prisoners. Twenty-four barely alive and one dead prisoner were returned to the prison some weeks later.

The railroad was required to give up its convicts, but it dragged its feet until 1880, when its contract had actually expired. No strong action was taken, nor was blame formally leveled at the lessees. The legislature went through the familiar ritual of cosmetic reform, passing a bill that permitted the governor to revoke contracts and require the superintendent to return the prisoners to the penitentiary when presented with evidence that lessees were abusing them—a bill in effect ratifying the actions already taken. Given the crowded and indeed deadly conditions within the penitentiary, however, there was little incentive for the governor or the superintendent to take such an action.[27]

Ironically, in fact, the Greenwood and Augusta investigation, which did much to bring leasing into bad repute, might stand as a useful milestone for the beginning of its most flourishing years in South Carolina. In 1880 the state took in $17,608, on top of a balance of just under $12,000, from prison operations. A New Jersey capitalist named A. C. Dibert leased 100 prisoners for a shoe factory inside the prison. He paid thirty-seven cents a day for the labor of women and boys and fifty cents for men's. The products of this venture had an excellent local reputation. In 1883 young Woodrow Wilson wrote in a story for the *New York Evening Post* that "The shoes made at the South Carolina Penitentiary are purchased all over that State as the best shoes made for ordinary wear."[28]

Other enterprises began to sprout, using convict labor as their edge over competitors. R. Pringle leased 120 prisoners at $10 per month to work in his phosphate mines; the competing firm of Cahill and Wise took 82 at $12.50. Seegers, the 1877 lessee whose farm had been worked on shares, took 25 at $5; and the Augusta and Knoxville Railroad leased 36—21 at $7 and 15 at $12.50 (all monthly rates). South Carolina, in manifest contrast to Tennessee, had its convicts serving diverse business interests in the state.[29]

Yet the numbers of convicts leased out were never large. In 1881, for instance, only 305 convicts were hired out; the other 385 were confined to the penitentiary—two and three to a cell—where they cost the state thirty-four cents per day to maintain. Of the 690 convicts 622 were black; 55 of them had died.[30]

Even allowing for the manifold shortcomings of public health and sanitation knowledge and for the arduous nature of life for almost all South Carolinians, imprisoned or free, in 1880, it must be acknowledged that these economies came at an enormous human price. Lipscomb, the superintendent, opened his 1881 report with a classic illustration of the qualities the Bourbons held most dear: "The appropriation of $23,600, made at the last session of the General Assembly, has not been drawn by us, and we take this method of returning it, with the further statement that we will not require any appropriation for the coming year, provided the General Assembly will allow us to use the earnings, as we have been doing for the last two years."[31]

But by 1885 this rosy financial picture had changed drastically. The major consequence of a new law of 1884 that made guards responsible to the state rather than the lessees was to make it financially impossible for the state to lease without vastly expanded appropriations. After years of making a point of not having to ask for appropriations, the Board of Directors was forced to request $100,000. There were 945 convicts that year, close to the peak population for the years of leasing. But only 76 of them were leased, while 874 were crammed together in the prison. It was just what the directors had feared would happen at the end of the contracts that had been in force earlier in the decade. In addition to asking for the appropriation, they appealed to the legislature to buy another farm[32]—*another*, for in 1883 South Carolina had cautiously purchased its first farm.

This 1883 purchase occurred at the same time that Tennessee entered on its contract with the TCI, Arkansas entered the mainstream of Southern convict management with its full-blown lease, Alabama regularized its convict operations by providing for an inspector and appointing R. H. Dawson to that position, and Texas tried but failed to undo its mistakes with the cancellation of Cunningham and Ellis's contract. While convict leasing entered the period when it became most entrenched, most fully institutionalized in the rest of the South, South Carolina took the steps that would guarantee its elimination.

The farm was located in present-day Richland County, then part of Lexington County, not far from the prison at Columbia, and cost only $4,250. At the same time a female prison was built by reallocating space on the top floor of the commissary. Because the farm was not a large enough concern to accommodate all that year's 896 prisoners, however, separate contracts were signed covering 400 convicts at $12.50 per month.[33]

The legislators responded to the Board of Directors' 1885 plea for appropriations and a farm with a mere trifle: permission to lease three farms close to the original Richland County site. One of them belonged to Seegers, the experienced lessee; the other two were owned by T. B. Aughty and James Sims. The contracts were for half shares. But this perfunctory arrangement threatened to come to grief, as well. The farms were almost completely flooded out in the first year. So relentless were the rains that the dam in the Columbia canal burst. Still, the leasing of the prisoners relieved the unbearable pressure in the penitentiary, as 366 convicts found themselves on the sodden plantations. Since the request for appropriations had been snubbed by the legislature, the prison reported a deficit of $3,911.41. Yet in spite of the floods and the business depression, the removal of the prisoners from the penitentiary walls and the small returns from the farms provided enough relief to bring the prison to the brink of solvency.[34]

V

During most of the 1880s, while South Carolina was inching toward the prison farm, North Carolina staunchly persisted in linking its convict labor policy with the fortunes of the state's railroads. By 1880 only 301 of the state's 996 convicts were in the prison, with all the rest on construction gangs, living in filthy converted cattle cars. By the latter part of the decade, however, the marriage began to go sour, as the business cycle combined with the saturation of North Carolina's transportation market to cause a sharp downward turn in railroad construction.

In 1887 the state's commissioner of labor solicited opinions from some of the state's leading citizens about the future of convict labor. The responses reveal a pattern of interconnected interests that opposed convict leasing. At least two labor leaders proposed the abolition of the penitentiary altogether. The Worthville Assembly of the Knights of Labor, for example, passed the following resolution: "*Resolved*, That we believe it would be to the best interests of the State to gradually do away with the penitentiary and adopt the whipping-post, pillory and stocks." More often, however, respondents pointed to the pitiful condition of the state's roads and to the efficiency of using prisoners for farm work. A black respondent from Wilmington, Coleman Twining, expressed the feelings of many:

> Now what shall we do with the convicts? If the authorities would buy a farm and work the farm with the convicts, it would feed all of them, and would be good healthy exercise for the convicts. . . . Then let each county use those prisoners for the purpose of building and repairing county roads. Then our expenses would be less by about one-half than under the present system, would have fewer convicts by three-fourths, and we would have county roads which we could travel over at all seasons of the year.[35]

The situation deteriorated still further in the next few years. The penitentiary's debt was $47,287.51 by November 1888, and the board

210

ascribed the financial hardship directly to the decline in demand for railroad work. By then only 354 out of 1,377 prisoners were working on railroads, the vast majority of them on the Western North Carolina.[36]

The definitive turn toward penitentiary farms in both states occurred early in the 1890s. In 1892 the number of prisoners in the Raleigh penitentiary led to overcrowding reminiscent of the 1870s. And with the prisoners being returned from the railroad camps, total cash earnings plummeted from $312,032.68 in 1890 to $88,514.63 two years later. "We have found no difficulty in making the Penitentiary fully self-supporting as long as we had Railroad work," the warden wrote. "But we have now been without railroad work for quite a while." That year the state leased, and in 1893 it purchased, the Caledonia plantation owned by the Futrell family of Edenton. The plantation had three cotton gins for its 1,500 acres planted in cotton, while about 2,000 acres were given over to other crops. Caledonia would be the state's prison farm until 1919.[37]

But just as it placed excessive reliance on railroads in the 1880s, North Carolina went overboard on farming in the 1890s. After the state purchased Caledonia, in 1893, the warden was enthusiastic about the farm's potential "to employ the entire force of able-bodied convicts, or practically all of them, in farming" in the coming year. In 1894 he confirmed the earlier expectations: "As indicated in my last annual report, the operations of the penitentiary have been confined almost entirely to farming." By 1898 the state had purchased three more farms. But when tricky bookkeeping turned actual cash deficits into apparent surpluses, the state began to move more in the direction of the second solution that Coleman Twining had advocated in 1887. It was the Good Roads Movement, at least as much as the prison farm, that led North Carolina to abandon convict leasing.[38] The Tarheel State's unique system of state-county prison management prevented any single solution to the management problem, so that both farms (for the state) and roads (for the county) would divert the course of convict labor.

South Carolina's farms were more modestly but more consistently successful. Although hosiers and shoemakers ceased their operations inside the prisons in 1890, the farms were developed by then to the point where they could take up the slack. They produced $20,000 in cotton that year. The state bought an additional farm in 1891 and the following year rented another on shares. By mid-decade yet another had been purchased, and sixty-eight mules were added to the eleven already on hand. In fact, so far along on the road to abolition was South Carolina with its use of prisoners for farm labor that these changes were conclusive. In 1897 the legislature effectively outlawed leasing by simply prohibiting the use of convict labor on private farms.[39]

PART THREE

ABOLITION

Thirteen

THE ABANDONMENT OF CONVICT LEASING

I

"Prison 'reform' is virtually contemporary with the prison itself: it constitutes, as it were, its programme." So writes Michel Foucault with characteristic, studied incongruity. The history of penology since the Enlightenment, Foucault contends, consists not in a neat sequence or progression of prisons–shortcomings–reforms, but in the repetitive application of the same disciplinary, punitive, normalizing elements of the same "carceral" program. "Penality," he argues, "would then appear to be a way of handling illegalities, of laying down the limits of tolerance, of giving free rein to some, of putting pressure on others, of excluding a particular section, of making another useful, of neutralizing certain individuals and of profiting from others."[1]

As an account of the rise and flourishing of the penitentiary, Foucault's work is not without its problems. Indeed some would say it is riddled with them: inaccuracy in his presentation of the historical facts, the imposition of wildly skewed interpretations on a limited body of evidence, and faulty logic, to name a few.[2] Yet if Foucault's reversals and paradoxes—"the soul is the prison of the body," reform is the prison's program, "discipline 'makes' individuals"—drive some careful historians to distraction, his portrayal of the intimate interconnectedness of reform and oppression and his resolute, indeed bitter, opposition to "progressist" versions of penological history serve as indispensable correctives in a field that has been characterized by a progressive, sometimes triumphalist, humanitarianism.

With respect to this disposition—that is, the tendency to interpret prison history in general and Southern criminal punishments in par-

215

ticular as a drama of progressive enlightenment—the scattered, early historical accounts of convict leasing have a distinctly paradoxical flavor. The authors of these early studies deserve tributes, since it was they who first pried open the door of disclosure—and they opened it more than a crack. Or, to change the metaphor, historians such as Blake McKelvey, Vernon L. Wharton, Fletcher Melvin Green, and Green's students Hilda Jane Zimmerman and A. Elizabeth Taylor picked up the rock of Southern penal history in the 1930s and 1940s and discovered underneath it shocking contemporary accounts of barbarous cruelty in a prison system the like of which was unknown in the United States before or since. They took from these accounts not only the empirical evidence but also the rhetoric of humanitarian indignation they found there. Surely these pioneers should not be criticized too harshly for their use of this rhetoric. As readers of this book have seen before now, the present author has been deeply enough engaged by the evidence to respond to it in the same manner on occasion. Yet the shock they experienced led them to emphasize the most sensational, most awful, aspects of leasing—its most gruesome camps, highest mortality rates, most eloquent expressions of public outrage. Often they cite as evidence not only the data but also contemporary responses to it. The tenor of their work taken together is, like that of their sources, one of outraged humanity.

The paradoxical quality of their work comes to the fore when they bring up the subject of abolition. For while on the one hand they underscore the system's barbarism, on the other the impulse they single out as causing the abolition of leasing is an almost purely humanitarian one: leasing was abolished because of a great upsurge of public indignation over the cruelties of the system. To be sure, some of these historians were more sophisticated, and their accounts more nuanced, than this synopsis may indicate. Zimmerman, for instance, was the author of one of the best dissertations in Southern history that was never published. She consistently noted the effect of the movement for good roads and of the apparent success of state-owned prison farms. But her emphasis was nevertheless on humanitarian concerns, public pressure, the publicity surrounding abuses, and the Progressive Era's concern for social welfare. "The convict lease system began to break under the pressure of humanitarian demands," she wrote concerning the practice in Arkansas; and in an article on Southern prison reform she emphasized "the growth of humanitarianism" as the main source of such reform.[3]

Fletcher M. Green cited "those people who did see the degradation and feel shame" as the parties responsible for numerous reforms, and ultimately for abolition. Disclosing his sympathies with the Progressive Era, and revealing as well, perhaps, a certain regional shame, Green stressed how "liberal and progressive leaders, business men, ministers, and teachers condemned a system that advertised to the outside world that they were a barbarous people." More remarkable still, he credited abolition to publicity about cruelty: "These and many other whippings, 'the most brutal ever inflicted by one human being upon another,' forced the state governments to abandon the Lease." What is left obscure in this account is the fact that although the statement he quotes comes from an 1895 Georgia report, that state found it possible to continue the system for thirteen years after the brutal whippings were condemned.[4]

A. Elizabeth Taylor wrote two pathbreaking articles on Georgia leasing in the early 1940s. While conceding that the argument against abolition centered around the loss of revenue, she went on to credit the elimination of the practice to a vigorous abolition campaign conducted by the *Atlanta Georgian* in 1908. Like other scholars, she was influenced by contemporary opinion as to the reasons behind abolition. As Georgia reformer Alexander McKelway had asserted in a 1908 speech: "To the Atlanta Georgian, a newspaper of that city, is due the main credit for arousing the state over the evils of the convict lease system, though the entire press of the State took up the fight." And Hastings Hart of the Russell Sage Foundation told the American Prison Association eleven years later that "gradually the consciences of the Southern people were awakened in one State after another, and the convict lease system was abolished, often at a great financial sacrifice, because of the conviction that it was impossible to administer with any proper regard for human rights."[5]

Mississippi's Vernon L. Wharton was likewise a trailblazer, one of the first post–World War II historians of Southern blacks to include social and cultural institutions as well as political events in his narrative. Wharton's account of leasing was as horrific as Green's or Taylor's, and his explanation of abolition was equally ideological. He placed "public indignation" first among three major forces—the other two being Alliance and Prohibitionist pressures, themselves chiefly humanitarian in nature—that "convinced" the authors of the 1890 Mississippi constitution to terminate leasing.[6] Wharton, therefore, like Green, McKelway, Hart, and others, attributed the abandonment of convict leasing to the sudden development of a sentiment. In so doing he fostered two misconceptions: first, that Mississippi leasing was abolished in practice by the 1890 constitution; and second, that it ended because people were indignant over cruelty to prisoners.

The rhetoric of the early convict leasing historians has a distinct pedigree that dates from the turn of the century. It derives most directly from a 1902 article by J. H. Jones, "Penitentiary Reform in Mississippi." Jones's tone of civilized shock and determined reformism in this article was itself derivative, of course; most notably it has links to George Washington Cable and to Frank Johnston—especially the latter, a friend and informant of Jones during his political career. Johnston had written a long article that appeared in Mississippi newspapers in 1887 condemning leasing in the familiar terms as being barbaric, a disgrace to civilization, and a type of slavery: themes that would reappear in Jones's piece couched in more eloquent phrases. One such phrase in particular stood out, and would echo down the years in discussions of leasing. The system, Jones said, "left its trail of dishonor and death which could only find a parallel in some of the persecutions of the Middle Ages." In 1947 Wharton quoted this striking phrase in his section on the convict lease. Two years later Green also used it—but without benefit of quotation marks—and then added a coda that was pertinent to champions of civilization in 1949: the convict lease "left a trail of dishonor and death that could find a parallel only in the persecutions of the Middle Ages or in the prison camps of Nazi Germany."[7] The humanitarian tone, although with an inflection perhaps more tragic than outraged, persisted in the superior work of Green's students, Taylor and Zimmerman. Thus was the indignation originally expressed by Jones passed down to post–World War II historians.

The uncritical reception accorded Jones's short and somewhat obscure article had a lamentable effect on subsequent interpretations. A more cautious rendering would have taken into account the facts that J. H. Jones was the chairman of the House penitentiary investigating committee of 1888; that he was a member of the 1890 Mississippi constitutional convention that adopted an article prohibiting leasing after 1894; and that he had a considerable political stake in the proposition that Article 10 had been efficacious. Thus his essay opened, rather than closed, with the statement—merely remarkable to read today but almost preposterous in 1902—that "the final abandonment of the convict lease system in Mississippi was the work of the constitutional Convention of 1890." Wharton, Green, and Zimmerman all accepted this version of events. "Thus passed the convict lease," Wharton incredibly remarked of the 1890 constitution. "Mississippi led off in 1890," echoed Green in his treatment of abolition. This interpretation would remain standard until the late 1960s, when William Holmes reconstructed the events leading to James K. Vardaman's political attack on the lessees.[8]

More recent historians have been more circumspect, but many of them also rely on explanations for abolition that are largely subjective, interior, and humanitarian in character. Donald Walker's thorough Texas study imputes abolition to the actions of "citizens of the South," who "pressured Southern legislatures to terminate the lease contracts," after having been "motivated by economic and humanitarian concerns and spurred into action by legislative investigations and newspaper disclosures of prison conditions." N. Gordon Carper's well-researched dissertation on Florida rather lamely invokes "the cause of humanity" which "had to wait until public opinion became so indignant that change was imperative." Paul W. Keve continually cites the infusion of "modern, sensible" ideas of prison management as the source of a steady improvement in Virginia's penological practices. Such "signs of progress" were especially evident in the twentieth century, he believes, and he attributes the elimination of such practices as involuntary sterilization to a "maturation of attitudes." John Dittmer's customary analytic penetration deserts him when he writes: "Exposure of camp conditions caused Georgians to abolish the lease system." Dewey W. Grantham refers to the "vigorous reform movement . . . led by the Atlanta *Georgian and News*" and "an increasingly indignant public" as central to the abolition of leasing in Georgia. And George B. Tindall simply points out that "South Carolina was fortunate to have the evils of the convict lease system exposed within two years of its inauguration in the state."[9]

But to say these things is merely to misstate the problem of causation, for the evils of convict leasing were pointed out in *every* state within two years of its inauguration, while newspaper disclosures and legislative investigations revealed horrible prison conditions for over forty years. Causation in history is always a question of timing, the question being: Why *then?* If awful conditions were revealed by investigating committees and if journalists and reformers publicized them throughout the history of leasing, why was it at one particular moment rather than another that leasing was abolished? As the *Birmingham Ledger* asked during another fruitless battle over abolition, this one in 1919: "What's the use of having the horror's [*sic*] of the convict leasing system presented to us at every quadrennial session of the general assembly if all that is accomplished is to fill our souls with chagrin, disgust and depression over man's inhumanity to man?"[10]

In 1900 Georgia, Alabama, and the Carolinas had over 90 percent of the child labor employed in Southern textiles. The number of children under sixteen in the mills had increased sixfold between 1880 and 1900. Some 87 percent of Southern cotton textile workers lived in company housing.[11] In Atlanta in 1906 there occurred one of the most shocking, brutal race riots in American history. It was followed by a successful legal campaign to disfranchise black voters. In short, the first decade of the twentieth century in the South is a period that epitomizes reaction, racism, brutality, and violence. How is it, then, that there could have been humanitarian motives behind leasing's abolition? How could leasing have been separated out from all other issues and given a separate, humane, treatment, while "the cause of humanity" had to wait for all the South's other, multifarious forms of oppression? The immediately preceding act of the legislature that abolished convict leasing in Georgia was to pass disfranchisement legislation. In spite of this abundantly evident historical context, most accounts of convict leasing leave the impression that at a certain point in Southern history citizens inexplicably developed humanitarian sentiments, and, that change once having taken place, they went on to effect the end of leasing—along, of course, with a profusion of other reforms derived from what Green called "the better penological trends of the North and West." As he summarized those trends: "First offenders were segregated from hardened criminals; reformatories were established; separate women's prisons were provided for; religious services were made available in the camps; books and schools were provided; the state boards of health began to take an interest in the health of the convicts; . . . Paroles were granted and long term sentences were shortened for good behavior."[12]

It is easy, indeed perhaps necessary, to be cynical about such superior Northern penological trends. A group of Tennessee legislators characterized lease camps in 1889 as "hell holes of rage, cruelty, despair, and vice,"[13] and certainly the same could be said of today's human warehouses, the products of endless cycles of reform dating from the Jacksonian period. This enduring institutional cruelty is what gives credence to Foucault's resolutely antiprogressive vision of penal history. The abolition of convict leasing is in a sense a key link in a meaningless chain, marking the transition from one distinct form of prison management to another, but it is always, despite such transitions, the same chain.

And yet it would be a distortion of another sort if the humanitarian motive were to be ignored altogether. Both Florida and Alabama present cases where sensational revelations about slain convicts—both of them white, both from out of state—did focus outside attention on those states and did produce a sense of shame and outrage. But humanitarianism, like any motive, requires certain enabling conditions to render it efficacious. In all cases those conditions included enough political pressure to overcome the massively entrenched interests of the lessees, or a set of economic circumstances that diminished the desire of lessees to retain this form of forced labor, or economic conditions promoting the use of convict labor in different areas altogether, or any combination of these.

That the pivot on which the lease began and ended was labor, not criminal punishment per se, can be seen in the fact that, except for the Carolinas and Tennessee, nowhere in the South did prison officials simply construct penitentiaries and install prisoners and rehabilitation programs in them after leasing was abandoned. Southern prison reform was essentially a reallocation of forced labor from the private to the public sector—from leasing to chain gangs and prison farms.

Two recent historians who look at abolition with clear-eyed, unsentimental directness are Mark T. Carleton and William F. Holmes. In his outstanding monograph on Louisiana prisons, Carleton takes particular pains to describe the end of leasing as an act for which a purely political explanation is both necessary and sufficient. "By 1901," he writes, "the practice of leasing convicts had been terminated in Louisiana—not primarily for humanitarian reasons nor because penal reformers had suddenly acquired genuine influence, but rather because the lessee . . . had become politically intolerable to the new ruling faction of the state Democratic Party." The governor who oversaw leasing, Murphy J. Foster, did so strictly "for reasons of political security and retaliation." Holmes, for his part, makes it clear that James K. Vardaman's role in finally terminating leasing in Mississippi was entirely due to his attempt to get even with his hated political enemies, the wealthy planters who leased the state's prisoners.[14]

Among other contemporary historians, Edward Ayers and Alex Lichtenstein most successfully avoid the category mistake of confusing expressed motivations with historical causation. Lichtenstein emphasizes the continuity between lease and chain gang, pointing out that chain-gang camps of the 1930s and 1940s seem virtually indistinguishable from their leasing predecessors of half a century earlier. And Ayers cautiously concludes that "in general, the Southern convict lease system ended the way it began—uncertainly, ambiguously."[15]

Leasing of prisoners did end uncertainly—and with many false starts along the way. The great *if* dominated Southern prison legislation for two generations: Leasing was declared illegal *if* it could be abandoned with no fiscal consequences. The *Austin Daily Statesman* reported on 17 March 1883 that opposition to the lease was "almost unanimous" in the capital. The legislature did indeed go ahead and terminate leasing. But it also said convicts could continue to work for private parties on contract if the state would be better served. Thirty years later convicts were still being leased. Alabama abolished leasing legislatively in 1893, as did Arkansas, but it continued. Alabama tried again in 1915, 1919, and 1923, and Mississippi outlawed it in the constitution of 1890. In all cases, the practice would not release its hold.

II

Georgia's story is particularly revealing. Although leasing of state prisoners was in fact dispensed with by a single law in 1908, many other aspects of the leasing system that were plainly illegal had continued for years before 1908 and had proven impossible to eradicate. Of these the most important was the leasing of county convicts.

The persistence of county leasing stands as a symbol of the immunity of all aspects of leasing to the full authority of legal institutions. Leasing county prisoners—misdemeanants with sentences of less than a year—to private individuals was illegal under an 1879 law, but counties could not keep their hands off such a steady and lucrative source of revenue, and for thirty years after the law was passed it was the common practice in the state for counties to lease such prisoners.

In December 1894, in *County of Walton* v. *Franklin et al.*, the Georgia Supreme Court ruled unequivocally that county leasing was impermissible. Walton County had contracted with Franklin to deliver all convicts to him in 1891 and 1892. In August 1892 Franklin refused to accept more prisoners and failed to meet his bond payment. The county filed suit to make Franklin accept the prisoners and pay the bond, but the supreme court dismissed the complaint on the grounds that the contract was illegal, merely observing in its brief opinion that "The county authorities have no power to hire out convicts."[16]

But this definite opinion had no discernible effect whatsoever on the counties' or the contractors' behavior. The year after the supreme court settled the issue, Gov. William Y. Atkinson commissioned R. F. Wright, a former principal keeper, to investigate the convict situation in the counties. The investigation turned up what Atkinson called a "burning shame." "Of the thirty-three camps visited twenty-six are worked by private individuals," Wright related; in other words they "are of that class which the Supreme Court has recently held to be illegal [in *County of Walton v. Franklin*]." Although Atkinson was sure "that comment by me is unnecessary to induce you to act," no legislation resulted from Wright's report.[17]

But in 1898 the state's supreme court would be given another chance to reaffirm its earlier decision. A county lessee named J. W. Tatum worked Will Russell on a private chain gang at Tatum's turpentine camp in Worth County. Tatum had hired Russell from the sheriff of Terrell County, for five dollars a month. In July 1897 Russell's mother filed a habeas corpus petition. Will had been sentenced to hard labor on public works in Terrell County, she contended, and Tatum's working him on a private chain gang two counties away was illegal. The supreme court granted Mrs. Russell's petition. "The whole arrangement was illegal," wrote Justice Cobb. It was not simply the fact of Russell's working in a different county from the one where he was sentenced but the county's act of entering into a contract with a private contractor that was at issue: "That convicts can not be worked in chain-gangs controlled by private individuals is the well-settled law of this State," Cobb affirmed.[18]

As a point of law it may have been settled, but as a matter of practice it continued. Ten years after *Russell* v. *Tatum*, fourteen years after *County of Walton* v. *Franklin*, and twenty-nine years after a statute made it illegal, county leasing continued to take place. The frustrated chairman of the Prison Commission wrote Gov. Hoke Smith in 1908: "The Prison Commission has for ten consecutive years, in each of its annual reports, reported such [illegal county] chaingangs to the General Assembly as being organized and conducted illegally, and contrary to law, and that it had no power or authority to break them up, or impose fines."[19]

County leasing would only be eliminated when the leasing of the state prisoners was abolished, and the state prisoners would be parceled out to the counties for their public works. The abolition of convict leasing in Georgia was an event that entailed many more factors than the indignation of an aroused public.

III

When on 21 December 1897 the legislature chose to continue leasing the state's convicts even after the twenty-year lease had expired, it instituted certain key changes. The most important was the provision for a lease of five years' duration. The new law also abolished the venerable office of principal keeper, replacing it with a three-man commission responsible for inspection and reports. The principal physician's office was eliminated as well; the camps themselves were to be responsible for engaging a local doctor for the convicts' needs. Aged and infirm men, women—who were to be segregated—and boys under fifteen would be sent to a state-operated prison farm. All other convicts were to be leased. In addition, the legislation contained a provision of the utmost significance: it mandated segregation by race.[20] This section of the law serves to indicate that the movement for the legal segregation of the races, which became in the 1890s a key element in the total strategy for racial subordination, was making its appearance in the prison system. Jim Crow legislation was one of the expedients which, in combination with disfranchisement, would eventually subvert the position of the lease system as a factor in Southern race relations. But it would take another decade before these changes would have their full effect.

As leasing entered its last decade in Georgia the prices of convicts rose dramatically. The general prosperity, combined with the fact that a lid had been kept on prices for a full two decades, meant that—until hard times came again in 1907 at least—convicts were a valuable commodity. For the 1899 leases, the state accepted bids from eight individuals or corporations at rates that varied from $98 to $102 per convict annually. These were certainly bargain prices, especially considering the fact that the 1897 legislation permitted subleasing. Still, they were a ninefold increase over those of 1874.

When this lease period ended in 1904, the next round of bids produced an average contract price of $225.52; in the next few years they continued to rise sharply and steadily. The fact that this price rise took place in spite of an equally steady population increase, which might be thought to have a depressing effect on prices, can be explained by two factors. First, the value of the commodities produced by convict labor was increasing. The Wholesale Price Index reveals that the index for farm products rose from 44.9 to 62.2, and that for building materials from 39.6 to 52.0, between 1898 and 1908.[21] However, wholesale prices continued their ascent during the year of the system's abolition. The value of convict labor commodities is only part of the reason for the costliness of a lease. The second, and more important, was that the inauguration of legal subleasing made the system more susceptible to genuine market forces, greatly increasing the pressure to pay close to the going rate for free labor.

While leasing was becoming less profitable to the individual firm, however, the state was making a parallel discovery: the cost-effectiveness of the chain gang. Chiefly comprising misdemeanants in what Alex Lichtenstein calls "a parallel, shadowy system of county and municipal road gangs," chain gangs were being used with increasing frequency. By 1901 there were 2,084 misdemeanor convicts being worked on sixty-one chain gangs. So useful were these prisoners to the counties that local politicians pressured for more. A 1903 act allowed counties to use felons on a prorated basis based upon the percentage of convicts they supplied to the prison system. This was a quid pro quo with a vengeance; the increase in population of this period can be attributed partly to this remarkable provision. In June 1904, 573 felons were being worked by twenty-nine counties.[22]

Meanwhile the cost of convicts continued to rise until, in 1907, the cost of a sublease reached $670, a free laborer's wage. The scales had been tipped, and they were tipped at the precise moment of a severe economic downturn, the Panic of 1907. Its effect on Georgia was critical, as lessees faced the prospect of being stuck with crews of laborers whom they had to feed, clothe, and attend to but whom they could not work.

By 1907, then, Jim Crow was established, disfranchisement was on its way (the 1906 Atlanta race riot is testimony to the fierceness of the campaign), the chain gang was on the rise, and convicts were becoming a burdensome expense to those who leased them. Thus the ground had been well and truly prepared for abolition when in the late summer of 1908 the General Assembly's convict investigating committee presented its withering report to the legislature, which had been called into special session by Gov. Hoke Smith for the explicit purpose of abolishing leasing. Among other abuses they uncovered, they found that Jake Moore, the state warden, had negotiated deals for the transfer of contracts among lessees in return for fees totaling $2,700. Furthermore, they related, Moore was the business partner of W. B. Hamby, the lessee of the greatest number of convicts; and, as if this were not enough, Moore was considerably in debt to Hamby. But Moore's peculations were not isolated. It had been a long- standing custom for deputy wardens to receive extra salaries from lessees, for instance. The lessees themselves were cited for numerous infractions of the lease statutes: they violated their contracts by working convicts at night; they whipped excessively; they worked on a quota system; their camps were overrun with vermin.[23]

While the committee was taking this testimony (from 20 July to 20 August 1908), the *Atlanta Georgian* ("that Yankee newspaper," Representative Butt of Fannin County grumbled[24]) mounted its aggressive editorial attack on the lease system, and on 2 August meetings were held in cities throughout the state to demand the termination of leasing. In Atlanta the legislature complied with Governor Smith's request and ended leasing effective with the expiration of the current contracts, in 1909.[25]

The final act of the General Assembly during its regular session had been the passage of disfranchisement legislation. Now, with disfranchisement having accomplished, the convict lease seemed redundant as well as unprofitable. On 7 October the state's voters ratified disfranchisement by a margin of two to one. One Georgia progressive explained its appeal in 1907: "I am convinced that at least 90 per cent of all [whites] who are free from corporate influence strongly favor this measure. It becomes more and more desirable to see the whites divide upon political issues without danger. This cannot be as long as the negro vote is considerable."[26]

Was public indignation a mighty tide that compelled the legislature to eliminate convict leasing then? Clearly not. The wrath of high-minded citizens had agitated the state with regularity during the previous four decades, and critical reports by investigating committees had been issued in 1878, 1881, 1890, and 1896, while the practice continued to brutalize prisoners and their keepers. It was not until the system lost its profitability to the lessees that it was finally abandoned.

Moreover, even the expressed motives of the abolitionists encompassed more than humanitarian concern. The public's ire stemmed from the corruption of prison officials and the desire to see the convicts used for public projects instead of the enrichment of individuals. That was why citizens prominent in the burgeoning "good roads" movement were at the forefront of the abolition campaign. And that was why Governor Smith, in his message to the assembly at the special session, ignored the charges of cruelty altogether, focusing instead on the inefficient use of convict labor and its potential for public usefulness. "I believe," he told the legislators, "it would be better for all the convicts to be worked *by the state* upon farms, in mines, upon public roads, in the construction of public highways, and in the drainage and development of land not now capable of use."[27]

The economic value of Georgia's convict lease to private firms plunged at precisely the moment that other forces converged to deprive it of its social usefulness. Its demise occurred when both its economic and social utility were undermined. Black Georgians were being reminded of their place in society by Jim Crow laws and disfranchisement, while the state was beginning to comprehend the full value of chain gangs. Meanwhile, firms squeezed by large capital outlays made at the onset of a sharp, if brief, depression found leasing a costly burden rather than a competitive advantage.

IV

If abolition was an exhausting effort in Georgia, it was an ordeal of almost superhuman proportions in Alabama. A brief review of the abolition of leasing in Alabama shows the tenacity of the system at its most extreme. Alabama's history is instructive, too, because of the extent to which its reformers invoked the issue of the contribution of convict leasing to their state's and their region's "shame." The sense of mortification among Southern prison reformers is both widespread and unmistakable. The shame arose from the awareness that the South had not kept up with penal practices in the rest of the world, that it was therefore "backward" or susceptible to disparagement on the grounds of being barbaric or uncivilized. In the words of the *Atlanta Georgian*, the lease "advertised us to the outside world as a barbarous people." As with other rhetorical conventions, here too there was a continuity between contemporary opponents of leasing and leasing's early historians; Fletcher M. Green, for example, has already been quoted using precisely these words. Leasing thus took its place in the ignoble regional lineup that included, in Donald Davidson's words, "lynchings, shootings, chain-gangs, poor whites, Ku Kluxers, hookworm, pellagra." George B. Tindall attributed this notion primarily to outsiders, calling it "a kind of neo-abolitionist image." But he understated the extent to which Southern reformers also shared it. Southern newspapers, speeches, and pamphlets were full of an anguished defensiveness over leasing.[28]

More revealing, perhaps, is the fact that feelings of shame appeared in unpublished sources. Julia Tutwiler summarized the combined themes of outside scrutiny, regional disgrace, and barbarism when she wrote to a fellow reformer in 1913: "The world is now a great neighborhood, where every nation is subject to the inspection and criticism of all others. Alabama cannot afford to be ranked with Russia and Morocco by other civilized commonwealths."[29] And most privately of all, R. H. Dawson prayed in 1890: "May God give me strength to work on, and make the convict system something of which the people need not be ashamed."[30]

These and other, more purely humanitarian, motivations animated a group of Alabama's leading citizens to form the Statewide Campaign Committee for the Abolishment of the Convict Contract System in 1923. Its first chairman was Judge William E. Fort of Montgomery, and its president was the great jurist Hugo Black. The committee held meetings every Monday evening at 8:00 in Birmingham's Hillman Hotel. The case of Martin Tabert, the Florida convict who had been whipped to death in Florida that year, was very much on their minds. Tabert's death had shamed Florida deeply, and had, with other factors, helped to bring about the elimination of leasing in that state. In 1923 a campaign to abolish leasing was yet again before the Alabama legislature: state senator Walter S. Brower submitted a bill to abolish the lease as of 30 September 1925. The Tabert case was prominent in his campaign. As Senator Brower told the *Birmingham Age-Herald,* "The Tabert boy, who was killed in a Florida convict camp was a short time man. He was convicted of riding a train. . . . Yet in reality he paid the death penalty for the offense of riding a train. There can be a repetition of the Florida affair in Alabama."[31]

The Tabert family's lawyer, Gudmunder Grimson, fresh from a victory in Florida, wired Judge Fort on 8 July 1923: "Congratulations on your campaign against convict leasing. Would it help if on my way home I stopped at Montgomery with some of Tabert evidence. Please wire me here today. We would like to see system causing his death driven absolutely out of our country." Six days later he wrote from Chicago: "You can readily see what criticism there would be on Alabama now if anything should happen while they permitted this leasing system to exist." With a sharp sense of the importance of the state's honor, he wrote of "this fight to pervent [sic] Alabama suffering from the publicity such as that Florida received."[32] The sectional issue was always present in Southern penology. When Hastings Hart wrote from New York City to South Carolina's Lawrence Orr Patterson, who as a newly appointed member of the Board of Charities was preparing a speech on prison reform, he took the opportunity to recommend Joseph Byers as the board's secretary. Byers possessed sterling credentials. Currently the president of the American Prison Association, he was just stepping down as commissioner of charities and corrections in New Jersey. He would have been an ideal candidate. But, Hart added, "I do not know whether he could be induced to go south." Hart was unaware of a previous exchange between Patterson and D. D. Wallace on the unsuitability of a "Yankee" for the position. "I should think that if we go out of the State," Wallace had written just two weeks previously, "it would be better to go to some Southern State, as there is such a widespread prejudice among our people against 'Yankees' that to get one would materially interfere with the influence and benefit of the office."[33]

The Statewide Campaign Committee boasted an impressive roster of support, but it was broad rather than deep. Among the attendees at the convict leasing conference that the committee sponsored on 21 May 1923 were representatives from church clubs, the Women's Christian Temperance Union, the Women's Republican Club, the Women's Trade Union Club, the Birmingham Trades Council, the Junior Chamber of Commerce, the American Legion Auxiliary, and the Shakespeare Club.[34] Support obviously came disproportionately from women's groups. In fact, the committee seems to have been chiefly a women's movement, with prominent male Alabama citizens, who were certainly sincere and hardworking, as cover.

The gender imbalance was not lost on some opponents of reform. Gov. William Brandon's correspondence on the matter contained a majority of letters from citizens opposed to reform; much of the opposition was based on a hostility to women's involvement in public issues. Women had only been enfranchised three years earlier, and the specter of their votes was discomfiting to some men. Fred W. Vaughan wrote in support of Brandon (who had abandoned his promise to work for abolition): "I guess old Judge Fort has his eye on your chair and wants the Petticoats to support him. . . . Please show this to the next gang of Petticoats that infest your office." H. A. Holt also wrote to express his disgust with "the Weeping Willow women and sobbing sissy men."[35]

However broad the committee's reach, however prominent and respected the men and women who led it, it had no discernible effect on the legislature. If a more responsible, indignant, humanitarian public opinion in opposition to convict leasing had ever arisen in the South, it does not appear in the historical record. But it was to no avail. In July 1923 the Alabama House and Senate adopted the so-called Long Resolution, saying that it was the sense of the legislature that no legislation concerning the convict lease system would be considered in that session.

In the following year the Knox case hit the Alabama and national headlines. Probably it did have some effect on the abandonment of leasing, but more important were the demands for good roads and the passage in 1928 of a gasoline tax to fund road gangs in the state. As citizens of the last state to continue leasing its convicts, Alabamians did undoubtedly feel shame at their prison system's backwardness. After all, neighboring Georgia and Mississippi had abolished leasing twenty and twenty-one years earlier, while the other major convict mining state, Tennessee, had done so in 1893. But the system in Alabama outlived Julia Tutwiler by twelve years.

*   *   *

And so the beast of convict leasing was finally slain in its seventh decade. But what was the real significance of its abolition? As is often the case, an observation by Abraham Lincoln might serve to put historical change in a proper perspective. On a freezing January night in 1865 Lincoln met his old congressional colleague Alexander H. Stephens, the Confederacy's vice president, for a secret peace negotiation aboard a steamer in the James River. Stephens was a tiny knot of a man who weighed but ninety-five pounds. When he arrived on board, Stephens first divested himself of his numerous cloaks, coats, and scarves; then the towering Lincoln stepped forward and offered his hand, saying in a kindly way, "Never have I seen so small a nubbin come out of so much husk."[36] Lincoln's rustic metaphor pertains as much to students of the human past as it did to Stephens's small frame or to the attenuated nation he represented, for what historians must try to do is to separate the small nubbin of human agency from the capacious husk of contingency that envelops it, while at the same time identifying that husk for what it is.

Human intentionality remains the most deceptive and elusive of historical subjects. When convict leasing was finished, some may have thought that the mighty exertions of a generation of reformers had borne fruit at last. But the truth was more complicated and less inspiring. A historic departure had certainly been achieved when states' prisoners were no longer available so private individuals could accumulate capital through the exploitation of their labor. But that achievement would have been little noticed by prisoners themselves, who continued to endure difficult conditions and callous or even cruel treatment on work gangs. Moreover, the abolition of leasing itself was only tangentially connected to the efforts of reformers.

Leasing's abolition thus brings up one of the enduring questions of the philosophy of history: namely, whether history has significance—whether historical transformations are the product of more or less blind forces that happen to people, or whether men and women shape such forces and events to their own purposes. Convict labor reformers worked for a distinct purpose in the late nineteenth and early twentieth centuries, and their objective was achieved. What would be misleading, if understandable, would be to link those two phenomena too closely. Leasing certainly would not have ended if no one had opposed it: that is a tautology. But its demise came about as a consequence of other, quite differently motivated actions than those of its opponents. And even though leasing died, the corruption and mistreatment accompanying convict forced labor did not die with it.

Similar ambiguities accompany all historic changes, including those of today. In spite of the implosion of the repellent regimes of Central and Eastern Europe, for example—surely one of the most significant historical events of this century—the lives of many ordinary people there remained suffused with a deep dissatisfaction. Czech president Václav Havel spoke of this disquiet with his usual forthrightness in a December 1994 speech in Budapest:

> I cannot help feeling that the birth of a new and genuinely stable European order is taking place more slowly, and with greater difficulty and pain than most of us had expected five years ago. Many countries that shook off their totalitarian regimes still feel insufficiently anchored in the community of democratic states. They are often disappointed by the reluctance with which that community has opened its arms to them. The demons we thought had been driven for ever from the minds of people and nations are dangerously rousing themselves again, and are surreptitiously but systematically undoing the principles upon which we had begun to build the peaceful future of Europe.[37]

And while "most dissidents tend to be a bit impractical," as Havel once observed, former communists seemed to be eminently pragmatic. Thus every country in the former Soviet satellite system witnessed a remarkable resurrection of former communists. Five years after the fall of the Berlin Wall Hungary's cabinet ministers had a combined 224 years of membership in the Communist Party, while the great Polish poet Adam Michnik noted what he called a "velvet restoration" of communism.[38]

But no matter how ambivalent the fall of European communism turns out to be, it remains a great advance, a genuine if clouded and uncertain form of progress. And just as this attainment owed at least as much to heroic intellectuals like Havel and to thousands of ordinary citizens who joined together in mass demonstrations in favor of equality and human dignity as it did to the calculating autocrat Mikhail Gorbachev, so also the heroic figures of the convict leasing era were not only those who sought its overthrow but also those who worked within it and maintained their integrity. These included officials like Dawson and Carroll and reformers like Cable and Tutwiler, as well as tens of thousands of prisoners who endured that purgatory and returned to their families and communities, and the chaplains, physicians, and inspectors who refused to consider the squalor and violence of the camps as normal or acceptable conditions in a nation that aspired to civilized norms of behavior.

NOTES

Introduction

1. *Houston Post*, 8 October 1990, 3; *New York Times*, 7 January 1991, A-14; "Prison Population Reaches Record High," *Trial* 29 (July 1993): 113–14.

2. Bernard Lonergan, *Method in Theology* (New York: Herder and Herder, 1970), Chap. 8.

3. Hastings H. Hart, "Prison Conditions in the South," *Proceedings of the National Prison Association*, 1919, 200, hereafter cited as NPA *Proceedings* [year].

4. Ward M. McAfee, "The Formation of Prison-Management Philosophy in Oregon, 1843–1915," *Oregon Historical Quarterly* (Fall 1990): 259–84.

5. Gary R. Kremer, "Politics, Punishment, and Profit: Convict Labor in the Missouri State Penitentiary, 1875–1900," *Gateway Heritage* (Summer 1992): 28, 29.

6. Paul W. Keve, *The History of Corrections in Virginia* (Charlottesville: University Press of Virginia, 1986), 72.

7. John F. Stover, "Northern Financial Interests in Southern Railroads, 1865–1900," *Georgia Historical Quarterly* 39 (June 1955): 205–20; Keve, *History of Corrections*, 80–94; quote 82.

8. James Tice Moore, *Two Paths to the New South: The Virginia Debt Controversy, 1870–1883* (Lexington: University Press of Kentucky, 1974), 87–89; Virginius Dabney, *Virginia: The New Dominion* (New York: Doubleday, 1971), 376–99.

9. Fred Helsabeck, "Convict Labor Systems in Virginia (1858–1907)," M.A. thesis, George Peabody College for Teachers, 1932, 5–6, 10.

10. Keve, *History of Corrections*, 75–77; death rates on 81.

11. Helsabeck, "Convict Labor Systems in Virginia," 98–102.

12. Quoted in Dabney, *Virginia*, 390.

13. See, for example, Wilson Nicholas Ruffin to Lewis E. Harvie, 11 January 1883, Harvie family papers, Virginia Historical Society, Richmond. I am grateful to Professor Jane Dailey for this reference.

14. Helsabeck, "Convict Labor Systems in Virginia," 122–43.

Chapter 1—Categories

1. Amos W. Butler, "President's Address," NPA *Proceedings*, 1910, 16 n.1a.

2. *Twentieth Annual Report of the Commissioner of Labor, 1905: Convict Labor*

(Washington, D.C., 1906), 22.

3. John Peter Altgeld, *Our Penal Machinery and Its Victims,* new and rev. ed. (Chicago: A. C. McClurg, 1886), 95; Glen A. Gildemeister, "Prison Labor and Convict Competition with Free Workers in Industrializing America, 1840–1890," Ph.D. diss., Northern Illinois University, 1977, 32.

4. E. T. Hiller, "Development of the Systems of Control of Convict Labor in the United States," *Journal of the American Institute of Criminal Law and Criminology* 5 (July 1914): 241–69 [part one]; (March 1915): 851–79 [part two]; quotation 878.

5. Altgeld, *Our Penal Machinery,* 95–96; Blake McKelvey, "The Prison Labor Problem: 1875–1900," *Journal of the American Institute of Criminal Law and Criminology* 25 (July 1934): 256–57; Hiller, "Development of the Systems," 250; Gildemeister, "Prison Labor," 33–38.

6. Altgeld, *Our Penal Machinery,* 111.

7. Gustave de Beaumont and Alexis de Tocqueville, *On the Penitentiary System and its Application in France* (1833; rpt. Carbondale: Southern Illinois University Press, 1964), 41.

8. John R. Commons and Helen L. Sumner, eds., *A Documentary History of American Industrial Society,* 11 vols. (Cleveland: A. H. Clark, 1910), V: 51.

9. "Commissioner Wright on Convict Labor," *Nation* 45 (4 August 1887): 89; Gildemeister, "Prison Labor," 159.

10. Hiller, "Development of the Systems," 253–54.

11. Governor's Message, *Alabama House Journal,* 1882, 173; R. H. Dawson, [Report from Alabama], NPA *Proceedings,* 1888, 82, 83.

12. J. H. Jones, "Penitentiary Reform in Mississippi," *Publications of the Mississippi Historical Society* 6 (1902): 111; Edward H. Hobbs, ed., *Yesterday's Constitution Today: An Analysis of the Mississippi Constitution of 1890* (University: University of Mississippi Press, 1960), 135; Penitentiary Report, *Mississippi Departmental Reports,* 1900–1901, 5; Fletcher Melvin Green, "Some Aspects of the Convict Lease System in the Southern States," in *Essays in Southern History,* ed. Green (1949; rpt. Westport, Conn.: Greenwood, 1976), 121; Vernon L. Wharton, *The Negro in Mississippi, 1865–1890* (New York: Harper Torchbooks, 1965), 242; U.S. Department of Labor, "Convict Labor," *Bulletin of the Department of Labor* 1 (July 1896): 446.

13. Quoted in Elizabeth Bonner Clark, "The Abolition of the Convict Lease System in Alabama," M.A. thesis, University of Alabama, 1949, 60.

14. U.S. Department of Labor, "Convict Labor," 446; U.S. Industrial Commission, *Report . . . on Prison Labor* (Washington, D.C., 1901), 7; Bureau of the Census, *Compendium of the Tenth Census* (Washington, D.C., 1883), 1693.

15. Bureau of the Census, *Compendium of the Eleventh Census* (Washington, D.C., 1894), Part 2: 163, 180.

16. NPA *Transactions,* 1873, 375–89; "Annual Report of the Secretary," ibid., 1874, 290.

17. Tom Finty Jr., "The Texas Prison Investigation," *Survey* 23 (18 December 1909): 390, 389.

18. [E. Stag Whiten], "Prison Labor," *American Labor Legislation Review* 1 (October 1911): 122; Charles Edward Russell, "A Burglar in the Making," *Everybody's Magazine* 18 (June 1908): 760.

19. See, for example, Green, "Some Aspects," 113–14; Mark T. Carleton, *Politics and Punishment: A History of the Louisiana State Penal System* (Baton Rouge: Louisiana State University Press, 1971), 22; Edward L. Ayers, *Vengeance and Justice: Crime and Punishment in the Nineteenth-Century American South* (New York: Oxford University Press, 1984), 327 n.11; Donald R. Walker, *Penology for Profit: A History of the Texas Prison System, 1867–1912* (College Station: Texas A&M University Press, 1988), 8–12.

20. George Brown Tindall, *South Carolina Negroes, 1877–1900* (Baton Rouge: Louisiana State University Press, 1977), 267; Bureau of the Census, *Historical Statistics of the United States, Colonial Times to 1970* (Washington, D.C., 1972), 34.

21. Orlando Patterson, *Slavery and Social Death: A Comparative Study* (Cambridge, Mass.: Harvard University Press, 1982), 13 (the phrase is italicized in the original). The limitations of the attempt to seek a universally valid definition spanning many cultures and eras are ably pointed out in Paul Finkelman's review of *Slavery and Social Death* in *Journal of Interdisciplinary History* 15 (Winter 1985): 508–11.

22. David Brion Davis, *"Slavery and Progress,"* in *Anti-Slavery, Religion, and Reform: Essays in Memory of Roger Anstey*, ed. Christine Bolt and Seymour Drescher (Hampden, Conn.: Archon, 1980), 355.

23. Charles L. Flynn Jr., *White Land, Black Labor: Caste and Class in Late Nineteenth-Century Georgia* (Baton Rouge: Louisiana State University Press, 1982), 8, 27.

24. Henry Colvin Mohler, "Convict Labor Policies," *Journal of the American Institute of Criminal Law and Criminology* 15 (February 1925): 583.

25. Robert William Fogel and Stanley L. Engerman, *Time on the Cross: The Economics of American Negro Slavery*, 2 vols. (Boston: Little, Brown, 1974), I: 107–57; Elizabeth Fox-Genovese and Eugene Genovese, *Fruits of Merchant Capital: Slavery and Bourgeois Property in the Rise and Expansion of Capitalism* (New York: Oxford University Press, 1983), 152–56.

26. R. H. Dawson to Thomas Seay, 16 January 1888, Board of Inspectors of Convicts, administrative correspondence, Alabama Department of Archives and History (hereafter cited as ADAH).

27. Whereupon the resourceful Miss Stewart filed a habeas corpus petition and actually won her release. The duty of the hirer, the Alabama Supreme Court ruled with a hint of annoyance, "was to receive her [from the jail], and put her to hard labor. It could not substitute therefor another and different punishment, to wit, imprisonment in the county jail." *Ex parte Stewart*, 13 So. 661 (1893). But this case is unique, and most lessees exercised considerable leeway in the placement

and grouping of the prisoners they hired.

28. Stanley L. Engerman, "Some Considerations Relating to Property Rights in Man," *Journal of Economic History* 33 (1973): 45–46; Jennifer Roback, "Southern Labor Law in the Jim Crow Era: Exploitative or Competitive?," *University of Chicago Law Review* 51 (Fall 1984): 1184.

29. Governor's Message, *Mississippi House Journal*, 1906, 19.

30. Fogel and Engerman, *Time on the Cross*, I: 54.

31. Quoted in Alrutheus Ambush Taylor, *The Negro in Tennessee, 1865–1880* (1941; rpt. Spartanburg, S.C.: The Reprint Company, 1974), 43.

32. Walter Wilson, "Chain Gangs and Profit," *Harper's* 166 (April 1933): 538.

33. Governor's Message, *Louisiana Documents*, 1886, 41.

34. Christopher R. Adamson, "Punishment After Slavery: Southern State Penal Systems, 1865–1890," *Social Problems* 30 (June 1983): 556, 559, 566; Thomas C. Holt, "'An Empire over the Mind': Emancipation, Race, and Ideology in the British West Indies and the American South," in *Region, Race, and Reconstruction: Essays in Honor of C. Vann Woodward*, ed. J. Morgan Kousser and James M. McPherson (New York: Oxford University Press, 1982), 288; Jonathan Wiener, *Social Origins of the New South: Alabama, 1860–1885* (Baton Rouge: Louisiana State University Press, 1978), 36–37; Roger L. Ransom and Richard Sutch, *One Kind of Freedom: The Economic Consequences of Emancipation* (New York: Cambridge University Press, 1977), 56–60.

35. James L. Roark, *Masters Without Slaves: Southern Planters in the Civil War and Reconstruction* (New York: Norton, 1977), 201, 108.

36. Harold D. Woodman, "Post–Civil War Southern Agriculture and the Law," *Agricultural History* 53 (January 1979): 321; Pete Daniel, "The Metamorphosis of Slavery," *Journal of American History* 66 (June 1979): 88, 89.

37. *Ruffin v. The Commonwealth*, 62 Va. 795, 796 (1871).

38. *Westbrook v. The State*, 133 Ga. 579–580 (1909).

39. *Westbrook v. The State*, 585.

40. *Davis v. Laning*, 85 Tex. 39 (1892), cited in 9 Tex. D. 515; *Willingham v. King*, 23 Fla. 478 (1887), cited in 6 S. D. 16.

41. By the Code of 1907. *Quick v. Western Ry. of Alabama*, 207 Ala. 376, cited in 6 S. D. 16.

42. The following paragraphs are based on Robert Hughes, *The Fatal Shore* (New York: Knopf, 1987); Stephen Nicholas, ed., *Convict Workers: Reinterpreting Australia's Past* (New York: Cambridge University Press, 1989); Ian Donnachie, "The Convicts of 1830: Scottish Criminals Transported to New South Wales," *Scottish Historical Review* 65 (April 1986): 34–47; J. B. Hirst, *Convict Society and Its Enemies* (Sydney: Allen & Unwin, 1983); Stephen Nicholas and Peter R. Shergold, "Internal Migration in England, 1818–1839," *Journal of Historical Geography* 13 (1987): 155–68; L. L. Robson, *The Convict Settlers of Australia* (Melbourne: Melbourne University Press, 1965).

43. Hughes, *Fatal Shore*, 303.

44. Donnachie, "Convicts of 1830," 36.

45. Nicholas and Shergold, "Internal Migration," 155.

46. [Georgia] *Report of the Principal Keeper of the Penitentiary*, 1897, 4–16.

47. Stephen Nicholas, "The Care and Feeding of Convicts," in *Convict Workers*, 180–98.

48. Report of Special Committee, *Alabama House Journal*, 1888–1889, 47.

49. Stephen Nicholas, "The Organization of Public Work," in *Convict Workers*, 152–66.

50. Population in [Georgia] *Principal Keeper's Reports*, 1882, 1896.

51. Penitentiary Report, *Louisiana Documents*, 1869–1870, 6; 1871–1872, 25; *First Annual Report of the Board of Public Charities of North Carolina*, 1870, 106; [North Carolina] *Penitentiary Report*, 1888–1890, 14; [Florida] *Report of the Adjutant General*, 1881, 267; [Florida] *Report of the Commissioner of Agriculture*, 1903–1904, 326; Penitentiary Report, *Mississippi House Journal Appendix*, 1872, 113; *Mississippi Departmental Reports*, 1878–1879, 125; Governor's Message, *Alabama House Journal*, 1869, 20; 1903, 30.

52. Nicholas, *Convict Workers*, 155; Hughes, *Fatal Shore*, 242.

53. U.S. Department of Labor, Second Annual Report, 1886, *Convict Labor*, 381.

54. Woodrow Wilson, "Convict Labor in Georgia," in *The South Since Reconstruction*, ed. Thomas D. Clark (Indianapolis: Bobbs- Merrill, 1973), 415; Alexis de Tocqueville to Francisque de Corcelle, 17 September 1853, in *Oeuvres complètes*, ed. J. P. Mayer, 15 vols. to date (Paris: Gallimard, 1951–), XV, pt. 2: 81.

55. George Frost Kennan, "Introduction" to George Kennan, *Siberia and the Exile System* (1891; rpt. Chicago: University of Chicago Press, 1958), xiii.

56. J. C. Powell, *The American Siberia, or Fourteen Years' Experience in a Southern Convict Camp* (1891; rpt. New York: Arno Press, 1969), 3, 121.

57. On one rather minor subject, Powell has been shown by a careful scholar to have exaggerated his claims: see Mildred L. Fryman, "Career of a 'Carpetbagger': Malachi Martin in Florida," *Florida Historical Quarterly* 56 (January 1978): 318.

58. Anton Chekhov, *The Island: A Journey to Sakhalin*, trans. Luba and Michael Terpak (New York: Washington Square Press, 1967), 9, 34, 40, 52.

59. Patterson, *Slavery and Social Death*, 112.

60. M. I. Finley, "Was Greek Civilization Based on Slave Labour?," in *Slavery in Classical Antiquity: Views and Controversies*, ed. M. I. Finley (Cambridge: W. Heffer and Sons, 1960), 55; Davis, *Slavery*, 9–22, et passim.

61. Fogel and Engerman, *Time on the Cross*, I: 129.

62. Chekhov, *The Island*, 64; emphasis added.

63. Hooper Alexander, "The Convict Lease and the System of Contract Labor—Their Place in History," in James E. McCulloch, ed. *The South Mobilizing for Social Service* (Nashville: Southern Sociological Congress, 1913), 164; Wilson,

"Convict Labor," 415; Green, "Some Aspects," 122.

64. N. Gordon Carper, "The Convict-Lease System in Florida, 1866–1923," Ph.D. diss., Florida State University, 1964, 132.

65. Patterson, *Slavery and Social Death*, 112.

66. Quotes in James Seay Brown Jr., *Up Before Daylight: Life Histories from the Alabama Writers' Project, 1938–1939* (University: University of Alabama Press, 1982), 111; Tindall, *South Carolina Negroes*, 268; [Georgia] *Report of the Principal Keeper*, 1875, 16; North Carolina Bureau of Labor Statistics, *First Annual Report* (1887), 199; James Oakes, *The Ruling Race: A History of American Slaveholders* (New York: Oxford University Press, 1982), 174.

Chapter 2—Labor

1. Kenneth Stampp, *The Peculiar Institution: Slavery in the Ante- Bellum South* (New York: Vintage, 1956), 54.

2. Fogel and Engerman, *Time on the Cross*, I: 203–6.

3. Stampp, *Peculiar Institution*, 54, 55.

4. See especially: Wiener, *Social Origins of the New South*, 34–72; Ralph Shlomowitz, "The Origins of Southern Sharecropping," *Agricultural History* 53 (July 1979): 557–75; Woodman,"Post–Civil War Southern Agriculture and the Law," 319–37; Ransom and Sutch, *One Kind of Freedom*, 67.

5. Herbert S. Klein, *African Slavery in Latin America and the Caribbean* (New York: Oxford University Press, 1984), 258–59.

6. Wiener, *Social Origins*, 35–73; Charles L. Flynn Jr., *White Land, Black Labor: Caste and Class in Late Nineteenth- Century Georgia* (Baton Rouge: Louisiana State University Press, 1982), 70–78.

7. Ralph Shlomowitz, "The Squad System on Postbellum Cotton Plantations," in *Toward A New South? Studies in Post–Civil War Southern Communities*, ed. Orville Vernon Burton and Robert C. McMath Jr. (Westport, Conn.: Greenwood, 1982), 265–80; Gerald David Jaynes, *Branches Without Roots: Genesis of the Black Working Class in the American South, 1862–1882* (New York: Oxford University Press, 1986), 173–90; quote on 173.

8. Stanley L. Engerman, "Coerced and Free Labor: Property Rights and the Development of the Labor Force," *Explorations in Economic History* 29 (1992): 18–19; Ralph Shlomowitz, "On Punishments and Rewards in Coercive Labour Systems," *Slavery and Abolition* 12 (September 1991): 97–102.

9. Monroe Work, "Negro Crime" (1906), rpt. in *Review of Black Political Economy* 16 (Summer–Fall 1987): 60; for the relation between vagrancy and contract laws and labor in the early postbellum period see William Cohen, *At Freedom's Edge: Black Mobility and the Southern White Quest for Racial Control, 1861– 1915*, passim, but esp. 28–34, 221–36.

10. Joseph P. Reidy, *From Slavery to Agrarian Capitalism in the Cotton Plantation South: Central Georgia, 1800–1880* (Chapel Hill: University of North Carolina Press, 1992), 225; I. A. Newby, *Black Carolinians: A History of Blacks in South Carolina from 1895 to 1968* (Columbia: University of South Carolina Press, 1973), 65–68.

11. Stefano Fenoaltea, "Slavery and Supervision in Comparative Perspective: A Model," *Journal of Economic History* 44 (September 1984): 635–68; quotes on 636, 667.

12. Nicholas, "Organisation of Public Work," 161, 162.

13. Shlomowitz, "On Punishments and Rewards," 100.

14. Quoted in Shlomowitz, "Squad System," 269.

15. Texas State Investigating Committee, *Report and Proceedings*, 1902, 415, 420.

16. [Anon.] *Story of the Arkansas Penitentiary* (n.p., n.d.; in Special Collections Department, Mullins Library, University of Arkansas, Fayetteville), 65.

17. Warden's Report, *Alabama House Journal*, 1882, 5; Governor's Message, ibid., 1919, 160. George Korson reported a ten-ton task for Alabama's convict miners; but this huge amount was for the squad, not an individual. George Korson, *Coal Dust on the Fiddle: Songs and Stories of the Bituminous Industry* (Hatboro, Pa.: Folklore Associates, 1965), 168.

18. *Messages of the Governors of Tennessee*, ed. and comp. Robert H. White and Stephen V. Ash, 10 vols. to date (Nashville: Tennessee Historical Commission, 1952–),VII: 485; Report of Special Committee, *Alabama House Journal*, 1888–1889, 447; *Tennessee House Journal Appendix*, 1893, 3.

19. For a description of the labor performed in the convict brickyards see David Berry, "Free Labor He Found Unsatisfactory: Convict Lease Labor at the Chattahoochee Brick Company, 1885–1909," *Atlanta History* 36 (Winter 1993): esp. 8–9.

20. Russell, "A Burglar in the Making," 755.

21. Jerrell H. Shofner, "Forced Labor in the Florida Forests, 1880–1950," *Journal of Forest History* 25 (January 1981): 17; Powell, *The American Siberia*, 27–30.

22. Quotes in N. Gordon Carper, "The Convict-Lease System," 392, 396; George Waverly Briggs, *The Texas Penitentiary* (San Antonio: San Antonio Express, [1909]), 11; Daniel A. Novak, *The Wheel of Servitude: Black Forced Labor after Slavery* (Lexington: University Press of Kentucky, 1978), 33.

23. See, for example, *Biennial Report of Texas Penitentiary*, 1880, 17.

24. D. M. Short to O. M. Roberts, 19 July 1879, Penitentiary Records (RG 22), Archives Division, Texas State Library, Austin. Hereafter cited as TSL-A. Photographs of woodcutter squads of the 1960s, squads essentially similar to those of eighty years before, can be found in Bruce Jackson, ed., *Wake Up Dead Man: Afro-American Worksongs from Texas Prisons* (Cambridge: Harvard University Press, 1972), between 44 and 47.

25. Warden's Report, *Alabama House Journal*, 1882, 5; [Georgia] *Report of the Principal Keeper*, 1875, 10.

26. *Tennessee House Journal*, 1885, 787; George W. Ford, *Special Report of the Commissioner of Labor and Inspector of Mines* (Nashville, 1891), 94.

27. *Tennessee House Journal Appendix*, 1894, 4, 3.

28. Robert Norrell, ed., *James Bowron: The Autobiography of a New South Industrialist* (Chapel Hill: University of North Carolina Press, 1991), 70; Justin Fuller, "History of the Tennessee Coal, Iron, and Railroad Company, 1852–1907," Ph.D. diss., University of North Carolina at Chapel Hill, 1966, 306.

29. *Tennessee House Journal Appendix*, 1886, 8.

30. James Bowron to R. H. Edmonds, ed., *Manufacturers Record*, 28 July 1923, copy to Gov. W. W. Brandon in Gov. W. W. Brandon unprocessed administrative records, Alabama Department of Archives and History (hereafter ADAH). Emphasis added. Portions of the letter are reprinted in Norrell, ed., *James Bowron*, 241–42.

31. *Sloss Iron & Steel Co.* v. *Harvey*, 116 Ala. 656 (1898); *Birmingham Post*, 23 March 1926, 1, reprinting a *New York World* story of the same date.

32. Sidney Mintz, *Sweetness and Power: The Place of Sugar in Modern History* (New York: Viking Penguin, 1985), 49; for valuable descriptions and illustrations of the process see also Manuel Moreno Fraginals, *The Sugarmill: The Socioeconomic Complex of Sugar in Cuba, 1760–1860*, trans. Cedric Belfrage (New York: Monthly Review Press, 1983), esp. 101–22.

33. Stanley L. Engerman, "Contract Labor, Sugar, and Technology in the Nineteenth Century," *Journal of Economic History* 43 (September 1983): 656.

34. *Proceedings of the Joint Committee Appointed to Investigate the Condition of the Georgia Penitentiary*, 1870, 5.

35. Extra Work. February 1889–May 1889, Penitentiary Records, TSL-A.

36. Texas State Investigating Committee, *Report and Proceedings*, 1902, 429, 430.

37. *Lipscomb* v. *Seegers*, 19 S. C. 431–32 (1883).

38. *Atlanta Constitution*, 9 September 1887, 5; 11 September 1887, 11; 22 September 1887, 5.

39. "Proceedings of the Convict Lease System Investigation," (Stenographic report), typescript in Georgia Department of Archives and History (hereafter cited as GDAH),1908, vol. 4, 1242–43; Fuller, "History of TCI," 306.

40. "Convict Lease System Investigation," vol. 2, 501–3.

41. Texas State Investigating Committee, *Report and Proceedings*, 1902, 441, 440, 439.

42. C. Vann Woodward, *Origins of the New South, 1877–1913* (Baton Rouge: Louisiana State University Press, 1951), 234.

43. *Birmingham Age-Herald*, 8 August 1889, quoted in Woodward, *Origins*, 232.

44. Gavin Wright, *Old South, New South: Revolutions in the Southern Economy*

since the Civil War (New York: Basic Books, 1986), 182–83; idem., "Postbellum Southern Labor Markets," in *Quantity and Quiddity: Essays in U.S. Economic History*, ed. Peter Kilby (Middletown, Conn.: Wesleyan University Press, 1987), 126.

45. Jennifer Roback, "Southern Labor Law in the Jim Crow Era: Exploitative or Competitive?," *University of Chicago Law Review* 51 (Fall 1984): 1191.

46. Ayers, *Vengeance and Justice*, 212.

47. Powell, *American Siberia*, 27.

48. Robert S. Starobin, *Industrial Slavery in the Old South* (New York: Oxford University Press, 1970), 28–30; Fuller, "History of TCI," 280; Rebecca Hunt Moulder, "Convicts as Capital: Thomas O'Conner and the Leases of the Tennessee Penitentiary System, 1871–1883," *East Tennessee Historical Society's Publications* 48 (1976): 50.

49. J. Carlyle Sitterson, *Sugar Country: The Cane Sugar Industry in the South, 1753–1950* (1953; rpt. Westport, Conn.: Greenwood, 1973), 237–39; Moulder, "Convicts as Capital," 58.

50. New Iberia *Louisiana Sugar Bowl*, 30 September 1880, 2 March 1882, quoted in Sitterson, *Sugar Country*, 250.

51. Edward L. Ayers, *The Promise of the New South: Life After Reconstruction* (New York: Oxford University Press, 1992), 125; Penitentiary Report, [Florida] *Messages and Documents*, 1905, 307; Governor's Message, *Alabama House Journal*, 1903, 32; 1911, 31.

52. Governor's Message, [Florida] *Messages and Documents*, 1901, 26–27; *Hamby & Toomer v. Georgia Iron & Coal Company*, 127 Ga. 792 (1906).

53. U.S. Department of Labor, *Twentieth Annual Report of the Commissioner of Labor*, 1905, 29; R. H. Dawson, [Report from Alabama], NPA *Proceedings*, 1888, 83, 85.

54. Chekhov, *The Island*, 107.

55. U.S. Department of Labor, *Convict Labor* (Washington, D.C., 1887), 303.

56. Quotes in Carper, "Convict-Lease System," 392; Robert D. Ward and William W. Rogers, *Convicts, Coal, and the Banner Mine Tragedy* (University: University of Alabama Press, 1987), 50.

Chapter 3—Camps

1. Woodward, *Origins of the New South*, 213; Wharton, *The Negro in Mississippi*, 239; McKelvey, "A Half Century of Southern Penal Exploitation," 117.

2. W. L. Spoon Papers, Southern Historical Collection, University of North Carolina, Chapel Hill.

3. *Columbus Ledger*, 31 October 1897, quoted in "What Shall We Do With Our County Convicts?," pamphlet in Rare Book Collection, University of North Carolina, Chapel Hill.

4. George W. Donaghey, "Why I Could Not Pardon the Contract System,"

Annals of the American Academy of Political and Social Science 46 (March 1913): 23.

5. *Marion M. Noble Manuscript,* Special Collections Division, Mullins Library, University of Arkansas, Fayetteville, 9; untitled clippings concerning convict pardons, George W. Donaghey papers, Special Collections, Mullins Library.

6. Russell, "A Burglar in the Making," 755; A. Elizabeth Taylor, "The Convict Lease System in Georgia," M.A. thesis, University of North Carolina at Chapel Hill, 1947, 122; [Anon.], *Story of the Arkansas Penitentiary,* 6; *Nashville Daily American,* 17 May 1877, quoted in Fuller, "History of TCI, 302.

7. [Texas] State Investigating Committee, *Report and Proceedings,* 1902, 429–30; Blake McKelvey, "Penal Slavery and Southern Reconstruction," *Journal of Negro History* 20 (April 1935): 172; Florida *House Journal,* 1899, 836; [Georgia] *Principal Keeper's Report,* 1868, 22–28; see also *Rules and By-Laws for the Government of the Texas State Penitentiary, Revised and Amended* (Galveston: Shaw and Blaylock, 1877).

8. *Mississippi House Journal,* 1888, 13; [Texas] State Investigating Committee, *Report and Proceedings,* 419.

9. [Texas] State Investigating Committee, *Report and Proceedings,* 419; Governor's Message, *Alabama House Journal,* 1919, 160.

10. Blake McKelvey, *American Prisons: A History of Good Intentions* (Montclair, N.J.: Patterson Smith, 1977), 181; *Knoxville Journal,* 10 March 1894, quoted in A. C. Hutson Jr., "The Overthrow of the Convict Lease System in Tennessee," *East Tennessee Historical Society's Publications* 8 (1936): 101; *Special Message of the Governor of Georgia,* 1895, 3, 7–9.

11. "Fire at Flat Top Prison Investigation by State Fire Marshal and Deputies," Department of Corrections and Institutions, administrative correspondence, 25, 35, ADAH.

12. Monthly Report of Mississippi Penitentiary, July 1899, Penitentiary Records, Mississippi Department of Archives and History. Hereafter cited as MDAH.

13. [Texas] State Investigating Committee, *Report and Proceedings,* 419.

14. Florida Penitentiary Report, *Messages and Documents,* 1903–1904, 327; [Georgia] *Principal Keeper's Report,* 1869, 6–7; Penitentiary Report, *Arkansas Public Documents,* 1895, 12.

15. [Anon.], "The New Slavery in the South—An Autobiography," *Independent,* 25 February 1904, 411; Ford, *Special Report of the Commissioner of Labor,* 44–45.

16. J. H. Jones, "Penitentiary Reform in Mississippi," *Publications of the Mississippi Historical Society* 6 (1902): 128; Governor's Message, *Alabama House Journal,* 1882, 4; Penitentiary Report, North Carolina *Legislative Documents,* 1884, 49, 3; R. H. Dawson, [Report from Alabama], NPA *Proceedings,* 1888, 84–85; *Biennial Report of the Texas Penitentiary,* 1880, 17; Mississippi Penitentiary Report, 1891, 13; Thomas Goree, "Some Features of Prison Control in the South," NPA *Proceedings,* 1897, 135.

17. J. K. P. Campbell to Richard Coke, 1 March 1875, 9 July 1875, Peniten-

tiary Records, TSL-A; [Georgia] Report of the Principal Physician, 1893; Penitentiary Report, *Arkansas Public Documents*, 1890, 43; Woodward, *Origins*, 214; George Washington Cable, *The Silent South, Together with the Freedman's Case in Equity and the Convict Lease System* (New York: Scribners, 1885), 171.

18. "Proceedings of the Convict Lease System Investigation," I: 25.

19. Penitentiary Report, *Arkansas Public Documents*, 1892, 19; [Georgia] *Principal Keeper's Report*, 1874, 7.

20. *Biennial Report of the Texas Penitentiary*, 1884, 17.

21. *Biennial Report of the Texas Penitentiary*, 1900, 34.

22. Mississippi Penitentiary Report, 1897–1899, 121.

23. "Proceedings of the Convict Lease System Investigation," 1908, 1079; A. J. McKelway, "Abolition of the Convict Lease System of Georgia," NPA *Proceedings*, 1908, 221.

24. *Arkansas Gazette*, 31 March 1888, 4.

25. [Georgia] *Principal Keeper's Report*, 1880, 10; Report of Special Committee to visit convict camps, *Florida House Journal*, 1903, 1152; Report of House Investigating Committee, *Mississippi House Journal*, 1888, 6, 32; [Texas] State Investigating Committee, *Report and Proceedings*, 425, 427, 433; Ford, *Special Report of the Commissioner of Labor*, 45; R. H. Dawson diary (SPR 95), 3 June 1883; 13 July 1883, ADAH.

26. Report of House Investigating Committee, *Mississippi House Journal*, 1888, 19–21, 16.

27. [Texas] State Investigating Committee, *Report and Proceedings*, 425, 405, 401.

28. [Anon], *Story of the Arkansas Penitentiary*, 5; Hutson, "The Overthrow," 101; *Messages of the Governors of Tennessee*, VII: 489; [Texas]]State Investigating Committee, *Report and Proceedings*, 427.

29. Quoted in Cable, *The Silent South*, 132.

30. Rebecca A. Felton, "The Convict System of Georgia," *The Forum* 2 (January 1887): 486, 485; *Atlanta Constitution*, 9 September 1887, 5; *Report of the Principal Keeper*, 1869, 9; Penitentiary Committee Report, *Arkansas Public Documents*, 1871, 9; *Arkansas Gazette*, 26 July 1874, 4; Penitentiary Report, *Mississippi Departmental Reports*, 1876, 9; Brian Steel Wills, *A Battle from the Start: The Life of Nathan Bedford Forrest* (New York: HarperCollins, 1992), 373.

31. *Atlanta Constitution*, 3 December 1900, 1; 8 December 1900, 2; *Report of the Prison Commission*, 1901, 22–23; 1902, 5.

32. W. B. Lowe and J. W. English to Geo. H. Jones, n.d., "Correspondence" in Miscellaneous Records, 1816–1916, Records of the Georgia Prison Commission, GDAH; Philip McIntyre, *Two Years in the Texas Hell at Huntsville* (n.p., n.d. [c.1895]), 19, Thomason Room, Sam Houston State University Library, Huntsville.

33. *Biennial Report of the Texas Penitentiary*, 1876, 9, 8; 1880, 18; minutes of penitentiary board, 5 May 1883, Penitentiary Records, TSL-A.

34. *Atlanta Constitution*, 2 September 1877; *Mississippi House Journal*, 1888, 10.

35. Carper, "Convict-Lease System," 19; Florida Penitentiary Report, *Messages and Documents*, 1905, 307; Marc N. Goodnow, "Turpentine: Impressions of the Convict Camps of Florida," *Survey* 34 (1 May 1915): 107; *Mississippi House Journal*, 1888, 7; Payroll Ledger, Mississippi State Penitentiary, February 1902, Penitentiary Records, Mississippi Department of Archives and History; State Investigating Committee, *Report and Proceedings*, 406.

36. George Orwell, *1984* (New York: Harcourt Brace Jovanovich, 1977), 267.

37. Michel Foucault, *Discipline and Punish: The Birth of the Prison*, trans. Alan Sheridan (New York: Pantheon, 1977), 54.

38. *Dallas Morning News*, 11 February 1990, 56; *Marion M. Noble Manuscript*, 9; Donaghey, "Why I Could Not Pardon," 23; *Davis* v. *State*, 81 Miss., 59 (1902); *Tennessee House Journal*, 1885, 786–87.

39. Governor's Message, *Alabama House Journal*, 1919, 160; *Marion M. Noble Manuscript*, 9.

40. [Texas] State Investigating Committee, *Report and Proceedings*, 433; Monthly Reports of Mississippi Penitentiary, July 1899, Penitentiary Records, MDAH; *Cornell* v. *The State*, 74 Tenn. 624 (1881).

41. Nicholas, "The Care and Feeding of Convicts," esp. 180–83; J. B. Hirst, *Convict Society and Its Enemies* (Sydney: Allen & Unwin, 1983), 58.

42. [Texas] State Investigating Committee, *Report and Proceedings*, 421; Walker, *Penology for Profit*, 60; testimony on treatment of convicts, Penitentiary Records, TSL-A.

43. Carper, "Convict-Lease System," 214.

44. "Proceedings of the Convict Lease System Investigation," I: 4, 9; *Atlanta Constitution*, 24 June 1891, 6.

Chapter 4—Georgia: That Sundown Job

1. Lawrence Gellert, "Negro Songs of Protest," *New Masses* 7 (May 1932): 11.

2. E. C. Wines, *The State of Prisons and of Child-Saving Institutions in the Civilized World* (1880; rpt. Montclair, N.J.: Patterson Smith, 1968), 191.

3. Georgia *Laws*, 1866, 155–56.

4. *Report of the Principal Keeper of the Penitentiary*, 1868, 8, 7, hereafter cited as *Report of the Principal Keeper* [date].

5. *Report of the Principal Keeper*, 1869, 6, 7, 10, 11.

6. *Report of the Principal Keeper*, 1868, 22–28.

7. *Report of the Principal Keeper*, 1878, 9.

8. *Atlanta Herald*, 27 March 1874, in "Scrapbook of a Black Republican in Georgia 1860s–80s: W. A. Pledger," John Emory Bryant Papers, Special Collections Department, Duke University Library, Durham, North Carolina.

9. Derrell Roberts, "Joseph E. Brown and the Convict Lease System," *Georgia Historical Quarterly* 44 (December 1960): 399–400.

10. Derrell C. Roberts, "Joseph E. Brown and His Georgia Mines," *Georgia Historical Quarterly* 52 (September 1968): 285–92.

11. *Report of the Principal Keeper,* 1874, 1–7.

12. Joseph H. Parks, *Joseph E. Brown of Georgia* (Baton Rouge: Louisiana State University Press, 1977), 575.

13. John E. Talmadge, "Joseph E. Brown's Missing Correspondence," *Georgia Historical Quarterly* 44 (December 1960): 411–18.

14. *Report of the Principal Keeper,* 1875, 1–10; Judson C. Ward Jr., "Georgia Under the Bourbon Democrats," Ph.D. diss., University of North Carolina at Chapel Hill, 1947, 385–86; Account Book of Convicts Leased, 1872–1876, Georgia Department of Archives and History (hereafter GDAH).

15. Account Book of Convicts Leased, 1872–1876; *Report of the Principal Keeper,* 1874, 11; 1875, 14.

16. *Report of the Principal Keeper,* 1896; Matthew J. Mancini, "Race, Economics, and the Abandonment of Convict Leasing," *Journal of Negro History* 63 (Fall 1978): 343–44.

17. Georgia *Laws,* 1876, 40–45; *Report of the Principal Keeper,* 1876, 9.

18. Derrell Roberts, "Duel in the Georgia State Capitol," *Georgia Historical Quarterly* 48 (December 1963): 420–24; Ward, "Georgia," 394–97.

19. *Report of the Principal Keeper,* 1878-1880, 1,2, 10–15.

20. Bond contract of Georgia Penitentiary Company Number Two, 28 August 1877, GDAH.

21. *Georgia House Journal,* 1897, Part 2, 1522–24; Roberts, "Brown and the Convict Lease," 401.

22. *Report of the Principal Keeper,* 1880, 9; Roberts, "Brown and the Convict Lease," 407.

23. *Report of the Principal Keeper,* 1880, 74; 1882.

24. *Report of the Principal Keeper,* 1853, 1870, 1875, 1880, 1886, 1890, 1896, summarized in Mancini, "Race, Economics, and Leasing," 345.

25. Rebecca A. Felton, "The Convict System of Georgia," *Forum* 2 (January 1887): 486.

26. David Berry, "Free Labor He Found Unsatisfactory: James W. English and Convict Lease Labor at the Chattahoochee Brick Company," M.A. thesis, Georgia State University, 1991, 5, 34–37.

27. Roberts, "Brown and the Convict Lease," 403; *Report of the Principal Keeper,* 1886, 10.

28. Mrs. William H. Felton, *My Memoirs of Georgia Politics* (Atlanta, 1911), 581; Felton, "A Petition from the Women's Christian Temperance Union of the State of Georgia," [1887], pamphlet, Rebecca Latimer Felton papers, Hargrett Library, University of Georgia, Athens; Felton, "Convict System," 485.

29. Reverend H. H. Tucker, "Prison Labor," NPA *Proceedings,* 1886, 245–64; quotes on 255, 258, 260, 262.

30. Rebuttals follow Tucker, "Prison Labor," on 264–69; quote on 269.

31. Monthly Reports of Corporal Punishment, Diet, and Condition of Convicts ("Whipping reports") for 1886, GDAH.

32. *Atlanta Constitution*, 27 August 1887, 7.

33. *Atlanta Constitution*, 2 September 1887, 5; 28 September 1887, 5; see also 28 August 1887, 11; 9 September 1887, 5; 22 September 1887, 5; 23 September 1887, 5; 30 September 1887, 7.

34. *Report of the Principal Keeper*, 1888, 4–5.

35. *Atlanta Constitution*, 23 June 1891, 5.

36. *Atlanta Constitution*, 17 April 1892, 13.

37. *Report of the Principal Keeper*, 1894, 1–6.

38. *Report of the Principal Keeper*, 1893, 4–5; *Report of the Principal Physician*, 13–30.

39. *Report of the Principal Keeper*, 1886, 122–25.

40. E. Merton Coulter, *James Monroe Smith: Georgia Planter* (Athens: University of Georgia Press, 1961), 63–93.

41. *Principal Physician's Report*, 1897, vi.

42. *Report of the Principal Keeper*, 1897, 30.

43. Barton C. Shaw, *The Wool-Hat Boys: Georgia's Populist Party* (Baton Rouge: Louisiana State University Press, 1984), 133; Woodward, *Origins of the New South*, 257.

44. Georgia *Laws*, 1897, 71–78; *Report of the Principal Keeper*, 1898, 13.

45. *Prison Commission Report*, 1904, 8.

46. "Georgia's Revenue from Convicts," *Outlook* 75 (7 November 1903): 522–23.

47. *Prison commission Report*, 1907, 6.

48. *Prison Commission Report*, 1908, 10.

49. A. Elizabeth Taylor, "The Convict Lease System in Georgia," M.A. thesis, University of North Carolina at Chapel Hill, 1947, 75–76; *Brown v. Barnes*, 99 Ga. 1 (1896); Roberts, "Brown and His Georgia Mines," 291.

50. Quoted in Hilda Jane Zimmerman, "Penal Systems and Penal Reforms in the South Since the Civil War," Ph.D. diss., University of North Carolina at Chapel Hill, 1947, 282.

51. For a fuller discussion of the abolition of leasing in Georgia, see Chapter 13.

Chapter 5—Alabama: Her Most Indefensible Shame

1. Wines, *State of Prisons*. 191.

2. Alabama *Laws*,, 1845–1846, 9–13; Governor's Message, *Alabama House Journal*, 1882–1883, 156–60; Malcolm C. Moos, *State Penal Administration in Alabama* (Tuscaloosa: University of Alabama Press, 1942), 1–6.

3. Dan T. Carter, "Prisons, Politics and Business: The Convict Lease Sys-

tem in the Post–Civil War South," M.A. thesis, University of Wisconsin, 1964, 67–68.

4. Governor's Message, *Alabama House Journal*, 1869, 20.

5. Annual Report of the Inspectors of the Alabama Penitentiary, *Alabama State Documents*, 1870.

6. Governor's Message, *Alabama House Journal*, 1882, 162.

7. Governor's Message, *Alabama House Journal*, 1882, 162.

8. Penitentiary Report, *Alabama State Documents*, 1873, 3; Governor's Message, *Alabama House Journal*, 1882, 164.

9. Governor's Message, *Alabama House Journal*, 1875, 15–16.

10. Allen J. Going, *Bourbon Democracy in Alabama, 1874–1890* (University: University of Alabama Press, 1951), 82; Carter, "Prisons, Politics and Business," 92.

11. Penitentiary Report, *Alabama State Documents*, 1878, 5, 11; 1880, 77; Governor's Message, *Alabama Senate Journal*, 1880, 33; Alabama *Laws*, 1878–1879, 42–43; P. D. Sims, remarks, NPA *Proceedings*, 1886, 266.

12. J. G. Bass to Gaius Whitfield, 30 November 1876; 6 January 1877; 6 December 1876, Gaius Whitfield Papers, Alabama Department of Archives and History (hereafter cited as ADAH). For the annual problem of collecting the contract payments, see also letters of 3 September 1878 and 2 September 1879.

13. Bass to Whitfield, 6 January 1877; 11 May 1877; 13 September 1877; 16 April 1877; 8 May 1877; 30 November 1878, Gaius Whitfield papers, ADAH.

14. Report of Joint Committee to Enquire into the Treatment of Convicts, *Alabama State Documents*, 1880–1881, 4–5.

15. House Committee to Investigate Warden Bankhead, *Alabama House Journal*, 1882–1883, 848.

16. Governor's Message, *Alabama House Journal*, 1882, 168.

17. Georgia *Laws*, 1881–1882, 106–7; Alabama *Acts*, 1882–1883, 134.

18. *Acts of Alabama*, 1882–1883, 25–26; 134–41; Governor's Message, *Alabama House Journal*, 1886, 26; R. B. Rhett to Emmett O'Neal, 17 April 1882, quoted in William Warren Rogers, *The One- Gallused Rebellion: Agrarianism in Alabama, 1865–1896* (Baton Rouge: Louisiana State University Press, 1970), 45.

19. R. H. Dawson, [Report from Alabama], NPA *Proceedings*, 1888, 82, 83.

20. *Montgomery Advertiser*, 4 January 1888, 7.

21. Contract in *Alabama House Journal*, 1888–1889, 470–71; Report of Special Committee, *Alabama House Journal*, 1888–1889, 447 (hereafter cited as Special Committee, *Alabama House Journal*, 1889); Robert Norrell, ed., *James Bowron: The Autobiography of a New South Industrialist* (Chapel Hill: University of North Carolina Press, 1991), 102.

22. Governor's Message, *Alabama House Journal*, 1890–1891, 26.

23. Special Committee, *Alabama House Journal*, 1889, 447; George Korson, *Coal Dust on the Fiddle:*, 164–71; R. M. Cunningham, M.D., "The Convict System

of Alabama in its Relation to Health and Disease," NPA *Proceedings*, 1889, 132; *Birmingham Post*, 23 March 1926, 1.

24. Special Committee, *Alabama House Journal*, 1889, 449.

25. Quoted in Archie Green, *Only a Miner* (Urbana: University of Illinois Press, 1974), 210.

26. Quoted in James Seay Brown Jr., *Up Before Daylight: Life Histories from the Alabama Writers' Project, 1938–1939* (University: University of Alabama Press, 1982), 111.

27. "Lone Rock Song" was taught to William Ely "Uncle Jesse" James by black convict miners at Tracy City, Alabama, when he was a young miner in the 1880s. Green, *Only a Miner*, 210.

28. R. H. Dawson diary, 7 March 1883; 6 March 1883; 13 March 1883, ADAH.

29. R. H. Dawson diary, 18 April 1883; 17 April 1883, ADAH.

30. R. H. Dawson diary, 22 May 1883; 25 October 1883; 1 May 1891; 27 August 1883, ADAH.

31. R. H. Dawson diary, 30–31 December 1890, ADAH.

32. Quoted in Robert D. Ward and William W. Rogers, *Convicts, Coal, and the Banner Mine Tragedy* (University: University of Alabama Press, 1987), 50.

33. Special Committee, *Alabama House Journal*, 1889, 453; Hooper quoted in *Alabama: A Documentary History to 1900*, rev. and enl. ed., ed. Lucille Griffith (University: University of Alabama Press, 1972), 618; income in Governor's Message, *Alabama House Journal*, 1892–1893, 29.

34. Alabama *Acts*, 1892–1893, 194–218; quotes on 209–10, 213.

35. Zimmerman, "Penal Systems," 75; Dawson in Penitentiary Report, 1888, 15; on Tutwiler's career see especially Paul M. Pruitt Jr., "Julia S. Tutwiler, Part One, Years of Innocence," *Alabama Heritage* 22 (Fall 1991): 37–44; "Julia S. Tutwiler, Part Two, Years of Experience," *Alabama Heritage* 23 (Winter 1992): 31–39.

36. Alabama *Acts*, 1886–1887, 84; Penitentiary Report, 1888, 15; R. H. Dawson to Julia Tutwiler, 20 February 1888; 20 March 1888, Board of Inspectors of Convicts letterbook, ADAH.

37. Robert David Ward and William Warren Rogers, *Labor Revolt in Alabama: The Great Strike of 1894*, Southern Historical Publication #9 (University: University of Alabama Press, 1965), esp. 105–20; Governor's Message, *Alabama House Journal*, 1894–1895, 34–50.

38. Governor's Message, *Alabama House Journal*, 1895–1896, 10, 22; 1896–1897, 11–12.

39. Governor's Message, *Alabama House Journal*, 1903, 32.

40. Quoted in Ward and Rogers, *Convicts, Coal*, 119.

41. Ronald L. Lewis, *Black Coal Miners in America: Race, Class, and Community Conflict 1780–1980* (Lexington: University Press of Kentucky, 1987), 32.

42. U.S. Industrial Commission, *Report of the Industrial Commission on Prison Labor* (Washington, D.C., 1900), 62; Special Committee, *Alabama House Journal*, 1889, 461.

43. Governor's Message, *Alabama House Journal*, 1915, 25–27, 45; 1911, 31; 1903, 32; Isidore Shapiro, "The Prison Problem in Alabama," American Prison Association *Proceedings*, 1917, 89.

44. Elizabeth Bonner Clark, "The Abolition of the Convict Lease System in Alabama," M.A. thesis, University of Alabama, 1949, 38–49.

45. Clark, "Abolition," 51–70.

46. Governor's Message, *Alabama House Journal*, 1919, 160; Report of the Legislative Investigating Committee on Convicts and Highways to the Legislature of 1919, ibid, 849.

47. Report of the Legislative Investigating Committee on Convicts and Highways to the Legislature of 1919, *Alabama House Journal*, 1919, 851.

48. Governor's Message, *Alabama House Journal*, 1919, 48.

49. Alabama *General Acts*, 1919, 1117–22.

50. Alabama *General and Local Laws*, 1921 Special Session, 30–31; Governor's Message, *Alabama House Journal*, 1923, 67–81; Clark, "Abolition," 83.

51. Quoted in Clark, "Abolition," 86.

52. Clark, "Abolition," 88.

53. Quoted in "Alabama's Convict System Under Fire," *Literary Digest*, 10 April 1926, 10.

54. Powell, *The American Siberia*, 8–9.

55. Zimmerman, "Penal Systems," 401–7. For additional discussion of the abolition of leasing in Alabama, see Chapter 13.

Chapter 6—A Hell in Arkansas

1. George Washington Cable, *The Silent South, Together with the Freedman's Case in Equity and the Convict Lease System* (New York: Scribners, 1885), 169.

2. Report of the Committee on the Penitentiary, *Arkansas House Journal*, 1871, 4–8.

3. *Arkansas Gazette*, 30 November 1872, 3–4.

4. Arkansas *Acts*, 1871, 301–8; *Arkansas Gazette*, 1 April 1871, 4.

5. Harry Williams Gilmore, "The Convict Lease System in Arkansas," M.A. thesis, George Peabody College for Teachers, 1930, 9; Eric Foner, *Reconstruction: America's Unfinished Revolution, 1863–1877* (New York: Harper and Row, 1988), 362, 353, 538.

6. *Arkansas Gazette*, 1 February 1873, 2.

7. *Arkansas Gazette*, 13 March 1873, 2.

8. Arkansas *Acts*, 1873, 92–100; *Arkansas Gazette*, 6 May 1873, 4; 9 May 1873, 4.

9. Gilmore, "Convict Lease," 24; for an example see *Arkansas Gazette*, 27 February 1979, 4.

10. Arkansas *Acts*, 1881, 144–45; Garland Bayliss, "The Arkansas State Peni-

tentiary under Democratic Control, 1874–1896," *Arkansas Historical Quarterly* 34 (1975): 198; *Laws of Mississippi*, 1876, 51–52; Penitentiary Report, 1888–1890, *Arkansas Public Documents*, 43.

11. Governor's Message, *Arkansas Public Documents*, 1887, 16, 20.

12. George Washington Cable to Louise Cable, 24 November 1883, different portions printed in Lucy Leffingwell Cable Bickle, *George W. Cable, His Life and Letters* (1928; rpt. New York: Russell & Russell, 1967), 110; and Arlin Turner, *George W. Cable: A Biography* (Durham: Duke University Press, 1956), 149.

13. *Arkansas Gazette*, 24 March 1888, 5; 4 April 1888, 2; 13 March 1888, 1.

14. *Arkansas Gazette*, 13 March 1888, 1; 31 March 1888, 1.

15. Gilmore, "Convict Lease," 40–41.

16. Report of the Secretary of State, *Arkansas Public Documents*, 1887–1888, 25.

17. Penitentiary Report, *Arkansas Public Documents*, 1888–1890, 12, 6.

18. *Genealogies of Kentucky Families* (Baltimore: Genealogical Publishing Co., 1981), II: 598; Ward quoted by Cable in *Silent South*, 123.

19. Gilmore, "Convict Lease," 28–29; Physician's Report, 1880, 3–5; Committee on the Penitentiary, *Arkansas House Journal*, 1881, 423.

20. *Arkansas Gazette*, 31 March 1888, 1.

21. *Arkansas Gazette*, 7 April 1888, 3.

22. *State ex rel. Arkansas Industrial Co. v. Neel*, 48 Ark. 283 (1886); Gilmore, "Convict Lease," 33–34.

23. Report of Secretary of State, *Arkansas Public Documents*, 1887–1888, 261–62.

24. *Biennial Report of the Board of Penitentiary Commissioners*, 1891, 16–17.

25. *Marion M. Noble Manuscript*, Special Collections Division, Mullins Library, University of Arkansas, Fayetteville, 8–9.

26. Committee on the Penitentiary, *Arkansas House Journal*, 1881, 424.

27. Penitentiary Report, *Arkansas Public Documents*, 1892, 15.

28. Jane Zimmerman, "The Convict Lease System in Arkansas and the Fight for Abolition," *Arkansas Historical Quarterly* 7 (Autumn 1949): 175–76.

29. Raymond Arsenault, *The Wild Ass of the Ozarks: Jeff Davis and the Social Bases of Southern Politics* (Philadelphia: Temple University Press, 1984), 40–56; quote on 43; J. Morgan Kousser, *The Shaping of Southern Politics: Suffrage Restriction and the Establishment of the One-Party South, 1880–1910* (New Haven: Yale University Press, 1974), 123–30.

30. *Biennial Report*, 1892, 15–16.

31. *Acts of Arkansas*, 1893, 121–44; quote on 124.

32. Penitentiary Report, *Arkansas Public Documents*, 1891–1892, 6, 12.

33. Report of Secretary of State, *Arkansas Public Documents*, 1896, 10.

34. *State of Mississippi, ex rel. J. B. Greaves, District Attorney, v. John J. Henry, Warden of the Penitentiary* (Sandy Bayou Mandamus Case) 87 Miss. 138 (1906).

35. Report of the Committee to Investigate the Management of the Arkansas State Penitentiary, *Arkansas Public Documents,* 1895, 4; Biennial Report of the Penitentiary, 1896, 58; 1898, 8.

36. *Acts of Arkansas,* 1899, 205–12; *McConnell v. Arkansas Brick & Mfg. Co.,* 70 Ark. 568 (1902); Arsenault, *Wild Ass of the Ozarks,* 131–34; Zimmerman, "Convict Lease System in Arkansas," 178.

37. Biennial Report of the Penitentiary, 1902, 6, 43, 50–71.

38. George W. Donaghey, "Why I Could Not Pardon the Contract System," *Annals of the American Academy of Political and Social Science* 46 (March 1913): 23, 25.

39. *Acts of Arkansas,* 1911, 379–81.

40. George W. Donaghey, *Building a State Capitol* (Little Rock: Parke-Harper, 1937), 300.

41. Zimmerman, "Convict Lease System in Arkansas," 181–86.

Chapter 7—Mississippi: An Epidemic Death Rate without the Epidemic

1. Dumas Malone, ed., *Dictionary of American Biography* (New York: Scribners, 1935), XV: 565–66; William C. Harris, *The Day of the Carpetbagger: Republican Reconstruction in Mississippi* (Baton Rouge: Louisiana State University Press, 1979), 361.

2. William Banks Taylor (with R. E. Cooley and W. R. Edwards), *Brokered Justice: Race, Politics, and Mississippi Prisons, 1798–1992* (Columbus: Ohio State University Press, 1992), 34–35.

3. Paul B. Foreman and Julien R. Tatum, "A Short History of Mississippi's State Penal Systems," *Mississippi Law Journal* 10 (April 1938): 259–60; Penitentiary Report, *Mississippi House Journal Appendix,* 1871, 113.

4. Penitentiary Report, *Mississippi House Journal Appendix,* 1870, 58; Harris, *Day of the Carpetbagger,* 356; Governor's Message, *Mississippi House Journal Appendix,* 1872, 8–9.

5. Wills, *A Battle from the Start,* 373; Nathan Bedford Forrest to O. M. Roberts, 11 October 1877, Penitentiary Records (RG 22), Archives Division, Texas State Library, Austin.

6. Penitentiary Report, *Mississippi House Journal,* 1873, I: 555; contract on 604–6.

7. John C. Jay, "General N. B. Forrest as a Railroad Builder in Alabama," *Alabama Historical Quarterly* 24 (Spring 1962): 30; Harris, *Day of the Carpetbagger,* 356; Penitentiary Report, *Mississippi House Journal,* 1873, I: 562, 601, 563.

8. Penitentiary Report, 1872, 17–18.

9. Mississippi *Laws,* 1872, 67–86.

10. *Laws of Mississippi,* 1876, 51–52. The law specified a value of one dollar

for the stolen property as the threshold for the charge of grand larceny; in effect any such theft would qualify.

11. Wharton, *Negro in Mississippi*, 237–38.

12. Green, "Some Aspects of the Convict Lease System," 120; Woodward, *Origins of the New South*, 213; Taylor, *Brokered Justice*, 47, 63, 65, 46; Penitentiary Report, 1897–1899, 120–21.

13. Mississippi *Laws*, 1875, 107–8.

14. Harris, *Day of the Carpetbagger*, 360; Wharton, *Negro in Mississippi*, 239; Penitentiary Report, *Mississippi Departmental Reports*, 1876, 1–13.

15. Penitentiary Report, *Mississippi Departmental Reports*, 1877, 3, 4, 131; 1878–1879, v, 154 (the 1877 report records a population of 1,012; the 1897–1899 report, pp. 120–21, gives a figure of 1,003); Isabel Barrows, "Life in Southern Prisons," *Harper's Weekly* 34 (2 August 1890): 605 (her barb was directed at the system in Tennessee).

16. Penitentiary Report, *Mississippi Departmental Reports*, 1878–1879, vii; 1882–1883, 5.

17. Penitentiary Report, *Mississippi Departmental Reports*, 1882–1883, 5; Report of House Investigating Committee, *Mississippi House Journal*, 1888, 34.

18. Governor's Message, *Mississippi House Journal*, 1882, 30–31.

19. Penitentiary Report, *Mississippi Departmental Reports*, 1884–1885, vi; Governor's Message, *Mississippi House Journal*, 1886, 35.

20. Ruby E. Cooley, "A History of the Mississippi Penal Farm System, 1890–1935: Punishment, Politics, and Profit in Penal Affairs," M.A. thesis, University of Southern Mississippi, 1981, 17.

21. J. H. Jones, "Penitentiary Reform in Mississippi," *Publications of the Mississippi Historical Society*, 6 (1902): 114.

22. *Laws of Mississippi*, 1886, 73–82.

23. Cooley, "Mississippi Penal Farm," 24; Taylor, *Brokered Justice*, 61–63.

24. Frank Johnston, "The Penitentiary Lease," *New Mississippian*, 11 October 1887, 1, 4; Jones, "Penitentiary Reform," 115 (calling the attorney "Capt. Frank Johnson" [*sic*]); Cooley, "Mississippi Penal Farm," 24.

25. Johnston, "Penitentiary Lease," 1, 4.

26. Jones, "Penitentiary Reform," 114–15; Foreman and Tatum, "Mississippi's Penal Systems," 263; Governor's Message, *Mississippi House Journal*, 1886, 35; Penitentiary Report, *Mississippi Departmental Reports*, 1888–1889, 3–7, 21; quote on 4.

27. Woodward, *Origins of the New South*, 321–49; quote on 323; *Williams v. State of Mississippi*, 170 U. S. 225 (1898).

28. William F. Holmes, "James K. Vardaman and Prison Reform in Mississippi," *Journal of Mississippi History* 27 (1965): 230.

29. Penitentiary Report, *Mississippi Departmental Reports*, 1895–1896, 3–8; quote on 3.

30. Penitentiary Report, *Mississippi Departmental Reports*, 1900–1901, 4–5, 110.

31. Board of Trustees minute book, 1901–1906: 7 October, 11 October, 3 November, 17 November 1902, penitentiary records, MDAH; on the penitentiary investigating committee's work, see the *Jackson Daily Clarion-Ledger*, 6 February 1902, 3; 20 February 1902, 2–3, 6.

32. William F. Holmes, *The White Chief: James Kimble Vardaman* (Baton Rouge: Louisiana State University Press, 1970), 157–59.

33. Board of Trustees minute book, 1901–1906: 7 December 1905, penitentiary records, MDAH; *State of Mississippi, ex rel. J. B. Greaves, District Attorney* v. *John J. Henry, Warden of the Penitentiary* (Sandy Bayou Mandamus Case), 87 Miss. 125 (1906).

34. *State v. Henry*, 129.

35. *State v. Henry*, 145, 149, 127.

36. *State v. Henry*, 162–63, 166.

37. Holmes, *White Chief*, 164–67; quote on 166; *Laws of Mississippi*, 1906, 142–43. For an excellent review of the political context see also Taylor, *Brokered Justice*, 72–76.

Chapter 8—Louisiana: The Road to Angola

1. Mark T. Carleton, *Politics and Punishment: The History of the Louisiana State Penal System* (Baton Rouge: Louisiana State University Press, 1971), 7.

2. Mark T. Carleton, Review of Edward L. Ayers, *Vengeance and Justice, Louisiana History* 26 (Winter 1985): 110.

3. E. C. Wines, "Annual Report of the Secretary," NPA *Transactions*, 1874, 327; Wines, *State of Prisons*, 190–91; Cable, *Silent South*, 169.

4. Carleton, *Politics and Punishment*, 30. The Board of Control did issue a thin report in May 1888.

5. Report of the Board of Control, *Louisiana Legislative Documents*, 1867, 3, 4, 7. Hereafter cited as Report of the Board of Control [year].

6. Report of the Board of Control, 1869, 47, 51, 3.

7. *Louisiana Acts*, 1868, 270–71; Report of the Board of Control, 1869, 50, 52; Carleton, *Politics and Punishment*, 17.

8. *Louisiana Acts*, 1870, 84–85; Carleton, *Politics and Punishment*, 17–18, 23; Report of the Senate Committee on the Penitentiary, *Senate Journal*, 1878, 7–8.

9. Report of the Board of Control, 1874, 2; 1875, 4, 15.

10. *Louisiana Acts*, 1875, 54; 1878, 222–24; Carleton, *Politics and Punishment*, 24–28.

11. Governor's Message, *Louisiana Documents*, 1876, 17, 19; Report of the Board of Control, 1878, 47; Governor's Message, 1878, 13.

12. Carleton, *Politics and Punishment*, 39; accounts of the various bills' dispositions on 47–57.

13. Governor's Message, *Louisiana Documents*, 1886, 12.

14. Ralph V. Anderson and Robert E. Gallman, "Slaves as Fixed Capital: Slave Labor and Southern Economic Development," *Journal of American History* 44 (June 1977): 24–46; quotes on 24, 25; "Genovese's rule" is from Eugene Genovese, *The Political Economy of Slavery: Studies in the Economy and Society of the Slave South* (New York: Vintage, 1965), 49.

15. Anderson and Gallman, "Slaves as Fixed Capital," 32, 28.

16. Governor's Message, *Louisiana Documents*, 1888, 46.

17. Carleton, *Politics and Punishment*, 60.

18. Carleton, *Politics and Punishment*, 61–63.

19. Governor's Message, *Louisiana Documents*, 1894; Mark T. Carleton, "The Movement to End the Convict Lease System in Louisiana," *Louisiana Studies* 8 (Fall 1969): 214.

20. Sidney James Romero Jr.,"The Political Career of Murphy James Foster, Governor of Louisiana, 1892–1900," *Louisiana Historical Quarterly* 28 (1945): 1141–51.

21. *Louisiana Acts*, 1894, 253.

22. "Louisiana's Convicts," *Independent* 51 (2 February 1899): 362–63.

23. Carleton, *Politics and Punishment*, 81–82.

24. "The Delta Prisons: Punishment for Profit," typescript report, Southern Regional Council, March 1968, 20, 5–10.

Chapter 9—Tennessee: The Economics of Coercion

1. Woodward, *Origins of the New South*, 232.

2. C. W. Blackburn to Gov. DeWitt Clinton Senter, 23 April 1869, quoted in Rebecca Hunt Moulder, "Convicts as Capital: Thomas O'Conner and the Leases of the Tennessee Penitentiary System, 1871–1883," *East Tennessee Historical Society's Publications* 48 (1976): 45; *Tennessee House Journal Appendix*, 1867, 347; 1868, 13–18; Larry D. Gossett, "The Keepers and the Kept: The First Hundred Years of the Tennessee State Prison System, 1830–1930," Ph.D. diss., Louisiana State University, 1992, 71–75; George W. Ford, *Special Report of the Commissioner of Labor and Inspector of Mines* (Nashville, 1891), 78–86; *Messages of the Governors of Tennessee*, ed. and comp. Robert H. White and Stephen V. Ash, 10 vols. to date (Nashville: Tennessee Historical Commission, 1952–), VI: 70–71.

3. *Messages of the Governors of Tennessee*, VI: 166 (for 1872); *Tennessee House Journal Appendix*, 1875, 65; 1877, 324; 1879, 6; 1881, 8; 1883, 5; 1885, 139; 1887, 46; 1889, 64; 1891, 64.

4. Text of the contract appears in *Messages of the Governors of Tennessee*, VI: 160.

5. *Tennessee House Journal Appendix*, 1871, 264.

6. *Tennessee House Journal Appendix*, 1875, 65, 80; 1877, 321.

7. Cable, *Silent South*, 126–28.

8. *Tennessee House Journal Appendix*, 1881, 9; Cable, *Silent South*, 131.

9. Moulder, "Convicts as Capital," 58–60.

10. *Tennessee Acts*, 1873–1875, 114–16.

11. *Tennessee Acts*, 1877, 192–200; *Messages of the Governors of Tennessee*, VI: 466–67, 488, 617.

12. *Messages of the Governors of Tennessee*, VI: 548; Moulder, "Convicts as Capital," 53, 62.

13. Gov. James D. Porter to Ben F. Cheatham, 31 July 1877, quoted in Moulder, "Convicts as Capital," 61.

14. Message of Gov. William Bate, 12 January 1885, *Tennessee Governors' Messages*, VII: 115–19.

15. Message of Bate, 12 January 1885, *Messages of the Governors of Tennessee*, 118; *Tennessee House Journal*, 1893, 350.

16. *Tennessee House Journal Appendix*, 1885, 139; 161–62; *Tennessee House Journal*, 1889, 325.

17. Isabel Barrows, "Life in Southern Prisons," *Harper's Weekly* 34 (2 August 1890): 603–7; *Report and Proceedings of the State Investigating Committee* [27th Texas legislature] (Austin, 1902), 437.

18. *Tennessee House Journal*, 1893, 336; 1885, 787; 1893, 342, 333.

19. Fran Ansley and Brenda Bell, eds., "Miners' Insurrections/Convict Labor," *Southern Exposure* 1 (Winter 1974): 152, 153.

20. Quotes in Walter Wilson, "Historical Coal Creek Rebellion Brought an End to Convict Miners in Tennessee," *United Mine Workers Journal*, 1 November 1938, 10; and Woodward, *Origins of the New South*, 233.

21. Ford, *Special Report of the Commissioner of Labor and Inspector of Mines*, 14–16.

22. The ensuing paragraphs are based on A. C. Hutson Jr., "The Coal Miners' Insurrection of 1891 in Anderson County, Tennessee," *East Tennessee Historical Society's Publications* 7 (1935): 103–21; A. C. Hutson Jr., "The Overthrow of the Convict Lease System in Tennessee," *East Tennessee Historical Society's Publications* 8 (1936): 92–113; Pete Daniel, "The Tennessee Convict War," *Tennessee Historical Quarterly* 34 (1975): 273–92.

23. James Tice Moore, "Agrarianism and Populism in Tennessee, 1886–1896: An Interpretive Overview," *Tennessee Historical Quarterly* 42 (1983): 76–94; quote on 76.

24. Hutson, "Overthrow," 86.

25. Hutson, "Coal Miners' Insurrection," 113; Ansley and Bell, "Miners' Insurrections," 149.

26. Hutson, "Overthrow," 102; P. D. Sims, "The Lease System in Tennessee and Other Southern States," NPA *Proceedings*, 1893, 128.

27. *Tennessee House Journal Appendix*, 1879, 6; 1881, 8; 1883, 5; 1885, 139; 1887,

46; 1889, 64; 1891, 64; 1894, 25–79; 1897, 873; Governor's Message, *Alabama House Journal*, 1895, 34.

Chapter 10—Texas: Here Come Bud Russel

1. Minutes of the State Penitentiary Board, 3 April 1883, Penitentiary Records (RG 22), Archives Division, Texas State Library, Austin. Hereafter cited as TSL-A.

2. *Reports of the Superintendent and Financial Agent of the Texas State Penitentiaries, 1884* (Austin, 1885), 50–51. The non- "white" prisoners on the railroad might have been either Mexicans or Mexican Americans. I use the term *Mexican* to designate ethnic origin, not citizenship; and to make use of a category that contemporary Texas prison officials employed in classifying prisoners by race.

3. *Dallas Herald*, 12 February 1883, quoted in *Dallas News*, 12 February 1933, 7.

4. *Laws of Texas*, 1866, 192–95; Lawrence D. Rice, *The Negro in Texas, 1874–1900* (Baton Rouge: Louisiana State University Press, 1971), 6–8; Donald R. Walker, *Penology for Profit: A History of the Texas Prison System, 1867–1912* (College Station: Texas A&M University Press, 1988), 19–21.

5. Walker, *Penology for Profit*, 26–29; *Report of the Superintendent of the State Penitentiary*, 1871, 39, 11.

6. *Message from the Governor of Texas on the Financial Condition of the State* (Austin, 1874), 1.

7. Walker, *Penology for Profit*, 29.

8. *Laws of Texas*, 1871, 192–95.

9. Ward, Dewey and Company, "The Texas State Penitentiary," NPA *Transactions*, 1874, 236; Thomas J. Goree, "Some Features of Prison Control in the South," NPA *Proceedings*, 1897, 132.

10. *Biennial Report of the Texas State Penitentiary*, 1876, 8, 106.

11. Walker, *Penology for Profit*, 43–45; Rice, *Negro in Texas*, 9, 10.

12. *Governors' Messages, Coke to Ross* (Austin: Texas State Library, 1916), 84; Walker, *Penology for Profit*, 36–40.

13. *Rules and By-Laws for the Government of the Texas State Penitentiary, Revised and Amended* (Galveston: Shaw and Blaylock, 1877), 14, 13.

14. J. K. P. Campbell to [Gov.] Richard Coke, 1 July 1875; 9 July 1875; Directors' biennial report, 14 March 1876; Campbell to J. W. Bush, B. W. Walker, and T. J. Goree, 24 June 1875, Penitentiary Records, TSL-A.

15. *Governors' Messages, Coke to Ross*, 83; *Biennial Report of the Penitentiary*, 1876, 3, 21, 74; Burnett & Kilpatrick, Memorandum of Clothing issued, October, November 1877. Penitentiary Records, TSL-A.

16. G. W. Bush, Thomas J. Goree, B. W. Walker to Richard Coke, January 1875, Penitentiary Records, TSL-A.

17. J. S. Duncan, "Richard Bennett Hubbard and State Resumption of the Penitentiary, 1876–78," *Texana* 21 (1974): 49, 52.

18. Calculated from figures in *Biennial Report of Texas Penitentiary*, 1900, 34.

19. *Biennial Report of the Texas Penitentiary*, 1886, 24.

20. Harold M. Hyman, *Oleander Odyssey: The Kempners of Galveston, Texas, 1854–1980s* (College Station: Texas A&M University Press, 1990), 211; Bruce Jackson, ed., *Wake Up Dead Man: Afro-American Worksongs from Texas Prisons* (Cambridge: Harvard University Press, 1972), 92 (Bud Russel was the transfer agent for the Texas prison system from 1912 to 1952).

21. Sidney Mintz, *Sweetness and Power: The Place of Sugar in Modern History* (New York: Viking Penguin, 1985), 32–73; quotes on 32, 51, 70; David Brion Davis, *Slavery and Human Progress* (New York: Oxford University Press, 1987), 5–8.

22. *Biennial Report of the Texas Penitentiary*, 1880, 39; 1882, 27; Goree, "Some Features of Prison Control," 155; *Biennial Report*, 1910, 14; E. C. Wines quoted in Jane Zimmerman, "The Convict Lease System in Arkansas and the Fight for Abolition," *Arkansas Historical Quarterly* 7 (Autumn 1949): 187–88.

23. Contract between G. W. Butler and Ed H. Cunningham, 1 January 1878, Penitentiary Records, TSL-A; profit calculated from figures in *Biennial Report of the Texas Penitentiary*, 1880, 51–52. Besides the $3.01 per month for each prisoner, Cunningham and Ellis were also obligated to pay the state $729.16 2/3 for the salaries of the physician, chaplain, superintendent, and directors. *Governors' Messages, Coke to Ross*, 731.

24. *Biennial Report of the Texas Penitentiary*, 1880, 10, 28; *Governors' Messages, Coke to Ross*, 732.

25. *Message of Gov. O. M. Roberts*, 1879, 5; Woodward, *Origins of the New South*, 60.

26. *Laws of Texas*, 1879, 47–57.

27. D. M. Short to O. M. Roberts, 19 July 1879, Penitentiary Records, TSL-A; for a summary of the investigation see Walker, *Penology for Profit*, 58–63.

28. *Biennial Report of the Texas Penitentiary*, 1880, 11, 17, 21, 51–52; 1882, 7.

29. *Governors' Messages, Coke to Ross*, 395.

30. *Biennial Report of the Texas Penitentiary*, 1882, 7.

31. Walker, *Penology for Profit*, 73–75; *Biennial Report of the Texas Penitentiary*, 1882, 14.

32. *Biennial Report of the Texas Penitentiary*, 1884, 41.

33. *Biennial Report of the Texas Penitentiary*, 1886, 5, 6; 1894, 5, 6, 9.

34. Mike Fowler and Jack Maguire, *The Capitol Story: Statehouse in Texas* (Austin: Eakin Press, 1988), 54–55.

35. *Message of Gov. T. M. Campbell*, January 1909, 22.

36. *Biennial Report of the Texas Penitentiary*, 1910, 1.

37. The articles by Tom Finty Jr. appeared in the *Galveston- Dallas News* on 1 August to 5 August, 29 August to 19 September, and 17 October 1909; and were

published in book form as *Our Penal System and Its Purposes* (Galveston-Dallas *News*, 1909). See also Tom Finty Jr., "The Texas Prison Investigation," *Survey* 23 (18 December 1909): 387–91. Briggs's articles were published by the *San Antonio Express* between 5 December 1908 and 11 January 1909 and gathered in *The Texas Penitentiary* (*San Antonio Express*, [1909]). The best summary of the investigation occurs in Walker, *Penology for Profit*, 128–42 and 185–89; on the three reformers see also Jane Howe Gregory, "Persistence and Irony in the Incarceration of Women in the Texas Penitentiary, 1907–1910," M.A. thesis, Rice University, 1994, 60–70.

38. Walker, *Penology for Profit*, 93–95 provides an excellent summary of convict prices between 1884 and 1910 albeit without linking these rising prices to abolition.

Chapter 11—Florida: Leasing on the Frontier

1. Bureau of the Census, *Compendium of the Ninth Census* (Washington, D.C., 1872), 530–31.

2. Jerrell H. Shofner, "Forced Labor in the Florida Forests, 1880–1950," *Journal of Forest History* 25 (January 1981): 15–16.

3. *Laws of Florida*, 1906, 1315.

4. N. Gordon Carper, "The Convict-Lease System in Florida, 1866–1923," Ph.D. diss., Florida State University, 1964, 304–25; Pete Daniel, *The Shadow of Slavery: Peonage in the South, 1901–1969* (New York: Oxford University Press, 1973), 82–109.

5. Joe M. Richardson, "The Freedmen's Bureau and Negro Labor in Florida," *Florida Historical Quarterly* 39 (October 1960): 167.

6. *Laws of Florida*, 1868, 35–43.

7. Carper, "Convict-Lease System," 16; *Annual Message of Governor Harrison Reed*, 1869, 7; 1870, 13.

8. Richardson, "The Freedmen's Bureau," 168; Mildred L. Fryman, "Career of a 'Carpetbagger': Malachi Martin in Florida," *Florida Historical Quarterly* 56 (January 1978): 321–25.

9. *Laws of Florida*, 1877, 92–95.

10. Carper, "Convict-Lease System," 25–33; Powell, *American Siberia*, 8–9; *Report of the Adjutant-General*, 1877, 138.

11. Carper, "Convict-Lease System," 63; *Report of the Adjutant- General*, 1879, 231; Powell, *American Siberia*, 12.

12. *Report of the Adjutant-General*, 1877, 130; 1879, 231.

13. A mistake repeated by Hilda Jane Zimmerman in her outstanding dissertation, "Penal Systems and Penal Reforms in the South Since the Civil War," University of North Carolina, 1947, 150. Powell, *American Siberia*, 14, 42.

14. Powell, *American Siberia*, 50.

15. Carper, "Convict-Lease System," 70–73; Governor's Message, *Journal of*

the General Assembly, 1881, 40–41.

16. Governor's Message, *Journal of the General Assembly,* 1883, 26; 1885, 18; *House Journal,* 1889, 35.

17. Report of the Adjutant-General, *Journal of the General Assembly,* 1881, 257–67; Governor's Message, *Journal of the General Assembly,* 1883, 27; 1885, 18–19; Report of the Adjutant-General, *House Journal,* 1889, 36, 41, 45; Report of the Commissioner of Agriculture, 1903–1904, 326.

18. Carter, "Prisons, Politics, and Business," 95.

19. Carper, "Convict-Lease System," 81, 96.

20. Penitentiary Report, *Messages and Documents,* 1893, 119.

21. Powell, *American Siberia,* 341.

22. Carper, "Convict-Lease System," 97–100; Zimmerman, "Penal Systems and Penal Reforms," 152; Prison Report, *Messages and Documents,* 1893, 119, 126.

23. Prison Report, *Messages and Documents,* 1895, 61–62; Governor's Message, *Messages and Documents,* 1901, 24. While the 1895 report gives an annual figure of $26,000, the later Governor's Message reports $21,000. Since the contract terms did not vary between 1894 and 1902, and all others were for $21,000, the latter figure is the more reliable.

24. Governor's Message, *Messages and Documents,* 1901, 26–27.

25. Carper, "Convict-Lease System," 137; Prison Report, *Messages and Documents,* 1899, 69.

26. Carper, "Convict-Lease System," 132, 168–69.

27. The 1900 value of turpentine calculated from figures in U.S. Bureau of the Census, *Historical Statistics of the United States, Colonial Times to 1970* (Washington, D.C., 1972), 208, 209n.6, 545; phosphate value ibid., 584; turpentine and pitch exports in *Yearbook of the United States Department of Agriculture for the Year 1905* (Washington, D.C., 1906), 776; *Yearbook . . . for 1910* (Washington, D.C., 1911), 668; Florida convicts in Penitentiary Report, *Messages and Documents,* 1905, 307.

28. *Laws of Florida,* 1899, 141–42; Governor's Message, *Messages and Documents,* 1901, 27; Prison Report, ibid., 48.

29. Governor's Message, *Florida House Journal,* 1905, 30.

30. Richard Barry, "Slavery in the South Today," *Cosmopolitan* 42 (March 1907): 481–91; quote on 484.

31. Carper, "Convict-Lease System," 263; Governor's Message, *Florida House Journal,* 1913, 19.

32. Carper, "Convict-Lease System," 209–10, 213, 229.

33. Governor's Message, *Florida House Journal,* 1909, 10; Albert W. Gilchrist, "Prison Reform in the South," NPA *Proceedings,* 1909, 126–30; idem, "The Jails and Prisons of Florida," APA *Proceedings,* 1911, 261.

34. Prison Report, *Messages and Documents,* 1905, 307–8, 311, 322; Carper, "Convict-Lease System," 204–5, 209.

35. Report of Special Committee to visit convict camps," *Florida House Jour-*

nal, 1901, 1150; Prison Report, *Messages and Documents*, 1905, 327; Dr. R. S. Blitch, "Condition of Penitentiary Affairs in Florida," NPA *Proceedings*, 1904, 288–89.

36. *Clyatt v. United States*, 197 U. S. 207 (1905); [Fred Cubberly], "Peonage in the South," *Independent* 60 (9 July 1903): 1616–18; Daniel, *Shadow of Slavery*, 3–18, 25; quote on 7.

37. *Clyatt v. United States*, 223.

38. Daniel, *Shadow of Slavery*, 3–18, provides a superb analysis; it is the definitive account of this case. Also useful is Carper, "Convict Lease System," 305–12. Carper criticizes Daniel for insufficient attention to the links between peonage and leasing in "Slavery Revisited: Peonage in the South," *Phylon* 37 (March 1976): 85–99.

39. Mary Church Terrell, "Peonage in the United States: The Convict Lease System and the Chain Gangs," *Nineteenth Century* 62 (August 1907): 321.

40. Carper, "Slavery Revisited," 85–99; Marc N. Goodnow, "Turpentine: Impressions of the Convict Camps of Florida," *Survey* 34 (1 May 1915): 103–8; Daniel, *Shadow of Slavery*, 24–25.

41. Shofner, "Forced Labor," 20–21.

42. The foregoing paragraphs are based on Gudmunder Grimson, "Whipping Boss," *North Dakota History* 31 (April 1964): 127–33; N. Gordon Carper, "Martin Tabert, Martyr of an Era," *Florida Historical Quarterly* 52 (October 1973): 115–31; Shofner, "Forced Labor," 21–22; "A Victim of Convict Slavery," *Literary Digest* 77 (21 April 1923): 40–45; "Florida 'Comes Clean' By Ending Convict Camps," *Literary Digest* 77 (16 June 1923): 36–41. Carper's dissertation on the Florida convict lease was completed in 1964. That same year Grimson wrote a memoir of the Tabert case in *North Dakota History*. In 1973 Carper's Tabert article was published in the *Florida Historical Quarterly*. The Grimson account is not mentioned in the 1973 article. This oversight would ordinarily be of no concern, but there is an important discrepancy between the two accounts. In the article, Carper writes of the Taberts' seeking help from the "family attorney, Norris Nelson," and he makes no mention of Grimson whatever. (Grimson *does* appear briefly in the dissertation [340].) Grimson, by contrast, says nothing about Nelson but claims the family asked him for help. The likelihood is that Nelson went to the older and more respected Grimson when he was unable to make headway on the matter. Both men were members of the North Dakota bar in 1922. Grimson was later a district judge. Communication from Carla Kolling, State Bar Board of North Dakota, 10 June 1993.

Chapter 12—The Carolinas: Paradigms for Abolition

1. Penitentiary Report, *Reports and Resolutions of the South Carolina General Assembly*, 1873, 116–18, 526–27, hereafter cited as *Reports and Resolutions* [year].

2. Penitentiary Report, *Reports and Resolutions*, 1880, 5; George Brown

Tindall, *South Carolina Negroes, 1877–1900* (Baton Rouge: Louisiana State University Press, 1977), 268; *Atlanta Constitution*, 2 September 1887, 1.

3. Albert D. Oliphant, *The Evolution of the Penal System of South Carolina from 1866 to 1916* (Columbia, S.C.: The State Company, 1916), 4; Ayers, *Vengeance and Justice*, 189.

4. Ayers, *Vengeance and Justice*, 59, 72, 188. Florida did not erect a penitentiary before the Civil War either, but its circumstances were peculiar: essentially a frontier state, it had a tiny population and became a state only fifteen years before Lincoln's election. See Ayers, 294 n.51.

5. Michael Hindus, *Prison and Plantation: Crime, Justice, and Authority in Massachusetts and South Carolina, 1767–1878* (Chapel Hill: University of North Carolina Press, 1980), 219; Ayers, *Vengeance and Justice*, 188; Oliphant, *Evolution of the Penal System*, 3.

6. Jesse F. Steiner and Roy M. Brown, *The North Carolina Chain Gang: A Study of County Convict Road Work* (1927; rpt. Montclair, N.J.: Patterson Smith, 1969), 22; Darnell F. Hawkins, "State Versus County: Prison Policy and Conflicts of Interest in North Carolina," *Criminal Justice History* 5 (1984): 93–94.

7. Wines, *State of Prisons*, 202–3.

8. Thomas Holt, *Black Over White: Negro Political Leadership in South Carolina During Reconstruction* (Urbana: University of Illinois Press, 1977), 96, 163.

9. North Carolina *Laws*, 1866–1867, 204–6; Hawkins, "State Versus County," 92–95; Steiner and Brown, *North Carolina Chain Gang*, 29–31.

10. Carter, "Prisons, Politics and Business," 35–38; quote on 38; Keve, *History of Corrections in Virginia*, 25; First Annual Report of the Board of Public Charities, North Carolina *Legislative Documents*, 1869–1870, 118; Zimmerman, "Penal Systems and Penal Reforms," 80–82.

11. North Carolina *Laws*, 1872–1873, 259–61; Penitentiary Report, North Carolina *Legislative Documents*, 1871–1872, 4, 19, 20; 1874, 37, 53.

12. Penitentiary Report, *Reports and Resolutions*, 1869–1870, 244–52.

13. Penitentiary Report, *Reports and Resolutions*, 1870, 110; Georgia *Principal Keeper's Report*, 1870, 5; (percentages calculated from sample of 70 of the 280 prisoners received).

14. Zimmerman, "Penal Systems and Penal Reforms," 83–84; Holt, *Black over White*, 169, 181.

15. Penitentiary Report, South Carolina *Reports and Resolutions*, 1872, 753–74; 1871, 253–55.

16. Report of the Commission Appointed to Examine into the Condition and Management of the Charitable and Penal Institutions of the State, *Reports and Resolutions*, 1877, 819; Donald R. Walker, *Penology for Profit: A History of the Texas Prison System, 1867–1912* (College Station: Texas A&M University Press, 1988), 24.

17. Penitentiary Report, South Carolina *Reports and Resolutions*, 1874, 143; 1875, 150.

18. Oliphant, *Evolution of the Penal System*, 4; Joel Williamson, *After Slavery: The Negro in South Carolina During Reconstruction, 1861–1877* (Chapel Hill: University of North Carolina Press, 1965), 325.

19. Penitentiary Report, North Carolina *Legislative Documents*, 1876, 30, 55.

20. North Carolina *Laws*, 1874–1875, 329–33.

21. Governor's Message, North Carolina *Legislative Documents*, 1877, 6; John F. Stover, *The Railroads of the South: A Study in Finance and Control* (Chapel Hill: University of North Carolina Press, 1955), 145; Zimmerman, "Penal Systems and Penal Reforms," 85–86, 128.

22. *Acts of South Carolina*, 1877, 263–64; revised 1878, 702.

23. Penitentiary Report, South Carolina *Reports and Resolutions*, 1877, 89–90.

24. Penitentiary Report, North Carolina *Legislative Documents*, 1876, 38–39.

25. Penitentiary Report, North Carolina *Legislative Documents*, 1880–1882, 7; Fred Olds, "History of the State's Prison," *Prison News* [inmate newspaper of the Raleigh State Prison], 15 November 1926, 4–7, North Carolina Collection, University of North Carolina Library, Chapel Hill; percentages calculated from Hawkins, "State Versus County," Table 2, p. 104.

26. Penitentiary Report, South Carolina *Reports and Resolutions*, 1878, 503–7.

27. *Acts of South Carolina*, 1879–1880, 469–70; South Carolina *Reports and Resolutions*, 1879, 891–92; Oliphant, *Evolution of the Penal System*, 6–7; Tindall, *South Carolina Negroes*, 269–73.

28. Penitentiary Report, South Carolina *Reports and Resolutions*, 1880, 6; 1881, 74; Oliphant, *Evolution of the Penal System*, 7; Woodrow Wilson, "Convict Labor in Georgia," *New York Evening Post*, 7 March 1883, rpt. in *The South Since Reconstruction*, ed. Thomas D. Clark (Indianapolis: Bobbs-Merrill, 1973), 413–14.

29. Penitentiary Report, South Carolina *Reports and Resolutions*, 1881, 67–75.

30. Penitentiary Report, South Carolina *Reports and Resolutions*, 1881, 97, 115.

31. Penitentiary Report, South Carolina *Reports and Resolutions*, 1881, 67.

32. *Acts of South Carolina*, 1884, 815; Penitentiary Report, South Carolina *Reports and Resolutions*, 1885, 538–39; 1884, 571; Tindall, *South Carolina Negroes*, 274.

33. Penitentiary Report, South Carolina *Reports and Resolutions*, 1883, 635–36.

34. Penitentiary Report, South Carolina *Reports and Resolutions*, 1886, 278–80; 1888, 54.

35. *First Annual Report of the Bureau of Labor Statistics of the State of North Carolina* (Raleigh, 1887), 195, 199. This Coleman Twining was likely the H. C. Twining who would later play a role in the black-dominated Wilmington city government that would be overthrown in one of the most horrible episodes of racial violence in American history. H. C. Twining was sworn in as an alderman in the aftermath of the crucial 1897 city election: see H. Leon Prather Sr., *We Have*

Taken a City: Wilmington Racial Massacre and Coup of 1898 (Teaneck: Fairleigh Dickinson University Press, 1984), 41.

36. Penitentiary Report, North Carolina *Legislative Documents,* 1890, 5, 13–14.

37. Penitentiary Report, North Carolina *Legislative Documents,* 1892, 6, 35; North Carolina *Public Laws,* 1893, 230–34. In 1830 the 1,000 slaves of James C. Johnston, who was of Scots ancestry, began to build a dike to reclaim new land for their master. The project took ten years. When it was finished, the sentimental Johnston named it for the land of his forbears. Fred A. Olds, "North Carolina's Prison Farms," *Charlotte Daily Observer,* 1 December 1911, in *Prisons in North Carolina,* clipping file through 1975, I: 276–77, North Carolina Collection, UNC.

38. Hawkins, "State Versus County," 111; Penitentiary Report, 1893, 8; 1894, 4; for the association between good roads and the abolition of convict leasing generally see Alex Lichtenstein, "Good Roads and Chain Gangs in the Progressive South," *Journal of Southern History* 51 (February 1993): 85–110.

39. Penitentiary Report, South Carolina *Reports and Resolutions,* 1890, 44; 1891, 94; 1892, 401; 1895, 726–27; Tindall, *South Carolina Negroes,* 276.

Chapter 13—The Abandonment of Convict Leasing

1. Michel Foucault, *Discipline and Punish: The Birth of the Prison,* trans. Alan Sheridan (New York: Pantheon, 1977), 234, 272.

2. Allegations deftly summarized in J. G. Merquior, *Foucault* (London: Fontana, 1985), 102–7.

3. Jane Zimmerman, "The Convict Lease System in Arkansas and the Fight for Abolition," *Arkansas Historical Quarterly* 7 (Autumn 1949): 181; idem., "The Penal Reform Movement in the South during the Progressive Era, 1890–1917," *Journal of Southern History* 17 (November 1951): 490.

4. Green, "Some Aspects," 121, 123.

5. A. Elizabeth Taylor, "The Abolition of the Convict Lease System in Georgia," *Georgia Historical Quarterly* 26 (September–December 1942): 273–87; quote on 277; idem, "The Origins and Development of the Convict Lease System in Georgia," *Georgia Historical Quarterly* 26 (June 1942): 113–28; A. J. McKelway, "Abolition of the Convict Lease System of Georgia," NPA *Proceedings,* 1908, 222; Hastings H. Hart, "Prison Conditions in the South," NPA *Proceedings,* 1919, 201.

6. Wharton, *Negro in Mississippi,* 242.

7. J. H. Jones, "Penitentiary Reform in Mississippi," *Publications of the Mississippi Historical Society* 6 (1902): 112; Wharton, *Negro in Mississippi,* 238; Green, "Some Aspects," 122. Green had grave problems with his quotation marks. His 1949 essay's opening sentence reads: "The problem of the control of convicts in such manner as to render them least troublesome and expensive to the govern-

ment and at the same time to insure them humane and proper treatment has always been a perplexing one." The 1942 article by his student A. Elizabeth Taylor—an article derived from an M.A. thesis done under his direction—opens with: "The problem of disposing of convicts in such a way as to render them least troublesome and expensive to the government and, at the same time, insure them humane and proper treatment has always been a perplexing one."

8. Jones, "Penitentiary Reform," 111; Wharton, *Negro in Mississippi*, 242; Green, "Some Aspects," 121; Zimmerman, "Penal Systems," 277; William F. Holmes, "James K. Vardaman and Prison Reform in Mississippi," *Journal of Mississippi History* 27 (1965): passim.

9. Walker, *Penology for Profit*, 194; Carper, "Convict-Lease," 218; Keve, *History of Corrections in Virginia*, 186, 226, 268; John Dittmer, *Black Georgia in the Progressive Era, 1900–1920* (Urbana: University of Illinois Press, 1977), 86; Dewey W. Grantham, *Southern Progressivism: The Reconciliation of Progress and Tradition* (Knoxville: University of Tennessee Press, 1983), 130–31; Tindall, *South Carolina Negroes*, 273.

10. *Birmingham Ledger*, 2 September 1919, quoted in Elizabeth Bonner Clark, "The Abolition of the Convict Lease System in Alabama," M.A. thesis, University of Alabama, 1949, 78.

11. Woodward, *Origins of the New South*, 416–20.

12. Green, "Some Aspects," 123.

13. *Tennessee House Journal*, 1889, 325.

14. Carleton, *Politics and Punishment*, 58, 74; see also idem., "The Movement to End," esp. 211–14; Holmes, "Vardaman," esp. 247–48.

15. Ayers, *Vengeance and Justice*, 221, 222; Lichtenstein, "Good Roads," 93, 107.

16. *The County of Walton v. Franklin et al.*, 95 Ga. 538 (1894).

17. *Special Message of the Governor of Georgia*, 1895, 3, 7.

18. *Russell v. Tatum*, 104 Ga. 332 (1898).

19. Joseph S. Turner to Hoke Smith, 16 September 1908, Hoke Smith papers, Russell Memorial Library, University of Georgia, Athens.

20. *Georgia Laws*, 1897, 71–78.

21. *Historical Statistics*, 115, 117, 123. For farm products 1926=100, for building materials 1910–1914=100.

22. Lichtenstein, "Good Roads," 93; *Georgia Laws*, 1903, 65–71; *Report of the Prison Commission*, 1904, 9.

23. "Report of Convict Investigating Committee," *Georgia Acts and Resolutions*, 1908, 1064–72.

24. *Atlanta Georgian*, 14 July 1908, 3.

25. Taylor, "The Origins and Development," 120–32, provides a good account of the state of public opinion.

26. Taylor, "Abolition," 277–79; Dewey W. Grantham Jr., *Hoke Smith and the*

Politics of the New South (Baton Rouge: Louisiana State University Press, 1958), 173–74, 161; John C. Reed, "The Recent Primary Election in Georgia," *South Atlantic Quarterly* 6 (January 1907): 33.

27. "Governor's Message," *Georgia Acts and Resolutions*, 1908, 1053; emphasis mine.

28. *Atlanta Georgian*, 26 June 1908; Green, "Some Aspects," 121; George B. Tindall, "The Benighted South: Origins of a Modern Image," *Virginia Quarterly Review* 40 (1964): 281; Davidson quote on 290.

29. Julia S. Tutwiler to Capt. Frank S. White, 13 June 1913, Statewide Campaign Committee for the Abolishment of the Convict Contract System records, ADAH, hereafter cited as Statewide Campaign records, ADAH.

30. R. H. Dawson diary, 30–31 December 1890, ADAH.

31. *Birmingham Age-Herald*, 25 July 1923, 1.

32. Telegram from G. Grimson to Judge William E. Fort, 8 July 1923; Grimson to Forte [sic], 14 July 1923, Statewide Campaign records, ADAH.

33. Hastings Hart to Lawrence Orr Patterson, 31 March 1915; D. D. Wallace to Patterson, 17 March 1915, Orr-Patterson Papers, Southern Historical Collection, University of North Carolina, Chapel Hill.

34. Wilson Kelley to Amibo Fisk, 5 July 1923, Statewide Campaign records, ADAH.

35. Fred W. Vaughan to W. W. Brandon, 3 June 1923; H. A. Holt to W. W. Brandon, 11 June 1923, Brandon unprocessed administrative correspondence, ADAH.

36. Edmund Wilson, *Patriotic Gore* (New York: Oxford University Press, 1962), 429.

37. Václav Havel, "A New European Order," *New York Review of Books* 42 (2 March 1995): 43.

38. *International Herald Tribune*, 25 October 1994, 1, 5.

SELECTED BIBLIOGRAPHY

This is a list of secondary works of direct relevance to this book, not a comprehensive inventory of all that has been written on the subject. Entries were selected on the basis of their significance and their accessibility.

Adamson, Christopher R. "Punishment after Slavery: Southern State Penal Systems, 1865–1890." *Social Problems* 30 (June 1983): 555–68.

"Alabama's Convict System Under Fire." *Literary Digest* 10 (10 April 1926): 10–11.

Altgeld, John Peter. *Our Penal Machinery and Its Victims*. Chicago: A. C. McClurg, 1886.

Anderson, Ralph V., and Robert E. Gallman. "Slaves as Fixed Capital: Slave Labor and Southern Economic Development." *Journal of American History* 44 une 1977): 24–46.

Ansley, Fran, and Brenda Bell, eds. "Miners' Insurrections/Convict Labor." *Southern Exposure* 1 (Winter 1974): 144–59.

Armes, Ethel. *The Story of Coal and Iron in Alabama*. New York: Arno Press, 1973. Reprint of 1910 edition.

Arsenault, Raymond. *The Wild Ass of the Ozarks: Jeff Davis and the Social Bases of Southern Politics*. Philadelphia: Temple University Press, 1984.

Ayers, Edward L. *The Promise of the New South: Life After Reconstruction*. New York: Oxford University Press, 1992.

_____. *Vengeance and Justice: Crime and Punishment in the 19th- Century American South*. New York: Oxford University Press, 1984.

Barr, Alwyn. *Reconstruction to Reform: Texas Politics, 1876–1906*. Austin: University of Texas Press, 1971.

Barrows, Isabel. "Life in Southern Prisons." *Harper's Weekly* 34 (2 August 1890): 603–7.

Barry, Richard. "Slavery in the South Today." *Cosmopolitan Magazine* 42 (March 1907): 481–91.

Baxley, Thomas L. "Prison Reforms During the Donaghey Administration." *Arkansas Historical Quarterly* 22 (Spring 1963): 76–84.

Bayliss, Garland. "The Arkansas State Penitentiary Under Democratic Control,

1874–1896." *Arkansas Historical Quarterly* 34 (1975): 195–213.

Beaumont, Gustave de, and Alexis de Tocqueville. *On the Penitentiary System and its Application in France.* Carbondale: Southern Illinois University Press, 1964.

Berry, David. "Free Labor He Found Unsatisfactory: Convict Lease Labor at the Chattahoochee Brick Company, 1885–1909." *Atlanta History* 36 (Winter 1993): 5–15.

_____. "Free Labor He Found Unsatisfactory: James W. English and Convict Lease Labor at the Chattahoochee Brick Company." Master's thesis, Georgia State University, 1991.

Boles, John B. "The New Southern History." *Mississippi Quarterly* 45 (Fall 1992): 369–83.

Briggs, George Waverly. *The Texas Penitentiary.* San Antonio: San Antonio *Express,* [1909].

Brown, James Seay, Jr. *Up Before Daylight: Life Histories from the Alabama Writers' Project, 1938–1939.* Tuscaloosa: University of Alabama Press, 1982.

Cable, George Washington. *The Silent South, Together with the Freedman's Case in Equity and the Convict Lease System.* New York: Scribners, 1885.

Carleton, Mark T. "The Movement to End the Convict Lease System in Louisiana." *Louisiana Studies* 8 (Fall 1969): 211–23.

_____. *Politics and Punishment: The History of the Louisiana State Penal System.* Baton Rouge: Louisiana State University Press, 1971.

Carper, Gordon N. "The Convict-Lease System in Florida, 1866–1923." Ph.D. diss., Florida State University, 1964.

_____. "Martin Tabert, Martyr of an Era." *Florida Historical Quarterly* 52 (October 1973): 115–31.

_____. "Slavery Revisited: Peonage in the South." *Phylon* 37 (March 1976): 85–99.

Carter, Dan T. "Prisons, Politics and Business: The Convict Lease System in the Post–Civil War South." Master's thesis, University of Wisconsin, 1964.

Chekhov, Anton. *The Island: A Journey to Sakhalin.* New York: Washington Square Press, 1967.

Cohen, William. *At Freedom's Edge: Black Mobility and the Southern White Quest for Racial Control, 1861–1915.* Baton Rouge: Louisiana State University Press, 1991.

_____. "Negro Involuntary Servitude in the South, 1865–1940: A Preliminary Analysis." *Journal of Southern History* 42 (1976): 31–60.

Commons, John R., and Helen L. Sumner, eds. *A Documentary History of American Industrial Society.* 11 vols. Cleveland: A. H. Clark, 1910.

Cooley, Ruby E. "A History of the Mississippi Penal Farm System, 1890–1935: Punishment, Politics, and Profit in Penal Affairs." Master's thesis, University of Southern Mississippi, 1981.

Coulter, E. Merton. *James Monroe Smith: Georgia Planter.* Athens: University of Georgia Press, 1961.

Cubberly, Fred. "Peonage in the South." *Independent* 60 (9 July 1903): 1616–18.

Daniel, Pete. "The Metamorphosis of Slavery." *Journal of American History* 66 (June 1979): 88–99.

_____. *The Shadow of Slavery: Peonage in the South, 1901–1969*. New York: Oxford University Press, 1973.

_____. "The Tennessee Convict War." *Tennessee Historical Quarterly* 34 (Fall 1975): 273–92.

Davis, David Brion. *Slavery and Human Progress*. New York: Oxford University Press, 1987.

Dittmer, John. *Black Georgians in the Progressive Era, 1900–1920*. Urbana: University of Illinois Press, 1977.

Donaghey, George W. *Building a State Capitol*. Little Rock: Parke- Harper, 1937.

_____. "Why I Could Not Pardon the Contract System." *Annals of the American Academy of Political and Social Science* 46 (March 1913): 22–31.

Donnachie, Ian. "The Convicts of 1830: Scottish Criminals Transported to New South Wales." *The Scottish Historical Review* 65 (April 1986): 34-47.

Duncan, J. S. "Richard Bennett Hubbard and State Resumption of the Penitentiary, 1876–78." *Texana* 21 (1974): 49–56.

"The End of Convict Leasing in Alabama." *Literary Digest* 98 (21 July 1928): 11.

Engerman, Stanley L. "Coerced and Free Labor: Property Rights and the Development of the Labor Force." *Explorations in Economic History* 29 (1992): 18–29.

_____. "Contract Labor, Sugar, and Technology in the Nineteenth Century." *Journal of Economic History* 43 (September 1983): 635–59.

_____. "Some Considerations Relating to Property Rights in Man." *Journal of Economic History* 33 (March 1973): 43–65.

Felton, Mrs. William H. *My Memoirs of Georgia Politics*. (Atlanta, 1911).

Felton, Rebecca A. "The Convict System of Georgia." *The Forum* 2 (January 1887): 484–90.

Fenoaltea, Stefano. "Slavery and Supervision in Comparative Perspective: A Model." *Journal of Economic History* 44 (September 1984): 635–68.

Finley, M. I. "Was Greek Civilization Based on Slave Labour?" In *Slavery in Classical Antiquity: Views and Controversies*. Cambridge: W. Heffer and Sons, 1960.

Finty, Tom, Jr. "The Texas Prison Investigation." *Survey* 23 (18 December 1909): 387–91.

"Florida 'Comes Clean' By Ending Convict Camps." *Literary Digest* 77 (16 June 1923): 36–41.

Flynn, Charles L., Jr. *White Land, Black Labor: Caste and Class in Late Nineteenth-Century Georgia*. Baton Rouge: Louisiana State University Press, 1982.

Fogel, Robert William, and Stanley L. Engerman. *Time on the Cross: The Economics of American Negro Slavery*. 2 vols. Boston: Little, Brown, 1974.

Foreman, Paul B., and Julien R. Tatum. "A Short History of Mississippi's State Penal Systems." *Mississippi Law Journal* 10 (April 1938): 255–77.

Foucault, Michel. *Discipline and Punish: The Birth of the Prison*, trans. Alan Sheridan. New York: Pantheon, 1977.

Fowler, Mike, and Jack Maguire. *The Capitol Story: Statehouse in Texas*. Austin: Eakin Press, 1988.

Fox-Genovese, Elizabeth, and Eugene Genovese. *Fruits of Merchant Capital: Slavery and Bourgeois Property in the Rise and Expansion of Capitalism*. New York: Oxford, 1983.

Fryman, Mildred L. "Career of a 'Carpetbagger': Malachi Martin in Florida." *Florida Historical Quarterly* 56 (January 1978): 317–38.

Fuller, Justin. "History of the Tennessee Coal, Iron, and Railroad Company, 1852–1907." Ph.D. diss., University of North Carolina at Chapel Hill, 1966.

"Georgia's Revenue from Convicts." *Outlook* 75 (7 November 1903): 522–23.

Gildemeister, Glen A. "Prison Labor and Convict Competition with Free Workers in Industrializing America, 1840–1890." Ph.D. diss., Northern Illinois University, 1977.

Gilmore, Harry Williams. "The Convict Lease System in Arkansas." Master's thesis, George Peabody College for Teachers, 1930.

Going, Allen J. *Bourbon Democracy in Alabama, 1874–1890*. University: University of Alabama Press, 1951.

Goodnow, Marc N. "Turpentine: Impressions of the Convict Camps of Florida." *Survey* 34 (1 May 1915): 103–8.

Gossett, Larry D. "The Keepers and the Kept: The First Hundred Years of the Tennessee State Prison System, 1830–1930." Ph.D. diss., Louisiana State University, 1992.

Grantham, Dewey W., Jr. *Hoke Smith and the Politics of the New South*. Baton Rouge: Louisiana State University Press, 1958.

_____. *Southern Progressivism: The Reconciliation of Progress and Tradition*. Knoxville: University of Tennessee Press, 1983.

Green, Archie. *Only a Miner*. Urbana: University of Illinois Press, 1974.

Griffith, Lucille, ed. *Alabama: A Documentary History to 1900*. Revised and enlarged ed. University: University of Alabama Press, 1972.

Grimson, Gudmunder. "Whipping Boss." *North Dakota History* 31 (April 1964): 127–33.

Harris, William C. *The Day of the Carpetbagger: Republican Reconstruction in Mississippi*. Baton Rouge: Louisiana State University Press, 1979.

Hawkins, Darnell F. "State Versus County: Prison Policy and Conflicts of Interest in North Carolina." *Criminal Justice History* 5 (1984): 91–128.

Helsabeck, Fred. "Convict Labor Systems in Virginia, 1858–1907." Master's thesis, George Peabody College for Teachers, 1932.

Hiller, E. T. "Development of the Systems of Control of Convict Labor in the United States." *Journal of the American Institute of Criminal Law and Criminol-*

ogy 5 (July 1914): 241–69 [part 1]; (March 1915): 851–79 [part 2].

Hindus, Michael. *Prison and Plantation: Crime, Justice, and Authority in Massachusetts and South Carolina, 1967–1978*. Chapel Hill: University of North Carolina Press, 1980.

Hirst, J. B. *Convict Society and Its Enemies*. Sydney: George Allen and Unwin, 1983.

Hobbs, Edward H., ed. *Yesterday's Constitution Today: An Analysis of the Mississippi Constitution of 1890*. University: University of Mississippi Press, 1960.

Holmes, William F. "James K. Vardaman and Prison Reform in Mississippi." *Journal of Mississippi History* 27 (1965): 229–48.

_____. *The White Chief: James Kimble Vardaman*. Baton Rouge: Louisiana State University Press, 1970.

Holt, Thomas. *Black Over White: Negro Political Leadership in South Carolina During Reconstruction*. Urbana: University of Illinois Press, 1977.

Hughes, Robert. *The Fatal Shore*. New York: Knopf, 1987.

Hutson, A. C., Jr. "The Coal Miners' Insurrection of 1891 in Anderson County, Tennessee." *East Tennessee Historical Society's Publications* 7 (1935): 103–21.

_____. "The Overthrow of the Convict Lease System in Tennessee." *East Tennessee Historical Society's Publications* 8 (1936): 82–103.

Hyman, Harold M. *Oleander Odyssey: The Kempners of Galveston, Texas, 1854–1980s*. College Station: Texas A&M University Press, 1990.

Jackson, Bruce, ed. *Wake Up Dead Man: Afro-American Worksongs from Texas Prisons*. Cambridge: Harvard University Press, 1972.

Jaynes, Gerald David. *Branches Without Roots: Genesis of the Black Working Class in the American South, 1862–1882*. New York: Oxford University Press, 1986.

Jones, Alton D. "Progressivism in Georgia, 1898–1918." Ph.D. diss., Emory University, 1964.

Jones, J. H. "Penitentiary Reform in Mississippi." *Publications of the Mississippi Historical Society* 6 (1902): 111–28.

Kennan, George. *Siberia and the Exile System*. Chicago: University of Chicago Press, 1958.

Kennan, George Frost. "Introduction" to George Kennan, *Siberia and the Exile System*. Chicago: University of Chicago Press, 1958.

Keve, Paul W. *The History of Corrections in Virginia*. Charlottesville: University Press of Virginia, 1986.

Klein, Herbert S. *African Slavery in Latin America and the Caribbean*. New York: Oxford, 1984.

Korson, George. *Coal Dust on the Fiddle: Songs and Stories of the Bituminous Industry*. Hatboro, Pa.: Folklore Associates, 1965.

Kousser, J. Morgan. *The Shaping of Southern Politics: Suffrage Restriction and the Establishment of the One-Party South, 1880–1910*. New Haven: Yale University Press, 1974.

Lewis, Ronald L. *Black Coal Miners in America: Race, Class, and Community Conflict 1780–1980.* Lexington: University Press of Kentucky, 1987.

Lichtenstein, Alex. "Good Roads and Chain Gangs in the Progressive South." *Journal of Southern History* 51 (February 1993): 85–110.

Link, William L. *The Paradox of Southern Progressivism, 1880–1930.* Chapel Hill: University of North Carolina Press, 1992.

"Louisiana's Convicts." *Independent* 51 (2 February 1899): 362–63.

Mancini, Matthew J. "Race, Economics, and the Abandonment of Convict Leasing." *Journal of Negro History* 63 (Fall 1978): 339–52.

McKelvey, Blake. *American Prisons: A History of Good Intentions.* Montclair, N.J.: Patterson Smith, 1977.

_____. "A Half Century of Southern Penal Exploitation," *Social Forces* 13 (October 1934): 112–123.

_____. "Penal Slavery and Southern Reconstruction." *Journal of Negro History* 20 (April 1935): 153–79.

_____. "The Prison Labor Problem: 1875–1900." *Journal of the American Institute of Criminal Law and Criminology* 25 (July 1934): 254–70.

Mintz, Sidney. *Sweetness and Power: The Place of Sugar in Modern History.* New York: Viking Penguin, 1985.

Mohler, Henry Colvin. "Convict Labor Policies." *Journal of the American Institute of Criminal Law and Criminology* 15 (February 1925): 583.

Moore, James Tice. "Agrarianism and Populism in Tennessee, 1886–1896: An Interpretive Overview." *Tennessee Historical Quarterly* 42 (1983): 76–94.

_____. *Two Paths to the New South: The Virginia Debt Controversy, 1870–1883.* Lexington: University Press of Kentucky, 1974.

Moos, Malcolm C. *State Penal Administration in Alabama.* Tuscaloosa: University of Alabama Press, 1942.

Moulder, Rebecca Hunt. "Convicts as Capital: Thomas O'Conner and the Leases of the Tennessee Penitentiary System, 1871–1883." *The East Tennessee Historical Society's Publications* 48 (1976): 40–70.

Nicholas, Stephen, ed. *Convict Workers: Reinterpreting Australia's Past.* New York: Cambridge University Press, 1989.

Norrell, Robert, ed. *James Bowron: The Autobiography of a New South Industrialist.* Chapel Hill: University of North Carolina Press, 1991.

Novak, Daniel A. *The Wheel of Servitude: Black Forced Labor after Slavery.* Lexington: University Press of Kentucky, 1978.

Oakes, James. *The Ruling Race: A History of American Slaveholders.* New York: Oxford, 1982.

Oliphant, Albert D. *The Evolution of the Penal System of South Carolina from 1866 to 1916.* Columbia: The State Company, 1916.

Parks, Joseph H. *Joseph E. Brown of Georgia.* Baton Rouge: Louisiana State University Press, 1977.

Patterson, Orlando. *Slavery and Social Death: A Comparative Study*. Cambridge, Mass.: Harvard University Press, 1982.

Powell, J. C. *The American Siberia, or Fourteen Years' Experience in a Southern Convict Camp*. New York: Arno Press, 1969.

Pruitt, Paul M., Jr. "Julia S. Tutwiler: Part One, Years of Innocence." *Alabama Heritage* 22 (Fall 1991): 37–44.

———. "Julia S. Tutwiler: Part Two: Years of Experience." *Alabama Heritage* 23 (Winter 1992): 31–38.

Rabinowitz, Howard N. *The First New South, 1865–1902*. Arlington Heights, Ill.: Harlan Davidson, 1992.

———. *Race Relations in the Urban South, 1865–1890*. Illini Books Edition. Urbana: University of Illinois Press, 1980.

Ransom, Roger L., and Richard Sutch. *One Kind of Freedom: The Economic Consequences of Emancipation*. New York: Cambridge University Press, 1977.

Reed, John C. "The Recent Primary Election in Georgia." *South Atlantic Quarterly* 6 (January 1907): 27–36.

Reidy, Joseph Patrick. *From Slavery to Agrarian Capitalism in the Cotton Plantation South: Central Georgia, 1800–1880*. Chapel Hill: University of North Carolina Press, 1992.

Rice, Lawrence D. *The Negro in Texas, 1874–1900*. Baton Rouge: Louisiana State University Press, 1971.

Richardson, Joe M. "The Freedmen's Bureau and Negro Labor in Florida." *Florida Historical Quarterly* 39 (October 1960): 167–74.

Roark, James L. *Masters Without Slaves: Southern Planters in the Civil War and Reconstruction*. New York: Norton, 1977.

Roback, Jennifer. "Southern Labor Law in the Jim Crow Era: Exploitative or Competitive?" *University of Chicago Law Review* 51 (Fall 1984): 1161–92.

Roberts, Derrell D. "Duel in the Georgia State Capitol." *Georgia Historical Quarterly* 48 (December 1963): 420–24.

———. "Joseph E. Brown and His Georgia Mines." *Georgia Historical Quarterly* 52 (September 1968): 285–92.

———. "Joseph E. Brown and the Convict Lease System." *Georgia Historical Quarterly* 44 (December 1960): 399–410.

Rogers, William Warren. *The One-Gallused Rebellion: Agrarianism in Alabama, 1865–1896*. Baton Rouge: Louisiana State University Press, 1970.

Romero, Sidney James, Jr. "The Political Career of Murphy James Foster, Governor of Louisiana, 1892–1900." *Louisiana Historical Quarterly* 28 (1945): 1129–1243.

Rothman, David. *Conscience and Convenience: The Asylum and its Alternatives in Progressive America*. Boston: Little, Brown, 1980.

———. *The Discovery of the Asylum: Social Order and Disorder in the New Republic*. Boston: Little, Brown, 1971.

Russell, Charles Edward. "A Burglar in the Making." *Everybody's Magazine* 18 (June 1908): 753–60.

Shaw, Barton C. *The Wool-Hat Boys: Georgia's Populist Party*. Baton Rouge: Louisiana State University Press, 1984.

Shlomowitz, Ralph. "On Punishments and Rewards in Coercive Labour Systems." *Slavery and Abolition* 12 (September 1991): 97–102.

_____. "The Origins of Southern Sharecropping." *Agricultural History* 53 (July 1979): 557–75.

_____. "The Squad System on Postbellum Cotton Plantations." In *Toward a New South? Studies in Post–Civil War Southern Communities*. Westport: Greenwood, 1982.

Shofner, Jerrell H. "Forced Labor in the Florida Forests, 1880–1950." *Journal of Forest History* 25 (January 1981): 14–25.

Sitterson, J. Carlyle. *Sugar Country: The Cane Sugar Industry in the South, 1753–1950*. Westport: Greenwood, 1973.

Smith, Albert C. "'Southern Violence' Reconsidered: Arson as Protest in Black-Belt Georgia." *Journal of Southern History* 51 (November 1985): 527–64.

Southern Regional Council. "The Delta Prisons: Punishment for Profit." Typescript, 1968.

Stampp, Kenneth. *The Peculiar Institution: Slavery in the Ante- Bellum South*. New York: Vintage, 1956.

Starobin, Robert S. *Industrial Slavery in the Old South*. New York: Oxford, 1970.

Steiner, Jesse F., and Roy M. Brown. *The North Carolina Chain Gang: A Study of County Convict Road Work*. Montclair, N.J.: Patterson Smith, 1969.

Talmadge, John E. "Joseph E. Brown's Missing Correspondence." *Georgia Historical Quarterly* 44 (December 1960): 411–18.

_____. "The Origins and Development of the Convict Lease System in Georgia." *Georgia Historical Quarterly* 26 (June 1942): 113–28.

Taylor, A. Elizabeth. "The Abolition of the Convict Lease System in Georgia." *Georgia Historical Quarterley* 26 (September-December 1942: 273-87.

Taylor, Alrutheus Ambush. *The Negro in Tennessee, 1865–1880*. Spartanburg, S.C.: The Reprint Company, 1974.

Taylor, William Banks. *Brokered Justice: Race, Politics, and Mississippi Prisons, 1798–1992*. Columbus: Ohio State University Press, 1992.

Terrell, Mary Church. "Peonage in the United States: The Convict Lease System and the Chain Gangs." *Nineteenth Century* 62 (August 1907): 306–21.

Tindall, George Brown. *South Carolina Negroes, 1877–1900*. Baton Rouge: Louisiana State University Press, 1977.

"Victim of Convict Slavery." *Literary Digest* 77 (21 April 1923): 40–45.

Walker, Donald R. *Penology for Profit: A History of the Texas Prison System, 1867–1912*. College Station: Texas A&M University Press, 1988.

Wallenstein, Peter. *From Slave South to New South: Public Policy in Nineteenth-Century Georgia*. Chapel Hill: University of North Carolina Press, 1987.

Ward, Judson C., Jr. "Georgia Under the Bourbon Democrats." Ph.D. diss., University of North Carolina, 1947.

Ward, Robert D., and William W. Rogers. *Convicts, Coal, and the Banner Mine Tragedy*. University: University of Alabama Press, 1987.

_____. *Labor Revolt in Alabama: The Great Strike of 1894*. Southern Historical Publication no.9. University: University of Alabama Press, 1965.

Wharton, Vernon Lane. *The Negro in Mississippi, 1865–1890*. New York: Harper Torchbooks, 1965.

White, Robert H., ed. *Messages of the Governors of Tennessee*. Nashville: Tennessee Historical Commission, 1963.

_____ and Stephen V. Ash, eds. and comps. *Messages of the Govenors of Tennessee*, 10 vol. to date (Nashville: Tennessee Historical Commission, 1952–).

Wiener, Jonathan. *Social Origins of the New South: Alabama, 1860–1885*. Baton Rouge: Louisiana State University Press, 1978.

Williamson, Joel. *After Slavery: The Negro in South Carolina During Reconstruction, 1861–1877*. Chapel Hill: University of North Carolina Press, 1965.

Wilson, Walter. "Chain Gangs and Profit." *Harper's* 166 (April 1933): 532–43.

_____. *Forced Labor in the United States*. New York: AMS Press, 1971. Reprint of 1933 edition.

_____. "Historical Coal Creek Rebellion Brought an End to Convict Miners in Tennessee." *United Mine Workers Journal* (1 November 1938): 10.

Wilson, Woodrow. "Convict Labor in Georgia." *The South Since Reconstruction*, Indianapolis: Bobbs-Merrill, 1973, 409–16.

Wines, E. C. *The State of Prisons and of Child-Saving Institutions in the Civilized World*. Montclair, N.J.: Patterson Smith, 1968.

Woodman, Harold D. "Post–Civil War Southern Agriculture and the Law." *Agricultural History* 53 (January 1979): 319–37.

_____. "Sequel to Slavery: The New History Views the Postbellum South." *Journal of Southern History* 43 (November 1977): 523–54.

Woodward, C. Vann. *Origins of the New South, 1877–1913*. Baton Rouge: Louisiana State University Press, 1951.

Work, Monroe. "Negro Crime." *Review of Black Political Economy* 16 (Summer–Fall 1987): 47–61.

Wright, Gavin. *Old South, New South: Revolutions in the Southern Economy Since the Civil War*. New York: Basic Books, 1986.

_____."Postbellum Southern Labor Markets." *Quantity and Quiddity: Essays in U.S. Economic History*. Middletown, Conn.: Wesleyan University Press, 1987.

Zimmerman, Jane. "The Convict Lease System in Arkansas and the Fight for Abolition." *Arkansas Historical Quarterly* 7 (Autumn 1949): 171–88.

_____. "The Penal Reform Movement in the South During the Progressive Era, 1890–1917." *Journal of Southern History* 17 (November 1951): 462–91.

_____. "Penal Systems and Penal Reforms in the South Since the Civil War." Ph.D. diss., University of North Carolina, 1947.

INDEX

276

215–19; and humanitarianism,
216–22; opposition to, 137–38, 193,
210, 222–32; prohibition of, 222–
32; as regional phenomenon, 3; as
retrograde, 36; revenue from, 9,
99, 102, 106, 109, 111–12, 137, 170,
174–75, 177, 179, 188, 192, 208, 211,
217; and shame, 217, 227–29; and
slavery, 20; outside the South, 5
convicts: Australian, 28–32; age of,
87; black, 92, 178; boys, 45, 86; as
capital, 23, 148; classification of,
13, 20, 105; demand for, 175;
intimidation of, 70; Mexican, 71,
176; race, 176; separation of, 73;
white, 176, 178
Cornell v. *The State*, 77
County of Walton v. *Franklin et. al.*, 222
Cox, Edward, 87
Cranford, J. A., 189, 190
Crawfish Springs, Georgia, 95
Crawford, George, 58, 108
criminal laws, 41, 120
Cubberly, Fred, 194–96
Cunningham, Edward, 149
Cunningham and Ellis, 174, 176–77,
178, 179, 209

Dade Coal Company, 82, 84, 85, 88,
94; rebellion at, 90, 95
Daniel, Pete, 25
Darden, G. T., 141
Darnell, John, 83
Davidson, Donald, 227
Davis, David Brion, 21, 35, 171
Davis, J. M., 27
Davis, Jeff, 128
Dawson, R. H., 57, 67, 70, 73, 105,
107–8, 209, 228, 232
Dean Brothers, 56
death rates, 66, 67, 86, 102, 134, 137,
139, 171, 178, 206, 207; non-leasing
states, 102

DeBardeleben, Henry, 106, 111
Deen, J. R., 195
Dennis, John, 198, 203, 206
depression of 1893, 96, 109, 111, 166
Dewey, E. C., 170
Dibert, A. C., 208
Dickinson, W. W., 128–29
diet, 125, 172
disease, 67, 202, 205, 207
disfranchisement, 126, 149, 196, 220,
224, 225, 226, 227
Dittmer, John, 219
Donaghey, George, 60, 127; pardons
convicts, 129–30
Donnachie, Ian, 29
Doss, M. L., 140
Dunkin, Thomas, 65
Dunnavant, W. P., 134, 135
Durham, T. E., 44
Dutton, Charles, 187, 188, 189, 193

Eagle, James, 126
East Florida Railway Company, 187–
88
elasticity of supply, 31
Ellis, C. G., 149
Ellis, C. W., 78
Engerman, Stanley L., 36
English, James W., 90, 94
escape, 68, 124, 171, 178, 206–7
Ex parte Stewart, 235 n.27

Felton, Rebecca Latimer, 89, 90
female prison, South Carolina, 209
Fenoaltea, Stefano, 42, 49
Finley, M. I., 35, 37
Finty, Tom, Jr., 19, 181
Fitzpatrick, L. A., 123, 124
Flat Top Mine, 65
Florida Naval Stores and Commis-
sion Company, 192, 194
Florida Pine Company, 193
Flynn, Charles L., Jr., 21

CPSIA information can be obtained
at www.ICGtesting.com
Printed in the USA
BVHW041430180920
589015BV00006B/14